Black Matriarchy: Myth or Reality?

A Wadsworth Series:
Explorations in the Black Experience

General Editors

John H. Bracey, Jr., Northern Illinois University
August Meier, Kent State University
Elliott Rudwick, Kent State University

American Slavery: The Question of Resistance
Free Blacks in America, 1800–1860
Blacks in the Abolitionist Movement
The Rise of the Ghetto
Black Matriarchy: Myth or Reality?
Black Workers and Organized Labor
The Black Sociologists: The First Half Century
Conflict and Competition: Studies in the Recent Black Protest
Movement

The anthologies in this series present significant scholarly work on particular aspects of the black experience in the United States. The volumes are of two types. Some have a "problems" orientation, presenting varying and conflicting interpretations of a controversial subject. Others are purely "thematic," simply presenting representative examples of the best scholarship on a topic. Together they provide guidelines into significant areas of research and writing in the field of Afro-American studies. The complete contents of all the books in the series are listed at the end of this volume.

Black Matriarchy: Myth or Reality?

Edited by

John H. Bracey, Jr.
Northern Illinois University

August Meier
Kent State University

Elliott Rudwick
Kent State University

Wadsworth Publishing Company, Inc.
Belmont, California

Acknowledgments

The authors wish to express their appreciation to Mrs. Barbara Hostetler, Mrs. Patricia Kufta, and Miss Eileen Petric at Kent State University, for helping in the preparation of this manuscript, and to Miss Linda Burroughs and Mrs. Helen Peoples of the Kent State University Library. They are especially indebted to James G. Coke, former Director of the Kent State University Center for Urban Regionalism.

July 1970   *JHB*
AM
ER

L. C. Cat. Card No.: 77–154815
ISBN–0–534–00049–5
Printed in the United States of America

1 2 3 4 5 6 7 8 9 10—75 74 73 72 71

For
Mrs. Anna H. Page,
my favorite aunt

JHB

Contents

Black Matriarchy:
Myth or Reality?

Introduction

Recent political controversy has refocused attention on an aspect of the black experience that has long been the subject of scholarly attention: the structure and functions of the black family. Scholars have tried to show that the black family was either a product of social conditions in the United States or has strong traces of African cultural survivals; that the black family was or was not female-dominated; that female dominance was a source of strength or of weakness; that the black family was a pathological expression of the American family or a product of a viable black subculture. The purpose of this volume is to illustrate the major points of view concerning the existence, extent, and nature of a black matriarchy. Students of the black family can then see what the issues are, what the evidence is, and what conclusions can be drawn.

The pioneering scholar of the Negro family was E. Franklin Frazier, a black sociologist trained at the University of Chicago under Robert E. Park and Ernest Burgess. Frazier's views on the black family were reiterated throughout his career in a number of articles and in three monographs: *The Negro Family in Chicago* (1932); *The Free Negro Family* (1932); and *The Negro Family in the United States* (1939). Frazier's main contention is that the Negro family contains no appreciable African influences and is a product of the condition of slavery and racial discrimination in the United States.

The first selection in this volume, written in 1959, traces the development of the black family over the entire period of the existence of blacks in the United States and sets the stage for the other selections in this volume. The second piece, a chapter from *The Negro Family in the United States,* is Frazier's classic statement on the subject. Frazier claims that the stresses of slavery resulted in a form of family life that he describes as matriarchal, and that social and economic conditions among lower-class blacks since emancipation have reinforced this pattern. Frazier's use of the term *matriarchy* — or what is today described by anthropologists and sociologists as *matrifocality* — embraces two distinct but interrelated concepts. First, the proportion of female-headed households is significantly higher among lower-class blacks than among lower-class whites. Second, the term *matrifocality* describes a household where the father is present but where the female exercises the dominant influence in family decisions. In Frazier's view, both of these manifestations of matriarchy can be characterized as pathological when compared to the "normal" American family. *It should be emphasized that the overwhelming majority of blacks live in two-parent households, but the proportion of female-headed households is about three times that among whites.* It should also be stressed that middle- and upper-class Negro families are characteristically patrifocal, and that matrifocality is part of the black lower-class subculture.

Frazier's life-long opponent on the question of West African cultural influences on the nature of the black family was Melville J. Herskovits, an anthropologist with a keen interest in West African and New World Negro cultures. Herskovits' *The Myth of the Negro Past* (1941), his classic study of West African cultures and their New World survivals, presents the view that concerning the black family: "the more prominent characteristics must be treated in terms of the cognate African sanctions which make them normal, rather than abnormal, and go far in aiding us to comprehend what must otherwise, after the conventional manner, be regarded as aberrant aspects of the family institution." In essence, then, Frazier views matrifocal tendencies as a response to the black man's experience in America, and Herskovits views them as rooted in West African cultures; Frazier regards matriarchy as a sign of social disorganization, Herskovits views it as playing an essential role in the survival of the black community in America.

Section Three presents the results from three empirical studies of Negro families in various contexts. The first selection is from Charles S. Johnson's *Shadow of the Plantation,* a sociological study of Macon County, Alabama, during the 1930s. Johnson echoes Frazier's views concerning the matrifocal character of the lower-class black family. He argues that the matriarchy is the product of the existence of a black subculture, saying that

The community tends to act upon the patterns of its own social heritage. This is true of sex relations as well as economic relations. The tradition of the plantation in relation to morals, sex relations, and marriage never has conformed to the world outside. Unique moral codes may develop from isolation. It has happened elsewhere.

The selections by Lee Rainwater and Elliot Liebow are case studies illustrating and amplifying Frazier's views on the matriarchal family. Rainwater's discussion focuses on mother-centered households in an urban public-housing project, and the chapter from Liebow's *Tally's Corner* examines the father-child relationship among a group of black streetcorner men. Referring to the group he has studied, Liebow says that "the majority of streetcorner men do not live in the same households as their children," and "the modal father-child relationship" is one of acknowledging paternity, but living separately and only grudgingly accepting any financial responsibility. Both Rainwater, a sociologist, and Liebow, an anthropologist, agree with Frazier's view that the situations they describe indicate serious social disorganization.

Section Four contains selections generated by the recent concern over the political and social problems posed by the existence of large numbers of oppressed blacks in the ghettos of the nation's cities. The first is the text of Daniel P. Moynihan's *The Negro Family: The Case for National Action* (1965). In apocalyptic tones, Moynihan contends that persuasive evidence exists to show that "the Negro family in the urban ghettos is crumbling," and that the resulting deterioration "is the fundamental source of the weakness of the Negro community at the present time." He then documents the breakdown of the family and the resulting ill effects on the black community in terms of crime, drug abuse, poor health, and illegitimacy. Concluding with a lengthy supporting quotation from Frazier, Moynihan calls for public action to meet this crisis. The "Moynihan Report" stirred up considerable controversy, the substance of which was that the breakdown in black family life, if indeed such a thing is happening, was a result and not a cause of the economic and social weakness of black Americans.

Hylan Lewis, a leading black sociologist, in his well-reasoned response, significantly shifts the emphasis from the black family as "cause" to the black family as "effect." Lewis' view is that despite some weaknesses, especially among the lower classes, the black family is on balance a "resource for change." Reviewing the work of Frazier and others, and updating the supporting data where necessary, Lewis reemphasizes the fact that female-headed households are less than one-third of the total, and that the two-parent household is as "normal" for blacks as for the society at large. Lewis concludes that socio-economic status and racial discrimination are the key factors responsible for the large amount of female domination, not the nature of the family itself.

The final section, "New Approaches," includes an article by Herbert H. Hyman and John Shelton Reed, which presents the results of their study of recent surveys of the proportion of female-headed black households, and of the extent to which the female exercises influence where the male is present. They acknowledge that blacks do have a larger proportion of female-headed households than whites, but not as large as is widely believed. Their tentative contention is that "there seems to be little evidence for any socio-psychological pattern of matriarchy peculiarly characteristic of the Negro family." The concluding article by Virginia Heyer Young, an anthropologist, begins by critically reviewing the previous literature on the nature of the black family. The bulk of her article presents the results of a detailed study of the childrearing practices, personality formation, and family relations of Southern Negro families, from which she concludes that the black family is "an internally consistent system" that is part of a viable American black subculture.

Scholars are now testing the hypothesis of the matriarchy at various periods in Afro-American history and exploring the matrifocal family as an adaptive mechanism that enables Negroes to cope with the inimical conditions of poverty and racism. The results of this research are not yet in. What the selections in this volume show, however, is the strength of a concept, the full validity of which has never been tested.

The Frazier Thesis

1

The Negro Family in America

E. Franklin Frazier

The evolution of the Negro family in the United States has a special significance for the science of culture. Within the short space of 150 years, the Negro family has telescoped the age-long evolution of the human family.[1] On the basis of concrete factual materials it is possible to trace the evolution of the Negro family from its roots in human nature to a highly institutionalized form of human association. During the course of its evolution, the Negro family has been forced to adjust itself to different forms of social organization and to the stresses and strains of modern civilization. In studying the adjustments which the Negro family has made to these changes, it is possible to gain a clearer understanding of the relation of human motivations to culture. Moreover, the evolution of Negro family life not only has provided additional evidence of the primary importance of the family in the transmission of culture but also has shown the role of the family in the building of new cultures.

Under the Institution of Slavery

As a result of the manner in which the Negro was enslaved, the Negro's African cultural heritage has had practically no effect on the evolution of his family life in the United States. The slave traders along the coast of Africa who were primarily interested in healthy young Negroes — generally males — had no regard for family relationships. In fact, the human cargo which they collected were the remnants of various tribes and clan organizations. The manner in which men and women were packed indiscriminately in slave ships during the Middle Passage tended to destroy social bonds and tribal distinctions. Then the process of "breaking" the Negroes into the slave system in the West Indies, where they often landed before shipment to the colonies and the United States, tended to efface the memories of their traditional culture. In the colonies and later in the southern United States, the slaves

"The Negro Family in America" by E. Franklin Frazier from *The Family: Its Function and Destiny,* Revised Edition, by Ruth Nanda Anshen, pp. 65–84. Copyright © 1959 by Ruth Nanda Anshen. Reprinted by permission of Harper & Row, Publishers, Inc.

were widely scattered on comparatively small plantations where there was little opportunity to reknit social bonds or regenerate the African culture.

Doubtless memories of African culture regarding mating survived, but these memories became meaningless in the New World. The mating or sexual associations which Negroes formed on American soil were largely in response to their natural impulses and the conditions of the new environment. There was, first, a lack of females in the slave population until the 1830's, and this caused the slaves in some sections to seek satisfaction of their sexual hunger among Indian women. Then there was the discipline of the plantation or the arbitrary will of the masters which regulated sexual association and the selection of mates among the slaves. Thus it came about that sexual selection and mating were no longer culturally defined or regulated by African mores.

Nevertheless, there was selection of mates on the basis of spontaneous impulses and mutual attraction. There was the wooing of females by males who attempted to win their favor by gifts and expressions of affection. The stability of these matings was dependent largely upon the temperaments of the mates and the strength of the mutual attraction and affection. Where the mates were inclined or were permitted to live together as husband and wife, mutual sympathies and understanding developed as the result of habitual association. Pregnancy and offspring sometimes resulted in the breaking of bonds, but they often provided a new bond of sympathy and common interest. A common interest in the relationship was more likely to develop where there were mutual services and the sharing of benefits, as for example in the cultivation of a garden. Under such conditions the Negro family acquired the character of a natural organization in that it was based primarily upon human impulses and individual wishes rather than upon law and the mores.

Under favorable conditions the family as a natural organization developed considerable stability during slavery. The first requirement for stable family life among the slaves was, of course, that the family groups should not be broken up through sale or arbitrary action on the part of the masters. Where the plantation became a settled way of life and a social as well as an economic institution, the integrity of the slave family was generally respected by the masters. Moreover, the social relations which grew up facilitated the process by which the Negro took over the culture of the whites. The close association between whites and Negroes, often from childhood, enabled the slaves to take over the language, manners, and ideas of the masters. These close contacts were enjoyed by the slaves who worked in and about the master's house. On many plantations the masters provided religious and moral instruction for the slaves. The moral supervision included, in some cases at least, the chaperonage of the female slaves. It was through those channels that the white man's ideas and sentiments in regard to sex and family relations were communicated to the slaves. These cultural advantages, which were restricted mainly to the house servant, became the basis of social distinctions among the slaves. The house servants enjoyed a certain prestige in the slave society which grew up abut the Negro quarters.

In the division of labor on the plantation there was some opportunity for the expression of talents and intelligence. This was especially true in regard to the black mechanics who were so necessary to the maintenance of self-sufficiency on the plantation. Often it was the son of a favored house servant who was apprenticed to a craftsman to learn a trade. In becoming a skilled craftsman or mechanic the intellectual powers as well as the manual dexterity of the slave were improved. In addition, because of his skill he was accorded recognition by the master and acquired a higher status among the slaves. The recognition which was accorded the personality of the skilled craftsman was reflected in his pride in his workmanship. What was more important was that it was a moralizing influence which was relected in the family life of the skilled artisans. The skilled mechanic often assumed the conventional role of husband and father and was recognized as the head of his family. The fruits of his skill, so far as a premium was placed upon good performance, were often shared with his family. Consequently, these family groups, which were without the support of law, often achieved the solidarity and stability of a legally sanctioned family.

The development of family life described above represents the development of the slave family under the most favorable conditions. Among the vast majority of slaves, the Negro mother remained the most stable and dependable element during the entire period of slavery. Despite a benevolent master, the slave family was often dispersed when the plantation was sold or an estate was settled. With indifferent or cruel masters the slave family was constantly being broken up and its members scattered. But in either case some regard had to be shown for the bond between the Negro mother and her children. The masters' economic interest in the survival of the children caused them to recognize the dependence of the young children upon the mother. Then, too, the master, whether out of humanity or self-interest, was compelled to respect the mother's often fierce attachment to her children. Wherever the charge that slave mothers were indifferent to their offspring has any factual support it can be explained by the forced pregnancies and harsh experiences attending motherhood. Most of the evidence indicates that the slave mother was devoted to her children and made tremendous sacrifices for their welfare. She was generally the recognized head of the family group. She was the mistress of the cabin, to which the "husband" or father often made only weekly visits. Under such circumstances a maternal group took form and the tradition of the Negro woman's responsibility for her family took root.

The development of the maternal family among the slaves was further encouraged by the sexual association between blacks and whites. In the cities, where slaves moved about freely and there were many free Negroes, the sexual relations between Negro women and white men were casual and often of a debased character. But it was not only in the cities that the races mixed. Although there is no way of measuring the extent of the sexual association between slaveholders and slaves, there is abundant evidence of concubinage and polygamy on the part of the masters. The character of the sexual associations between the two races ran the gamut of human relationships. At one extreme the slave woman or Negro woman was used to satisfy a fleeting impulse. At the other extreme the sexual association was supported by personal attachment and deep sentiment. In the latter case, the white father in rare instances might assume the role of a father which lacked only a legal sanction. Nevertheless, because of the ideas and sentiments embodied in the institution of slavery, the Negro or mulatto mother remained the responsible and stable head of the family group. On the other hand, it was from such associations that the free Negro population continued to increase until the Civil War.

The Family Among the Free Negroes

The free Negro population increased steadily from the time when Negroes were first introduced into the Virginia colony in 1619. For three or four decades the servitude of the Negroes was limited to seven years, as in the case of white servants. Even after the status of the Negro servants became one of perpetual servitude, or slavery, the free Negro population continued to increase. The increase in the free Negro population came from five sources: (1) children born of free colored parents; (2) mulatto children born of free colored mothers; (3) mulatto children born of white servants and of free white women; (4) children of free Negro and Indian parentage; and (5) manumitted slaves.[2] Although it is not possible to know the increase in the free Negro population through each of these sources, it appears that the manumission of slaves was relatively the most important source. Slaves achieved freedom through manumission both because of the action of their owners and because of their own efforts. A large number of the white fathers emancipated their mulatto offspring; as a result about three-eighths of the free Negroes were mulattoes, as compared with only one-twelfth of the slave population. In numerous cases the white fathers provided for the economic welfare and education of their colored offspring. Slaves were able to become free through their own efforts especially in Maryland, Virginia, and North Carolina, where the economic basis of slavery was being undermined. In these areas skilled artisans were permitted to hire out their time and save enough money to buy their freedom. Whether they were freed because of their relation to their white masters or because of their own efforts, the free Negroes possessed certain cultural advantages which were reflected in their family life.

It was among the free Negroes that the family first acquired an institutional character. This was possible primarily because the free Negroes were able to establish family life on a secure economic foundation. In the southern cities the free Negroes had a secure position in the economic organization. Partly on the basis of wealth and occupation, a class system emerged among the free Negroes. Among the wealthier free colored families in Louisiana and in Charleston, some of whom were themselves slaveholders, the family was similar to that of the white slaveholders. It was patriarchal in organization and the status of women was similar to that of the women among the white slaveholding class. Moreover, these families were founded upon traditions which had been built up over several generations. Those traditions were a measure, in a sense, of the extent to which the Negro had assimilated the American cultural heritage.

It has already been pointed out how the house servants and the slave artisans had been able because of their favored position to take over American culture. Here it should be pointed out how the free Negroes, who had come largely from these groups, incorporated the American culture and transmitted it through their families to succeeding generations. Because of their relationship to the white race the mulattoes generally had a conception of themselves different from that of the pure-blooded Negro. Where they were favored by their white fathers, the close association with their fathers or their position in the household enabled them to take over the attitudes and sentiments as well as the overt behavior of the father. As freedmen with some economic competence or with a mechanical skill which afforded a good income, they were able to maintain a way of life that accorded with their conception of themselves and with the patterns of behavior taken over from the whites. This led to the beginning of an institutional life within the free colored communities similar to that in the white communities. The free Negroes established schools, churches, literary societies, and organizations for mutual aid. The families with traditions formed the core of the organized social life in the free Negro communities. Not only did these families give support to the institutional life, but they were supported in turn by the institutions of the community. Although it is true that because of social isolation the culture of the free Negroes became provincial and ingrown, it nevertheless provided a heritage for their children.

Civil War and Emancipation

The Civil War and emancipation created a crisis in the family life of the Negro. This crisis affected the free Negro family as well as the slave family. It tended to destroy whatever stability the slave family had achieved under the slave regime. It tore the free Negro family from its moorings in a society where it occupied a privileged position. The distinction between slave and free was wiped out. How did the Negro family meet this crisis? How was its organization and stability influenced by its new relation to American culture? How, specifically, was its role or function in mediating American culture to the Negro affected by the Negro's new relation to American life? These are some of the questions which we shall attempt to answer in the present chapter.

As the Union armies penetrated the South, the plantation regime was disrupted and the slaves were uprooted from their customary way of life. Thousands of Negroes flocked to army camps and to the cities; thousands joined the march of Sherman to the sea. The disorder and confusion were a test of the strength and character of family ties. In many cases the family ties which were supported only by habit and custom were broken. Negro men deserted their families and even some Negro mothers deserted their children. On the other hand, many fathers took their families with them when they went in search of freedom. Many Negroes went in search of relatives from whom they had been separated through sale while they were slaves. Throughout this chaotic situation, the Negro mother held the family group together and supported her children. This devotion was based partly upon her traditional role and partly upon the deep emotional attachment to her young that was evoked in the face of danger.

The northern missionaries who went south to establish schools and hospitals and to assist the Negro during his first steps in freedom were faced with the problems of the Negro family. They encouraged the Negro to get a legal sanction for his marital relations and to settle down to orderly monogamous marriage. They had to contend with the confusion which slavery had caused by the selling away of "husbands" who returned to claim "wives" who had "married" other men. Then there was the problem of giving the Negro husband and father a status in family relations which he had not enjoyed during slavery. The missionaries depended chiefly upon exhortation and moralizing to establish conventional marital and familial relations among the freedmen. These methods had some effect but they did not determine the future development of the Negro family. The course of that development was determined by the dominant economic and social forces in the South as well as by the social heritage of the freedmen.

When conditions became settled in the South the landless and illiterate freedman had to secure a living on a modified form of the plantation system. Concessions had to be made to the freedman in view of his new status. One of the concessions affected the family organization. The slave quarters were broken up and the Negroes were no longer forced to work in gangs. Each family group moved off by itself to a place where it could lead a separate existence. In the contracts which the Negroes made with their landlords, the Negro father and husband found a substantial support for his new status in family relations. Sometimes the wife as well as the husband made her cross for her signature to the contract, but more often it was the husband who assumed responsibility for the new economic relation with the white landlord. Masculine authority in the family was even more firmly established when the Negro undertook to buy a farm. Moreover, his new economic relationship to the land created a material interest in his family. As the head of the family he directed the labor of his wife and children and became concerned with the discipline of his children, who were to succeed him as owners of the land.

As the result of emancipation the Negro was thrown into competition with the poor whites. At the same time he became estranged from the former slaveholding class, and the sympathetic relations which had been built up during slavery were destroyed. Since the nature of the contacts between whites and blacks was changed, the character of the process of acculturation was changed. The estrangement between the whites and blacks was inevitable when the color caste was established in the South. If the democratic aims set up during the Reconstruction Period had been achieved, this estrangement would not have occurred. But where race was made the basis of status the Negroes in defense withdrew from the whites and suspected even their attempts to help the freedmen. Consequently, there came into existence two separate social worlds and, as far as spatial separation permitted, two separate communities. Since the Negro's personal life was oriented toward the separate Negro world, he derived his values from that world. The patterns of behavior and ideals which he took over from the white man were acquired generally through formal imitation of people outside his social world. In their social isolation the majority of Negroes were forced to draw upon the meager social heritage which they had acquired during slavery.

In the world of the Negro folk in the rural areas of the South, there grew up a family system that met the needs of the environment. Many of the ideas concerning sex relations and mating were carried over from slavery. Consequently, the family lacked an institutional character, since legal marriage and family traditions did not exist among a large section of the population. The family groups originated in the mating of young people who regarded sex relations outside of marriage as normal behavior. When pregnancy resulted, the child was taken into the mother's family group. Generally the family group to which the mother belonged had originated in a similar fashion. During the disorder following slavery a woman after becoming pregnant would assume the responsibility of motherhood. From time to time other children were added to the family group through more or less permanent "marriage" with one or more men. Sometimes the man might bring his child or children to the family group, or some orphaned child or the child of a relative might be included. Thus the family among a large section of the Negro population became a sort of amorphous group held together by the feelings and common interests that might develop in the same household during the struggle for existence.

From the standpoint of marriage statistics the rural Negro population has shown a large percentage of illegitimacy. But these statistics have little meaning if they are not related to the folkways regarding sex and marriage relations which have grown up in those isolated rural areas. The type of sex and marital relations which have been described does not indicate that sex relations have been promiscuous and free from controls. There has been, in the first place, the general recognition of the obligation of the mother to her children. In fact, pregnancy has been regarded as a phase of the maturing or fulfillment of the function of a woman. On the other hand, marriage meant subordination to a man or the formation of a new type of relationship. Often, therefore, when a girl became pregnant and the man wanted to marry her, the girl's mother objected. Later the girl might marry the father of her child or some other man. But this meant forming a partnership in working a farm together and assuming other obligations. In a society of this type the mother continued to occupy a dominant position in the family. The grandmother enjoyed an even more important position and has always been a leading figure in the Negro family.

Statistics have always shown a large number of Negro families with women as heads. These statistics have reflected the conditions described above. It appears that about 10 percent of the Negro families in the rural areas, as compared with about 30 percent in urban areas, have had women as heads. This difference is doubtless due to the fact that in the rural areas of the South the Negro man and the woman with her children need each other more in the struggle for existence than do those in the city. In fact, the stability of these family groups in the rural areas has depended largely upon the coöperation of man and woman in the struggle for a livelihood. As the result of this coöperation, deep sentiments and attachments have developed not only between spouses but also between the fathers and their children. This has caused these family groups to have on the whole the stability of conventional family groups.

Not all rural Negro communities in the South have been characterized by the simple mores described above. The rural Negro communities have differed greatly, the differences being dependent upon both economic and cultural factors. Where, outside the plantation area, the Negro has been able to acquire land and a higher economic status, the family has achieved an organization closely resembling the American pattern. The economic factor, however, has not been the sole determinant of this difference. In the areas outside the plantation region the Negro has never been so isolated biologically, mentally, and socially as in that section. Dating from the time of slavery, the Negro in those outside areas, as we have pointed out, has lived in closer association with the whites and has enjoyed some opportunity for self-development. When the Negro began his career as a freedman, therefore, he had a richer cultural heritage as well as a greater opportunity for economic development than the Negro in the plantation South. Nevertheless, the high percentage of landownership among the families outside the plantation area has provided a basis for a stable family life. As we have seen, it has encouraged the growth of a patriarchal family system. Moreover, the church and other institutions in these communities have supported conventional family mores. Illegitimacy and unlegalized marriage relations have not been tolerated as among the isolated plantation folk.

The progressive stabilization of Negro family life continued throughout the nineteenth century and during the first decade of the twentieth. This process was associated with a gradual increase in home and landownership and has involved the intermarriage of the stable elements among the descendants of free Negroes with the more ambitious and successful freedmen with a background of slavery. The descendants of the free Negroes brought to these unions a rich cultural heritage, and the ambitious descendants of slaves brought new aspirations and a new outlook on life. Out of this process there emerged a class stratification of the Negro population which was based largely upon social distinctions, the principal one of which was the tradition of a stable and conventional family life. In placing a high value upon a stable and conventional family life, these elements in the Negro population were safeguarding the chief means through which the gains of the Negro in civilization were preserved and transmitted to future generations.

Urbanization and Negro Family Life

So far the discussion of the Negro family has been concerned mainly with the family in the agricultural South, where nine-tenths of the Negro population was concentrated until the first decade of the present century. Around the opening of the century the drift of rural Negroes to southern cities had begun to attract attention. Then came the mass migrations to northern cities during and following the First World War, and these dramatized the accelerated urbanization of the Negro population.

In the hundreds of towns and cities of the South, the Negro family had taken shape and the rural folk culture was attempting to adjust itself to new conditions. Many Negro women had been attracted to these urban areas because of the chance to gain a living in domestic service. Sometimes they carried their illegitimate as well as their legitimate offspring with them. The freedom from familial and community controls sometimes meant the sloughing off of the responsibilities of motherhood, and the sexual freedom of the rural areas lost much of its harmless character. Sex expression tended to become a purely individualistic affair in which the hedonistic element became the chief end. Yet the family continued to survive among the majority of the population in these towns and cities. Here its maternal character was even more conspicuous than among the rural folk, not only as a result of the high rate of illegitimacy but also because of desertion on the part of the male head of the family. Amid the general demoralization of family life in these urban areas, there were enclaves of families which because of deeply rooted traditions maintained conventional family life and held themselves aloof from the masses.

The effects of an urban environment upon the Negro family were accentuated among the masses who migrated to the metropolitan areas of the North. The inadequacy of the sex and familial folkways and mores which had given stability to life in the rural South was revealed in the problems of the Negro family in the city. First, there was the problem of illegitimacy. As we have seen, illegitimacy was not necessarily a social problem among the isolated folk in the rural South. It did not violate the mores and the ideal of motherhood, for there women enjoyed a certain social sanction in any case. In an urban environment sex and motherhood were given a new social definition. The bearing of children was an economic burden which placed a handicap upon the mother as well as upon the family group in the severe struggle for existence. Then, too, the community, through neighbors, schoolteachers, social workers, and others, frowned upon unmarried motherhood and defined it as immoral. As a consequence the unmarried mother's behavior lost its naïve character. Her growing sophistication with the ways of city life, together with the economic burden of childbearing and the moral disapproval of the community, changed her attitude toward motherhood. Although this resulted in much demoralization, it should not be overlooked that the new stimuli of the city awakened the imagination of men and women, and the romantic element became involved in the sex experience.

Desertion on the part of the husband and father has been another serious problem of the Negro family in the city. In the rural South fathers had often deserted their families when they had gone to work in turpentine and lumber camps or in the cities. When Negroes began migrating to the North, it was sometimes the man who went first, with the idea of sending for his wife and children. Once in the environment of the city, however, the father or husband developed new interests and formed new sexual associations. Even when the husband or father brought his wife or family to the city, he often deserted them. Though in many cases of desertion the couple had not been legally married, nevertheless desertion on the part of the man was equivalent to the breaking of marital ties. Desertion meant that the community of interests and the sympathies which had held families together in the rural South were dissolved in the cities. Moreover, the social control exercised by the church and lodge and neighborhood opinion no longer existed in the city. Desertion revealed one of the chief weaknesses of this type of family: the absence of family traditions deeply rooted in the mores of the group. The informal breaking of legal marriage ties and the confused notions concerning the marital status and divorce tended to emphasize how much the family folkways of the migrants differed from the American mores governing marital relations.

The inadequacy of the type of family organization to which the migrant was accustomed resulted in much juvenile delinquency. Although juvenile delinquency in our cities is primarily a community problem, the widespread juvenile delinquency among the children of Negro migrants has resulted largely from the failure of the family. The poverty of the Negro has required many mothers to seek employment outside the home. As we have pointed out, in a third of the Negro families in the cities the mother has been the sole head of the family. Consequently, Negro children have been denied the supervision of their parents. Even in families where the father has been present, there has been no cultural heritage that could be communicated to the children. The folk culture, which these families have brought from the South, lost its meaning in the cities of the North. However much these families attempted to isolate their children from the influences of the cities, they could not prevent them from being affected by the public school.

Although the public school has contributed to the disorganization of the Negro folk culture in the city, it has also brought the Negro into contact with the larger American culture and thereby helped in the reorganization of his family life. The reorganization of family life, however, has not been achieved merely by the acquisition of new ideas concerning family life. The new ideas have only become effective in behavior when they were related to changed economic and social conditions. In the northern metropolis the occupational differentiation of the Negro population has been accelerated. As the Negro man has become an industrial worker and has no longer been dependent entirely upon domestic service and casual unskilled labor, he has become subject to a discipline that has affected his home life. The fact that he has received a higher and a more steady remuneration has enabled him to assume full responsibility for the support of his family. As a consequence, he has received more recognition as the head of the family and as such has taken more interest in his children, whom he has wanted to see "get ahead" as a result of greater educational opportunities.

The occupational differentiation of the Negro population was accelerated as the result of the changes in the economic organization of American life and important changes in the racial policy of the American government during and following World War II. Before the war, the increasing occupational differentiation of the Negro population had become the basis of a new class structure. Before the mass migration to northern cities which began with World War I, there had been small enclaves of Negro families — generally of free ancestry and mixed blood — that constituted an upper social class. The social position of these families was not determined so much by their occupation and income as by their cultural heritage and tradition of conventional family life. Sometimes when confronted by the onrush of southern migrants who threatened their way of life, they retreated into an isolated circle of friends. On the other hand, the migrants with their new economic, political, and educational opportunities and their awakened ambitions competed for a place in the Negro communities. In the fierce competition of urban life many of the old social distinctions lost their meaning and new standards of behavior and symbols of status came into existence. Such new marks of distinction as money, education, and power were essentially the same as those in the larger American culture, but the isolation of the Negro had given them relatively a different value.

Three fairly well defined socioeconomic classes began to emerge in the Negro communities in the larger cities.[3] At the bottom of the social pyramid was the lower class. Among this class family life was a precarious affair, having no roots either in a fixed habitation and a secure income or in a traditional culture. The lower-class families were usually concentrated in slum areas and depended upon incomes derived from casual employment in the least desirable occupations. Because of the uncertain employment of the men, the women, who found less difficulty in securing employment, occupied a dominant position in the family. The marital relations among this class were unstable even when there had been legal marriage. When no children were involved the women were as mobile as the men, but when there were children the mother struggled to hold the family together. It was in this class that the socialization of the child had been based mainly upon the exigencies of daily living involving the interaction of the parents and their child. This interaction consisted mainly in the expression of emotional reactions and in the impulsive behavior of the members of the unstable household toward each other. These reactions were generally uninfluenced by a cultural tradition or by the cultural patterns of the American community.

As the result of improved economic and educational opportunities a middle class became differentiated from the lower class. The stable and conventional families forming this class were the core of the institutional life of the Negro community. Because of their attempt to maintain a conventional family life, these families placed much emphasis upon respectability. Some of these families had escaped from the lower-class status; thus they became the source of a tradition of conventional familial relations which was passed on to their children. Often, however, these middle-class families had a tradition of conventional family life which had its roots in the South. In fact, it was the families with some social heritage and with traditions of a stable family life which were most able to withstand the disintegrating effects of the urban environment.

The middle class has continued to expand in size and in influence as the Negro population has continued to become urbanized.[4] In the country as a whole about the same proportion — five-eighths — of Negroes as of whites live in cities. In the North and in the West where the Negro enjoys larger economic opportunities and political rights, about a fourth of the Negro families are able to maintain middle-class standards. On the other hand, in the South where there are racial barriers to the employment of Negroes in white-collar and professional occupations and Negroes lack political power, only an eighth of the Negro families are able to support a middle-class way of life. The emergence of a new middle class among Negroes which has been the result of urbanization and the improvement in the economic status of Negroes has had important social consequences in the development of the Negro family. Above all it has meant that a large section of the Negro population has broken with the two really vital cultural traditions in the social history of the Negro. On the one hand, the genteel tradition which flourished among the mulattoes who were free before the Civil War and their descendants has ceased to determine the character of the familial behavior of upper-class Negroes. On the other hand, it has resulted in the rejection of the familial behavior of the Negro folk. Although the disintegration of the genteel tradition has created greater instability in family relations, the rejection of the familial patterns of the Negro folk has brought about the institutionalization of marriage and family life.

The emergence of a relatively large and influential middle class which has been uprooted from its "racial" traditions has influenced in other ways the form and functioning of the Negro family. The Negro family has become largely oriented to the values of the American culture. This has tended to reduce the size of the Negro family and bring about a sense of equality among its members. Moreover, the Negro family has developed a new style of life and new goals for its members. One phase of this new orientation toward the values of American culture is seen in the great emphasis which the middle class places upon conspicuous consumption. The emphasis upon conspicuous consumption represents both an attempt to consolidate its superior status within the Negro community and to achieve identification with the white American community. This does not mean, however, that middle-class Negro families have discarded altogether their social heritage. In fact, the persistence of the genteel tradition and the folk tradition often creates a confusion of values and goals. This becomes evident in the behavior and general outlook of the so-called upper class which has tended to become differentiated from the middle class despite the fact that the so-called upper-class Negroes derive their incomes from professional and white-collar occupations and a comparatively few small businesses. Since this "upper-class" sector of the new middle class sets the patterns of behavior and aspirations of the new middle class, it has tended to create a "world of make believe" in view of the Negro's economic and social position in American life.

The Negro Family and Modern Civilization

Although this discussion has been concerned with the Negro family in American civilization, it has a broader significance. The problems which the Negro family has encountered in its development involve problems of acculturation and assimilation which other peoples as well as Negroes must face today as a result of the impact of Western civilization. In the United States Negroes are placed in a peculiar position with reference to Western civilization because they were practically stripped of their traditional culture. Consequently, there was scarcely any opportunity for cultural conflicts to develop in the United States as in other parts of the world.[5] However, as the result of the emergence of a new middle class among American Negroes, their changing relation to American society involves problems of culture and personality which are related to the family.

The character of the Negro family during the various stages of its development has been affected by the social isolation of Negroes in American society. The lack of opportunity for the Negro male to participate freely in the economic organization and his subordination to whites as well as the general exclusion of Negroes from political activities have all affected the organization and the functioning of the Negro family. This has entailed a waste of human life and human energy. It represents in a sense the price which the Negro has been forced to pay in order to survive in American society. But this survival has not been the survival of a biological group but of a sociologically defined group. And it has been the family which has assured the survival of the Negro in American society.

The emergence of a new middle class is evidence of the increasing integration of the Negro in American society. However, the increasing integration of the Negro has brought into relief problems of culture and personality. The new middle class is without roots because it is increasingly cutting itself loose from its roots in the segregated Negro community. Moreover, it still has no social roots in the white community since it has not become identified with the white middle class. Consequently, middle-class Negroes are experiencing considerable conflict and frustration, and this is being reflected in Negro families. What social heritage can Negro parents pass on to their children? What group identification can they provide their children? Sociologically, these conflicts and frustrations are manifesting themselves in social disorganization and personal disorganization. Formerly social and personal disorganization was confined almost exclusively to lower-class Negroes, but increasingly the problems resulting from disorganization are manifesting themselves among middle-class Negroes.

The survival of the Negro in American civilization is a measure, in a sense, of his success in adopting the culture of the whites or an indication of the fact that the Negro has found within the white man's culture a satisfying life and a faith in his future. His future survival in a highly mobile and urbanized society will be on a different basis. In the large metropolitan communities of the North, Negroes are increasingly intermarrying with whites. Thus the Negro family is incorporating new traditions, and the children of mixed marriages have a new view on American life. As the result of these developments the Negro will have to face greater stresses in his personal life, and the segregated groups and institutions will no longer provide an adequate refuge in the white man's world. During all these changes and crises the family will continue to play an important role in transmitting the new conception which the Negro will acquire of himself and of his place in American society.

Notes

[1] See the writer's *The Negro Family in the United States,* Chicago, University of Chicago Press, 1939.

[2] John H. Russell, *The Free Negro in Virginia,* Baltimore, Johns Hopkins University Press, 1913, pp. 40–41.

[3] See St. Clair Drake and Horace R. Cayton, *Black Metropolis,* New York, Harcourt, Brace and Company, 1945, pp. 494–715.

[4] See E. Franklin Frazier, *Black Bourgeoisie,* Glencoe, Ill., The Free Press, 1957.

[5] See, for example, I. Schapera, *Western Civilization and the Natives of South Africa,* London, George Routledge & Sons, 1934.

The Matriarchate

E. Franklin Frazier

Only women accustomed to playing the dominant role in family and marriage relations (if we may regard the slaves as having been married) would have asserted themselves as the Negro women in Mississippi did during the election of 1868. We are told that,

if a freedman, having obtained [a picture of Grant], lacked the courage to wear it at home on the plantation in the presence of "ole marsa and missus" or of "the overseer," his wife would often take it from him and bravely wear it upon her own breast. If in such cases the husband refused to surrender it, as was sometimes the case, and hid it from her or locked it up, she would walk all the way to town, as many as twenty or thirty miles sometimes, and buy, beg, or borrow one, and thus equipped return and wear it openly, in defiance of husband, master, mistress, or overseer.[1]

These women had doubtless been schooled in self-reliance and self-sufficiency during slavery. As a rule, the Negro woman as wife or mother was the mistress of her cabin, and, save for the interference of master or overseer, her wishes in regard to mating and family matters were paramount. Neither economic necessity nor tradition had instilled in her the spirit of subordination to masculine authority. Emancipation only tended to confirm in many cases the spirit of self-sufficiency which slavery had taught.

When emancipation came, many Negro mothers had to depend upon their own efforts for the support of themselves and their children. Their ranks were swelled by other women who, in seeking sex gratification outside of marriage, found themselves in a similar situation. Without the assistance of a husband or the father of their children, these women were forced to return to the plow or the white man's kitchen in order to make a livelihood for their families. From that time to the present day, as we have seen in the preceding chapter, each generation of women, following in the footsteps of their mothers, has borne a large share of the support of the younger generation. Today in the rural sections of the South, especially on the remnants of the old plantations, one finds households where old grandmothers rule their daughters and grandchildren with matriarchal authority. Sometimes their

From E. Franklin Frazier, *The Negro Family in the United States*, pp. 125–145. © 1939 by the University of Chicago Press. Reprinted by permission of the publisher.

authority dates from the days following emancipation when, in wandering about the country, they "found" their first child.

It is, of course, difficult to get a precise measure of the extent of these maternal households in the Negro population. The 1930 census showed a larger proportion of families with women heads among Negroes than among whites in both rural and urban areas.[2] Moreover, it also appeared that in the cities a larger proportion of Negro families were under the authority of the woman than in the rural areas. In the rural-nonfarm areas of southern states from 15 to 25 per cent of the Negro families were without male heads; while in the rural-farm areas the proportion ranged from 3 to 15 per cent. In the rural-farm areas tenant families had a much smaller proportion with woman heads than owners, except in those states where a modified form of plantation regime is the dominant type of farming. For example, in the rural-farm area of Alabama between 13 and 14 per cent of both tenant and owner families were without male heads. Although rural areas showed a smaller proportion of families without male heads than urban areas, still it is in the rural areas of the South that we find the maternal family functioning in its most primitive form as a natural organization. In spite of the fact that official statistics on the marital relations of these women are of doubtful accuracy, a closer view of census materials on the families in three southern counties in 1910 and 1920 throws additional light on the extent and character of these maternal households in this region.[3]

Table 1 indicates that from a fifth to a fourth of the families in the three counties — two in the Black Belt and the third in the coastal region — were without a male head. In each of the counties in 1910 the families in which the wife was a mulatto had a smaller proportion without a male head than the families with a black wife or mother.[4] The smaller proportion of families without a male head among the mulattoes was doubtless due to the relatively higher economic and cultural status of this class, which had less illiteracy and a higher rate of homeownership than the blacks. In 1920 the mulattoes in the North Carolina county still showed a smaller proportion of families without male heads; while in the Black Belt counties the standing of the mulattoes was reversed in one instance and was the same as the blacks in the other. The migrations during the war might have been responsible for the change in the relative position of the two classes in the Black Belt counties, since the population of both counties decreased between 1910 and 1920. This much, at least, is true: the increase in the proportion of families without a male head among the mulattoes in these latter counties was accompanied by a decrease in the number of homeowning families among this class.

We can get a better conception of the relation of homeownership to stable and normal family relations by examining the marital status of these women who are heads of families. Although our figures are not absolutely accurate, they reveal to a much greater extent the real nature of the conjugal relations of these women than the published statistics.[5] We have, in addition to the two usual classifications — wid-

Table 1: Number and Percentage of Negro Families with Female Heads in Three Southern Counties, 1910 and 1920

County	Color of Woman	1920			1910		
		Total Number Families	Families with Woman Head		Total Number Families	Families with Woman Head	
			Number	Per Cent		Number	Per Cent
Hertford County, N.C.	Black	1,270	243	18.9	1,093	266	24.3
	Mulatto	796	122	15.9	788	154	19.5
Macon County, Ala.	Black	939	274	29.1	840	240	28.5
	Mulatto	101	30	29.8	110	27	24.5
Issaquena County, Miss.	Black	1,940	372	19.1	2,595	636	24.5
	Mulatto	94	23	23.4	331	67	20.2

owed and divorced — two others: women who apparently had been married but were separated from their husbands and women who had had only irregular relations with men. For example, we find that in Issaquena County, Mississippi, in 1910, of the 671 women heads of families, 159, or 21 per cent, were separated from their husbands and 66, or about 10 per cent, had had only irregular relations with men. In Hertford County, North Carolina, for the same year, 14.1 per cent of the women heads of families were separated, and 34.6 per cent had had only irregular relations with men; while the separated and the irregular unions each comprised about 14 per cent of the women heads of families in Macon County, Alabama. After making allowance for the separated and those who have had only irregular associations with men, the majority of these women are classified as widows. This is true of the blacks as well as the mulattoes and of the tenants as well as of the homeowners. But an important difference appears between the women who own their homes and those who are renters or whose home tenure is unknown. Among the homeowners from 80 to 100 per cent of the women are included under widowhood, whereas for the renters and those of unknown tenure only from 50 to 70 per cent were in this class. This was true of both the blacks and the mulattoes and seems to indicate that widowhood among the homeowners was generally real widowhood.[6]

That these figures represent more truly the conjugal relations of these women than published statistics is apparent from the histories of their marital experiences. The divorced, and in some cases the widowed, in published statistics are often in fact merely separations, since divorce is regarded by many of these people as an individual affair not requiring legal sanction. As we shall see below, "divorce" in one case consisted in giving the man a "scrip." On the whole, these simple folk have vague notions concerning the legal requirements for divorce. One man said that he did not need a divorce from his wife because "she was in one county and me in another."[7] Another man considered himself divorced when his wife was sentenced to jail for cutting a woman. Many of the women who were heads of families have

Table 2: Marital Status of Women Heads of Families According to Tenure of Homes in Three Southern Counties, 1910 and 1920

Tenure of Homes	Total Families	1920				Total Families	1910			
		Separated	Widowed	Divorced	Irregular		Separated	Widowed	Divorced	Irregular
Hertford County, N.C.										
Owners	63	3	53	2	5	74	2	60	2	10
Renters	133	24	77	3	29	112	9	63	4	36
Unknown	165	30	119	3	13	126	33	127	4	62
Macon County, Ala.										
Owners	15	0	15	0	0	15	1	13	0	1
Renters	161	20	121	2	18	142	22	86	20	14
Unknown	127	20	100	3	4	108	15	62	11	20
Issaquena County, Miss.										
Owners	31	1	29	0	1	20	1	18	1	0
Renters	239	60	140	1	38	316	81	208	3	24
Unknown	118	28	82	1	7	340	77	211	10	42

been married and in some cases often married. They have often broken marital ties and remarried without a legal divorce. On a plantation in Alabama a woman near sixty, who worked a "one-horse farm" with her son, recounted the story of her three marriages. Her father, who had been "raised up under the hard task of slavery," had sent her as far as the fourth grade. Then her marriage career began. Of the first two husbands she said:

Me and him separated and he divorced me. Me and the second one got married and come down here. Then he fought me when this boy [her son] was six months old. We fought like cats and dogs. One night I had to call Uncle R —— P ——. He asked me for his 'vorce and I gi' it to him. I just wrote him a "scrip." I got a man to write it for him.

Her third husband, who had been dead seven years, died, according to her testimony, of high blood pressure, leakage of the heart, and kidney trouble. Another old woman had a similar story to tell. When she announced "all my children done married off," she was speaking of two sets of children — one by her husband and another by the man with whom she lived after having "divorced" her husband. According to her story, her husband had told her that he wanted a divorce, and she had replied that he was welcome to it. But as to the reason back of the breaking of the marriage bond, she explained: "He didn't work to suit me, and I didn't work to suit him."

This last naïve statement concerning divorce reveals much in regard to the nature of marriage and its dissolution among these simple folk. Among these people we come face to face with marriage as it probably existed in the early stages of social development. Marriage as an institution rooted in the mores does not exist in many places. Where it has developed any degree of permanency and the couples are seemingly bound by conjugal affection, more fundamental interests than mere sentiment have been responsible in the beginning for the continuance of the association in marriage. When one woman was asked whether she was married, her reply was: "Me and my husband parted so long, done forget I was married." What marriage means to many of these women was expressed by a woman who spoke of herself as "Miss," although she had been married twice, and wanted another husband to help her work. Her first husband, whom she had married when she was fifteen, was killed by lightning after they had been together twelve years. A second husband had been dead two years, and at present she was making a living by "hoeing and fertilizing" on a place that, she said, "they tells me it was here in slavery times." Her only idea indicating preference in regard to a husband was that he must be dark, for "if he is most too light, he looks too much like white folks." But the main factor in regard to the partner in marriage was that he should co-operate with her in farming. As she remarked, "I am looking for someone to marry, so I can get on a farm and kinda rest." She had hoped that her son in Cleveland, who had served in France during the war, would relieve her from going into the field each day in the hot sun; but he had written that he was sick, and she had sent for him to come home.

Where marriage is regarded chiefly as a means of co-operation in the task of making a living and does not rest upon an institutional basis, it is not surprising to find some of these women speaking of "working with a man" as a sufficient explanation of their living together. This was the explanation offered by an illiterate buxom black woman of forty or more who had been farming "right round twenty-five acres" for two years with a man who was separated from his wife a quarter of a mile away because they "just couldn't get along and separated." She had had several children without being married, the only living one being cared for by her mother. But some of these cases of irregular unions are not the result of the naïve behavior of simple folk. We have seen in the preceding chapter how in one case both the parents of the unmarried mother and the unmarried mother herself attempted to represent the man in the house as a "boarder."[8] Wherever we find this consciousness of the violation of the dominant mores or a certain sophistication, the couples will attempt to represent their union as some socially approved relationship or as conventional marriage. This was the case with a brickmason, forty-seven, who had been educated at Tuskegee Institute. He was living with a woman, twenty-two, on a "patch" of five acres for which they were paying sixty dollars rental a year. The woman was a mulatto who thought that she had some Indian blood. Her mother was farming with eight children, while her father had deserted the mother and gone to Detroit. This irregular union was especially convenient for the man, since it was outside the public opinion and censure of the group with whom he spent much of his time in town.

Some of these irregular unions are due to the association between white men and colored women. The prevalence of these associations is determined by several factors. They are found more frequently in the small towns of the South than in the isolated rural regions where large numbers of Negroes have been concentrated for nearly a century or longer. The proportion of mulattoes in the Negro population is a measure of the isolation of the Negro and of the amount of contacts between the races. In Issaquena County in the Yazoo-Mississippi Basin only 10 per cent of the families were mulattoes in 1910, while in Hertford County, North Carolina, 40 per cent of the families showed mixed blood. In Hertford County, where in 1910, as we have seen, about 35 per cent of the women who were heads of families had only irregular relations with men, the association between white men and colored women continued on a large scale for a long period after slavery. These irregular unions were generally formed by white men and mulatto women. According to our figures, 28 of the 108 women heads of families who had carried on irregular relations were mulattoes. In 1920 there were 19 mulattoes among the 47 women in this class. The change in these figures is indicative of an actual decrease in these types of associations; for in this community there has been a conscious effort on the part of the colored population to repress such associations and enforce conventional standards of conduct.[9]

A minister, who established a school in this county and has worked there nearly a half-century, related the following concerning these associations when he began his work there:

When I first came here I often heard mulatto women say that they would rather be a white man's concubine than a nigger's wife. The mulatto women and white men claimed that since the law did not allow them to marry and they had only one wife that it was all right. Conflict over this almost broke up P —— P —— Baptist Church. There was a scattering of families, many going north and passing for white. The feeling was such between mulattoes and blacks that they wanted me to place the mulattoes on the second floor and the blacks on the third floor of the school dormitory. I mixed them up in the school purposely and got black evangelists for the church.[10]

Although frequently the white man was not married and lived with his mulatto concubine as his wife, this was not invariably the case. It is also true that in many instances the economic advantages which these mulatto families enjoyed were due to the provision which the white father had made for his concubine and his mulatto children. In the following document, which was furnished by a woman who was born before emancipation, we have the case of a white man with a white family as well as a colored family. In this case, the white father made no provision for his colored family:

I wanted to be somebody and some account. I was ashamed of my black family [family background]. I hated that my mother did not marry a colored man and let me live like other folks with a father, and if he did not make much he could spend that with us. I despised my white father and his folks. I might have loved him if he had noticed and treated us like other folks. His wife died after a while, but she never fussed as I know of about his colored family. He had large children, some grown. He did not stay at home. He would have the work done by Negro slaves. He had lots of slaves and families of slaves. He must have had, with the children, fifty or seventy-five slaves in all. He was right good to them. He would eat at my mother's house. She called him "the man," and we called him "the man." He would come in at bed-time; and even before his wife died, he would come and stay with my mother all night and get up and go to his house the next morning. His children despised us and I despised them and all their folks, and I despised him. We had to work hard, get no education, and but a little to live on. He had plenty of property but didn't give mother one thing. Her uncle gave her home and field and we had to work it.[11]

The disgust which this woman felt toward her home life caused her to leave it and establish one based upon conventional moral standards. Referring to her home, she said, "It was so ugly and common that I meant to get married and leave that hateful place. It is true I loved the man I married; but I had as much in mind in getting married to leave that place as I had in marrying for love."[12]

While the association between white men and colored women in this community has been on a larger scale than in most southern communities, it is similar to many other areas in the South where there has been a long history of such associations dating from slavery. Just as the phenomenon in this community has declined because of the growing sentiment against it on the part of both blacks and whites, it has decreased in other areas of the South.

Let us turn our attention to these women in their role of mothers and as heads of their families. Some of the separated and widowed in Issaquena County in 1910 had given birth to as many as twenty children or more. Even among those who had had only irregular relations with men there were women with from ten to twelve children. But the actual number of children in these families was often small because of the numerous miscarriages and stillbirths and the high infant mortality which we find among them.[13] The following case of a woman who had two stillbirths and three miscarriages was not unusual, for some women had lost as many as nine or ten children.

This woman had no conception of her age for she thought that she might be about 20, although later she said that her husband had been dead nearly 20 years. She was living in a one-room shack, covered with sheet iron, with a daughter's illegitimate 12 year old son, and her own illegitimate 14 year old daughter. These two children were helping her to hoe and plow a "one-horse farm on halves," instead of attending school. The family was receiving an "advance" of $4.00 a month. Another daughter, who "had taken sick with a misery in the head and breast," died suddenly during the past year. The mother tried to get a doctor; but as she said concerning her landlord, "Dis white man don't gi' you doctor like talking." Although it was difficult to get a clear history of her pregnancies and children, it appeared that she had had three children while married and three illegitimate children after the death of her husband. Two of these latter children were stillborn and in addition she had three miscarriages. These stillbirths and miscarriages were evidently due to syphilitic infection since she showed a positive Wassermann reaction.

This woman and her children had been on the present location for three years; and, although she had moved away from her former landlord because she "got tired of working for nothing," she "hadn't seen a nickel for a year." With her "advance" of four dollars a month, she and the children were living on "dry meat and corn bread," with an occasional dinner of greens from her garden on Sundays. Her situation was not unlike that of many other women who were heads of families.

The struggle of these women to get a living for themselves and the children who are dependent upon them is bound up with the plantation system in the South. Most of the mothers, as we have seen (Table 2), are tenants; and many of the relatively large group of unknown home tenure are either living with their parents who are tenants or are themselves mere farm laborers. They work from year to year "on halves" or are supposed to pay a stipulated amount of cotton and receive in return an "advance" in food, and, occasionally, clothes at the store. Mothers living with their parents and mothers with grown sons to aid them are able to work larger farms than women depending solely on their own labor. Consequently, mothers with young children are generally only able to work a "patch," comprising four to six acres. The "advances" in food, which often consist of corn meal and fat bacon, are correspondingly small. They supplement this with vegetables from their gardens when the dry weather does not destroy them. As the result of this restricted diet, we find both mothers and children suffering from pellagra. Statistics indicate that eight Negroes in Macon County died in 1930 of pellagra, but we know little concerning the numerous cases that did not result in death.[14]

One could scarcely find a more depressing picture of abject poverty and human misery than that presented by a young black woman, who had had two illegitimate children by different fathers, living in a one-room shack on a plantation in Alabama not many miles from Tuskegee Institute. The father of one child was somewhere over the creek, while the father of the other was "in Montgomery or somewhere." One child had evidently died of undernourishment and neglect. The young mother sat on a broken stool in the middle of the room furnished only with an iron cot covered with filthy rags. From her dried-up breast a baby, half-strangled by whooping cough, was trying to draw nourishment. Barefooted and clothed only in a cotton waist and dress pinned about her, she was rocking the child as her body swayed listlessly to an inarticulate singsong tune. On the cold embers in the fireplace lay a skillet containing the remnants of corn bread made only with water, because the landlord had refused fat meat as a part of her "advance." That same morning he had driven her with blows from her sick child to work in the field.

Not all mothers with children depending upon them for support sink to the level of poverty and misery of the woman portrayed above. Although as tenants they receive no accounting from their landlords, many of them manage to get adequate clothing and food of sufficient variety to keep them in health. In the plantation area the relatively few owners are better off so far as the necessities of life are concerned. But ownership of land is not always an infallible sign of independence and comfort. The system of credit and the relations of the races in the former stronghold of slavery cause even landowning mothers to lead a precarious existence. In regions like the North Carolina county outside of the area where agriculture is still dominated by the plantation system, homeownership signifies much more independence and comfortable living. No single crop dominates the agricultural activities; and, consequently, even during times of economic stress there may be an abundance of food for consumption. Moreover, in situations like that in the North Carolina county, where colored women have lived with white men, the struggle for existence has been relieved by the provision which the white fathers often made for their concubines and children.

The maternal family is not held together solely by the co-operative activities incident to farming; it is also a natural organization for response. Although some women, after a brief marriage career, return to their mothers' households in order to work with them at farming, many others return to the family group for satisfactions of an emotional nature. There was, for instance, a thirty-eight-year-old woman who had left her husband after five years of marriage, because, as she said, she "got tired of staying with him" and preferred to "be with mamma and them." She was working on a "two-horse farm" with her brother, who took care of her until settlement was made at the end of the year. That she usually received nothing at the end of the year was of no importance to her as long as she lived with her mother and brother and sister. The same valuation which she placed upon the intimate and sympathetic contacts afforded by the family group was expressed by a man, when he remarked: "I'm rich; when you have mother and father, you're rich." In fact, in the relatively isolated world of these black peasants, life is still largely organized on the basis of the personal and sympathetic relations existing between the members of the various family groups.

As a rule, the mothers show a strong attachment for their children. This is evident even in the young mothers whose offspring could be mistaken for younger brothers or sisters and are frequently regarded as such. In fact, in this world where intimate and personal relations count for so much, the relation between mother and child is the most vital and is generally recognized as the most fundamental. The rumor that even a starving mother was giving up her children was received by some women as an unpardonable crime against the natural dictates of the human heart. The intense emotional interdependence between mother and child that one so often finds is encouraged by a long nursing period. According to their own testimony, some women have nursed their children until they were three or four years old. Of course, these elemental expressions of love and solicitude for their offspring are often detrimental to the welfare of the children. Many a woman who "jes' lives and wuks to feed her chillen" will give her child meat and bread when it is a few days old. This is done, they say, "to strengthen their stomachs." When one mother pointed to her overfed nineteen-year-old daughter as proof of the efficacy of such treatment, she never thought of the possible relation of such treatment to the death of ten of her children during infancy.

The dependence of the child upon the mother, who is the supreme authority in the household, often creates a solidarity of feeling and sentiment that makes daughters reluctant to leave home with their husbands and brings sons back from their wanderings. During the World War Negro soldiers who had been drafted in these rural areas and sent to camps often complained in the manner of children of being torn from their mothers. The mothers on their part show equally strong attachment for their grown sons and daughters. The reason which mothers frequently give for not permitting their daughters to marry the fathers of their illegitimate children is that they were unwilling to part with their daughters. No matter how long a wandering son or daughter has been away from home, mothers rejoice in their return; and if they hear that their children are sick, they will make great sacrifices to bring them back in order that they may have the ministrations that only a mother can give, or that they may die in the arms of the one who bore them.

As a rule, where we find mothers who do not want their children or neglect them, the sympathetic basis of family relations has been destroyed through the mobility of the population, or life and labor have made children a burden and a hardship. The isolation of these simple communities is being broken down, and "overproduction" in agriculture is sending women and girls to seek a living in town. The old relationships and traditional values are being destroyed, and new wishes, generally indicating an individualization of life-pattern, are becoming dominant. Sometimes children are left at home to be cared for by grandmothers. In spite of these changes, a large proportion of each generation of Negro mothers in these rural areas continue to bear patiently the burden of motherhood and assume responsibility for the support of their children. Their daughters still follow in their footsteps and bring their offspring to the maternal household. Then these mothers are elevated to the dignity of grandmothers, a position which gives them a peculiar authority in family relations and places upon them the responsibility for keeping kindred together.

Notes

[1] A. T. Morgan, *Yazoo; or, On the Picket Line of Freedom in the South* (Washington, D.C., 1884), p. 232.

[2] The 1930 census gave an enumeration of families with woman heads. The general situation in regard to Negro families may be briefly summarized as follows: (1) the proportion

of families with woman heads is higher in the South than in the North or West; (2) in all three sections it is higher in urban areas than in either rural-farm or rural-nonfarm areas; (3) it is higher among tenants than among owners in the urban areas but shows the opposite tendency in rural areas; and (4) it is lowest in the rural-farm areas of the North and the West.

[3] Statistical data on the families in these three counties represent approximately 100 families from each of the ten precincts in Macon County, Ala., and practically all the Negro families in Issaquena County, Miss., and Hertford County, N.C. These families were taken from the original census returns. They were not the "families" or households as defined by the census but included the following types of relationships: (1) a married couple and their children, adopted, and step-children, if any; (2) a married person whose spouse is not living at home and the children of that person, if any; (3) a widowed or divorced person and the children, if any; (4) a single man and woman who, from the information in the "relation to the head of the house" column, or from other information on the schedule, appear to be living as man and wife; and (5) a single girl who has an illegitimate child where this was clear. These families have been classified according to the color of the wife. The families in which no woman was present have been classified in the totals according to the color of the male head of the family.

[4] The writer is aware of the criticism which can be brought against the use of the census classification of blacks and mulattoes as an index to the extent of mixed-bloods among the Negroes. At the census of 1910 the term "black" included all persons who were "evidently full-blooded Negroes," while the term "mulatto" included "all other persons having some proportion or perceptible trace of Negro blood" (Bureau of the Census, *Negro Population, 1790–1915* [Washington, 1918], p. 207). The same definition of mulattoes and of full-blooded Negroes was used in 1920. Although the Census Bureau admits the uncertainty of the classification, since the distinction "depends largely upon the judgment and care employed by the enumerators," the classification probably contains on the whole as much accuracy as one could obtain.

[5] The Census Bureau made the following statement concerning the accuracy of data on marital condition of Negroes: "It is recognized that the error attaching to the return of marital condition may be considerable. In some cases males who are or have been married, but are living apart from their families, may return themselves as single; females who have never been married, especially mothers with young children dependent upon them, may return themselves as either married, widowed, or divorced; married females deserted by their husbands may return themselves as widowed, the deserting husbands returning themselves as single; widowed males may return themselves as single; divorced males may return themselves as either single or widowed; and divorced females may return themselves as widowed. Where the return of marital condition is made by a third person, who does not know the facts, it is probably commonly presumed, and in some cases erroneously, that persons living apart from their families, especially males, are single. The result of these errors in combination would be, as regards the classification of males, overstatement of the number single and understatement of the number married, widowed, or divorced, and as regards the classification of females, overstatement of the number married, and widowed, and understatement of the number single or divorced" (*Negro Population, 1790–1915,* p. 235).

[6] Concerning the accuracy of statistics on the widowed in the federal enumeration of 1900, the Census Bureau states that "among 1,000 negroes at least 15 years of age, 345 are single and 539 are married, while among 1,000 whites of the same age, 14 more are single and 20 more are married, the total difference of 34 being almost balanced by the fact that among the negroes 31 more in each 1,000 are widowed than among the whites. The relatively short life of the negro population would lead one to expect a rather large number in this class, but the difference between the two races seems to be too great to be accounted for in that way. One is disposed to believe that no small number of the 565,340 negro widows or widowers were persons whose conjugal relations had been ended by separation rather than by death and whose conjugal condition, therefore, has been inaccurately described" (Bureau of the Census, *Negroes in the United States* [Bull. 8 (Washington, 1904)], p. 48).

[7] Nearly a half-century ago Bruce made the same observations concerning the breaking of family ties among the plantation Negroes: "The instance very frequently occurs of a negro

who has deserted his wife in one county getting, by false statements, a license to marry in another county, and there establishing a new home with as much coolness as if he had been single when he obtained the second license; but so accustomed are the whites to the sexual freedom of their former slaves that when it comes to their ears that a certain negro who resides in their vicinity has two wives to whom he is legally bound, living, the rumor, however capable of substantial proof, is almost always winked at or not considered worthy of investigation" (Phillip A. Bruce, *The Plantation Negro as a Freeman* [New York, 1889], p. 22).

⁸ Bishop Coppin related the following concerning marital relations after the Civil War and attempts on the part of the church to break up such irregular unions: "Then there were other kinds of irregular living by Church members when there was no one to prefer 'charges and complaints,' and bring the transgressor to book. A man might be a member of the Church, and yet be 'stopping' with a woman to whom he was not married. Or, in the irregular union, the woman might be the Church member. These are cases where even common law marriage was not claimed. Both parties going for single. The man just a 'star boarder.' But, in this general clean up at Friendship, under the new regime, such parties had to choose between getting married, or facing charges for immoral conduct. Dear old Friendship now became the Ecclesiastical Court House, as well as the Church. For any of the above named lapses, hitherto unnoticed, a member was liable at any 'Quarterly Meeting' to be called to face charges and complaints" (L. J. Coppin, *Unwritten History* [Philadelphia, 1920], pp. 126–27).

⁹ Bishop Coppin (*op. cit.*, pp. 130–31) recites the following typical case in which a white man forced the Negro community to accept his colored concubine: "The father being a man of means and influence, defied public sentiment, and held family number one in servile submission. But his influence did not stop there; he would have it understood that his mistress must not be Churched, but rather must be regarded as a leading spirit at the Church to which she belonged, and which he gave her means to liberally support. If he had power enough to enslave his own legitimate family, forcing even the wife into unwilling silence, and besides, to so maintain himself in society as to prevent a general protest, it is not to be wondered at, that the Colored Community, dependent, perilous, would also hold its peace."

¹⁰ Manuscript document.

¹¹ Manuscript document.

¹² Manuscript document.

¹³ A study of Negroes on a plantation in Louisiana in the early part of the present century showed the following: "Of these 80 women 58 have had children. These 58 have had 268 children, or an average of 4.62 per woman, of which 154, or 57.5 per cent, are still living. In 34 cases out of 58, or 59 per cent, the first child is living. All those who were questioned on this subject, and who have lived with the Negroes all their lives, stated that the birth rate is diminishing rapidly and that stillbirths and miscarriages are becoming much more common" (J. Bradford Laws, *The Negroes of Cinclaire Central Factory and Calumet Plantation* [Louisiana Department of Labor Bull. 38 (January, 1902)], p. 103).

¹⁴ See Elbridge Sibley, *Differential Mortality in Tennessee* (Nashville, Tenn., 1930), pp. 91–95, concerning high death-rates among Negroes from pellagra in the cotton areas of Tennessee.

The Question of African Survivals

2

On West African Influences

Melville J. Herskovits

It is well recognized that Negro family structure in the United States is different from the family organization of the white majority. Outstanding are its higher illegitimacy rate and the particular role played by the mother. Certain other elements in Negro social organization also make it distinctive, and these will be considered later; but for the moment the more prominent characteristics must be treated in terms of the cognate African sanctions which make them normal, rather than abnormal, and go far in aiding us to comprehend what must otherwise, after the conventional manner, be regarded as aberrant aspects of the family institution.

At the outset, it is necessary to dismiss the legal implications of the term "illegitimate" and to recognize the sociological reality underlying an operational definition of the family as a socially sanctioned mating. In this case, illegitimacy is restricted to those births which are held outside the limits of accepted practice. The situation in the West Indies, projected against the African background of marriage rites and family structure, will here as elsewhere make for clarity. In West Africa, it will be remembered, preliminaries to marriage include negotiations between the families of the two contracting parties to assure all concerned that the young man and woman are ready for marriage, that they are competent to assume their obligations under it, and that no taboos in terms of closeness of actual or putative relationship stand in the way of the match. This done, the young man (and in some tribes the young woman) assumes certain obligations toward his prospective father- and mother-in-law, which in many instances continue after marriage. In all this area, it is further to be recalled, the family is marked by its polygynous character, and the manner of its extension into such larger kinship groupings as the extended family and the sib.

In the New World, these forms when brought into contact with European patterns of monogamy and the absence of wider social structures based on relationship have resulted in institutions which, however, though differing considerably from one region to another, have nonetheless become stabilized in their new manifestations. Thus the elaborateness of the betrothal mechanism has in several regions been translated into ceremonies which even when European in form are essentially African in feeling. The Haitian *lettre de demande*[1] and its counterpart in the British

West Indian islands are, in their form and mode of presentation, entirely in the tradition of Africa. The survival of the polygynous marriage pattern is likewise found in Haiti in the distinction made between marriage and what is termed *plaçage,* a system whereby a woman is given a man by her father but without legal or church sanction. The similar means whereby a man and woman in the British West Indies may form regularly constituted unions without the approval of church or government is seen in the institution of the "keeper."

In Haiti, at least, actual polygyny is found, though as a practical matter it can be practiced only by men who are wealthy and powerful enough to manage their plural wives. For while it is a delicate task, at best, for a man to manage a polygynous household — even in Africa, "a man must be something of a diplomat," as one Dahomean put it — where invidious distinctions are set up between legal and free matings, the tensions become greatly heightened. Therefore, even in Haiti, actual polygyny is rare, while elsewhere in the New World it takes the form of what may be termed "progressive monogamy," not unlike that developed by the whites in recent years, though in this latter type formal divorce must precede socially sanctioned remating. Thus, while a Trinidad woman, once legally married, is always called "mistress," the fact that her union is legal does not mean that it will be any more enduring than if she were to take up housekeeping with a keeper. Nor does it often occur that she or her husband will go to the trouble of securing a legal divorce should the match be broken. They merely separate, and subsequent keepers are taken without regard for the legal niceties. The children of matings previous to or subsequent upon the "marriage" are under no social handicap, despite their legal illegitimacy as compared to those born of regularly married parents. For as elsewhere in the Negro New World, a child is rarely handicapped because of the nature of the relationship under which he was brought into the world; he stands on his own feet, and his parentage figures but slightly in establishing his social position.

Another aspect of West African social organization having important implications for the study of New World Negro kinship groupings concerns the place of women in the family. By its very nature, a polygynous system brings about a different relation between mother and children than a monogamous type — a relationship that goes far in bringing about an understanding of the so-called "matriarchal" form of the Negro family in the United States, the West Indies, and South America. The question most often raised in accounting for any African derivation of this type of family, wherein, unlike most white groups, the importance of the mother transcends that of the father, is whether this may not reflect African unilateral canons of sib descent. But while this fact may enter into the traditional residue, it is not to be regarded as playing any considerable role. In West Africa, descent is counted more often on the father's than on the mother's side and, as in other portions of the continent, the parent socially unrelated to the child is as important from a personal and sentimental point of view as is the one to whose family the child legally belongs.

What is much more important for an understanding of the sanctions underlying this "matriarchal" Negro family type is the fact that in a polygynous society a child shares his mother only with his "true" brothers and sisters — everywhere recognized as those who have the same father and the same mother — as against the fact that in the day-to-day situations of home life he shares his father with the children of other women. This means that the attachments between a mother and her child are in the main closer than those between father and children; from the point of view of the parent, it means that the responsibilities of upbringing, discipline, and supervision are much more the province of the mother than of the father. In most parts of the African areas which furnished New World slaves, the conventions of inheritance are such that a man may, and often does, make an arbitrary selection of his heir from among his sons. Because of this, there is a constant jockeying for position among his wives, who are concerned each with placing her children in the most favorable light before the common husband. The psychological realities of life within such a polygynous household have yet to be studied in detail; but that the purely human situation is such as to make the relationship between a mother and her children more intimate than that between the family head and any but perhaps one or two of the offspring of the various wives who share this common husband and father, is a point which cannot be overestimated.

Against this background the patterns of marriage and family organization prevalent in the Negro communities of the United States may be projected, so as to indicate the points in the available literature at which the influence of African tradition can be discerned. The following summary statement as concerns mating and the family in the southern county studied by C. S. Johnson is to the point:

The postponement of marriage in the section . . . does not preclude courtship, but accentuates it, and gives rise to other social adjustments based on this obvious economic necessity. The active passions of youth and late adolescence are present but without the usual formal restraints. Social behavior rooted in this situation, even when its consequences are understood, is lightly censured or excused entirely. Conditions are favorable to a great amount of sex experimentation. It cannot always be determined whether this experimentation is a phase of courtship, or love-making without the immediate intention of marriage, or recreation and diversion. Whether or not sexual intercourse is accepted as a part of courtship it is certain no one is surprised when it occurs. When pregnancy follows, pressure is not strong enough to compel the father either to marry the mother or to support the child. The girl does not lose status, nor are her chances for marrying seriously threatened. An incidental compensation for this lack of censuring public opinion is the freedom for the children thus born from warping social condemnation. There is, in a sense, no such thing as illegitimacy in this community.[2]

In studying a community such as this, we are therefore faced with a situation where acculturation has brought on disintegration — disintegration due to slavery, to the present economic background of life, and to those psychological reactions which are the concomitants of life without security. Reinterpretation of earlier, pre-American, patterns has occurred, but readjustment to normal conditions of life has been inhibited. We thus must recognize that the elasticity of the marriage concept among Negroes derives in a measure, largely unrecognized, from the need to adjust a polygynous family form to patterns based on a convention of monogamy, in a situation where this has been made the more difficult by economic and psychological complications resulting from the nature of the historical situation.

A rich documentation exists in the way of indices which point to the aspects of Negro social organization that differ strikingly from white patterns. It is only necessary to turn to the general study of the problem by Frazier[3] or such a specialized analysis as that of Reed[4] to realize to what an extent the incidence of productive matings without legal status is out of line with white practices. Yet when the emphasis laid on the proper type of marriage proposal in the Sea Islands, where there is some measure of stability in Negro society,[5] is compared with Frazier's statement that 30 per cent of the births on that island are illegitimate, it is apparent that here, at least, sanctions other than those of the European type are operative. Johnson's summary of the various forms of union found among the Negroes of Macon County, Georgia, provides further illustrative material:

Children of common-law relationships are not illegitimate, from the point of view of the community or of their stability, for many of these unions are as stable as legally sanctioned unions. They hold together for twenty or thirty years, in some cases, and lack only the sense of guilt. Again, there are competent, self-sufficient women who not only desire children but need them as later aids in the struggle for survival when their strength begins to wane, but who want neither the restriction of formal marriage nor the constant association with a husband. They get their children not so much through weakness as through their own deliberate selection of a father. Sexual unions for pleasure frequently result in children. There is a term for children born under the two latter circumstances. They are called "stolen children." "Stolen children," observed one mother, "is the best." A woman with children and who has been married though later separated from her husband may add other children to her family without benefit of formal sanctions. These are "children by the way." The youthful sex experimentation, which is in part related to the late marriages, often results in children. These are normally taken into the home of the girl's parents and treated without distinction as additions to the original family. Finally, there are the children who result from the deliberate philandering of the young men who "make foolments" on young girls. They are universally condemned. These children, as circumstances direct, may be placed with the parents of the mother or father of the child, an uncle, sister, or grandmother. They are accepted easily into the families on the simple basis of life and eventually are indistinguishable from any of the other children. Even if there were severe condemnation of true "illegitimates," confusion as to origin would tend both to mitigate some of the offenses and to obscure them all from specific condemnation.[6]

What is recognizably African in all this? The "common-law relationship" is merely a phrase for the recognition of the fact that matings not legally sanctioned may achieve enough stability to receive equal recognition with regularly performed marriages. In Africa, and in the West Indies where Africanisms persist, marriage is not a matter requiring approval of the state or of any religious body. Only consent of the families concerned is needed, while marriage rites depart from the secular only to the extent that they are directed toward obtaining the benevolent oversight of the ancestors. Therefore Negro common-law marriages in the United States conflict in no wise with earlier practices, while in so far as they require the approval of the families of the principals, they are, indeed, directly in line with African custom.

The "competent, self-sufficient women" who wish to have no husbands are of especial interest. The social and economic position of women in West Africa is such that on occasion a woman may refuse to relinquish the customary control of her children in favor of her husband, and this gives rise to special types of matings that are recognized in Dahomey and among the Yoruba, and may represent a pattern having a far wider distribution. The phenomenon of a woman "marrying" a woman,[7] which has been reported from various parts of the African continent and in a part of this same complex, testifies to the importance of a family type which might well have had the vitality necessary to make of it a basis for the kind of behavior outlined in the case of the "self-sufficient" woman who, in the United States, desires children but declines to share them with a husband. The same traditional basis exists for "children by the way," those offspring of women, once married, by men other than their husbands.

In the community studied by Powdermaker, types of mating and attitudes toward them have likewise been differentiated:

For this group, there are three ways in which a man and woman may live together: licensed marriage, solemnized by a ceremony, usually in a church; common-law marriage; and temporary association, not regarded as marriage. For the large majority of the households the form is common-law marriage, which is legally valid in Mississippi. Of the remainder, temporary matings are probably more numerous than licensed marriages. Most of the latter are in the upper and the upper middle class. Temporary mating is most easily countenanced in the lower class, though it is not uncommon in the middle class. A licensed marriage in the lower or lower middle class is extremely rare. A common-law marriage in the upper class is even more so; and in this class for two people to live together with no pretense of real marriage would be extremely shocking.[8]

The approach to this problem through the analysis of mores which differ according to classes within the Negro community is especially pertinent, for these classes represent differing degrees of acculturation to majority patterns. This being the case, then the variations in attitude and behavior concerning the family from one class to another reflect differentials in accommodation in so far as this institution is concerned.

This is made even clearer by the discussion of attitudes toward divorce:

> Even the few members of the upper middle class who are regularly married do not as a rule consider it necessary to go through court procedure in order to be divorced from a former mate and free to marry another. It is not regarded as immoral to remarry without securing a divorce, since in this class the marriage license is not a matter of morals, and marriage itself is highly informal. Divorce proceedings are expensive, and involve dealing with a white court, which no Negro chooses if he can avoid them. Thus a legal divorce becomes something more than a luxury; it savors of pretension and extravagance.[9]

Here is evidence of lag under acculturation. Sanctioned divorce is a comparatively recent introduction into white mores, and has been superimposed upon a complex of quasi-puritanical religious social prohibitions. This antecedent patterning being absent from aboriginal and early New World Negro conventions, the attitude toward legal divorce as a pretension and an extravagance is understandable. For under Negro conventions, operative in Africa and in the New World generally, there is little social disapprobation of divorce. Consequently, in terms of a carry-over of this point of view, legal divorce is needless, since separation and subsequent remating (if not remarriage) is taken more or less for granted.

The other major difference between Negro family organization and that of the white majority touches on the position of women within the family. So important is the role of the woman when compared to that of the man, in terms of common American convention, that the adjective "matriarchal" has come to be employed in recent years when describing this family type. Statistical reports bear out common observation concerning the phenomenon:

> The 1930 census showed a larger proportion of families with women heads among Negroes than among whites in both rural and urban areas. Moreover, it also appeared that in the cities a larger proportion of Negro families were under the authority of the woman than in the rural areas. In the rural non-farm areas of the southern states from 15 to 25 per cent of the Negro families were without male heads; while in the rural-farm areas the proportion ranged from 3 to 15 per cent. In the rural-farm areas tenant families had a much smaller proportion with woman heads than owners, except in those states where a modified form of plantation regime is the dominant type of farming. For example, in the rural-farm area of Alabama between 13 and 14 per cent of both tenant and owner families were without male heads.[10]

Some further statistics are also relevant:

> In southern cities the disparity between whites and Negroes in respect to the proportion of families with woman heads is much greater. In the twenty-three

southern cities with a population of 100,000 or more in 1930, from a fifth to a third of all Negro families had a female head. However, in most of these southern cities, the difference between owner and tenant Negro families in this regard was much greater than in northern cities.[11]

Of the several classifications of Negro family types which take the position of the woman into account, two may be cited. The first concerns the family as it exists at the present time among the Negro urban workers:

The status of husband and wife in the black worker's family assumes roughly three patterns. Naturally, among the relatively large percentage of families with women heads, the woman occupies a dominant position. But, because of the traditional role of the black wife as a contributor to the support of the family, she continues to occupy a position of authority and is not completely subordinate to masculine authority even in those families where the man is present. . . . The entrance of the black worker in industry where he has earned comparatively good wages has enabled the black worker's wife to remain at home. Therefore, the authority of the father in the family has been strengthened, and the wife has lost some of her authority in family matters. . . . Wives as well as children are completely subject to the will of the male head. However, especially in southern cities, the black worker's authority in his family may be challenged by his mother-in-law.[12]

Johnson has differentiated family types in the rural region studied by him into another set of categories. Noting the fact that in terms of the commonly accepted pattern wherein the father is head of the family, "the families of this area are . . . considerably atypical," since, "in the first place, the role of the mother is of much greater importance than in the more familiar American group," he goes on to distinguish three kinds of families. First come those "which are fairly stable" and are "sensitive to certain patterns of respectability"; then there are those termed "artificial quasi-families" that "have the semblance of a normal and natural family, and function as one," except that "the members of the group are drawn into it by various circumstances rather than being a product of the original union"; and finally the form is found where "the male head remains constant while other types of relationship, including a succession of wives and their children by him, shift around him."[13] In addition to these, however, are the families headed by women:

The numbers of households with old women as heads and large numbers of children, although of irregular structure, is sufficiently important to be classed as a type. . . . The oldest generation is the least mobile, the children of these in the active ages move about freely and often find their own immediate offspring, while young, a burden, as they move between plantations. Marriages and remarriages bring increasing numbers of children who may be a burden to the new husband or a hindrance to the mother if she must become a wage-earner. The simplest expedient is to leave them with an older parent to rear. This is usually intended as a temporary measure, but it most often ends in the establishment of a permanent household as direct parental support dwindles down. The responsibility is accepted as a matter of course by the older woman and she thereafter employs her wits to keep the artificial family going.[14]

Powdermaker likewise notes the elasticity of families headed by women, and indicates how congenial this pattern is to Negroes living in various social and environmental settings:

The personnel of these matriarchal families is variable and even casual. Stepchildren, illegitimate children, adopted children, mingle with the children of the house. No matter how small or crowded the home is, there is always room for a stray child, an elderly grandmother, an indigent aunt, a homeless friend. . . . The pattern of flexibility, however, expanding and contracting the household according to need, is not restricted to the poorer and more crowded homes. A typical family of the upper middle class is headed by a prosperous widow, who in her early twenties married a man over sixty years old. He was considered very wealthy and had been married several times before. The household now includes his widow's eleven-year-old daughter (an illegitimate child born before she met her husband), the dead husband's granddaughter by one of his early marriages, and the granddaughter's two children, two and three years old. The granddaughter was married but is divorced from her husband. Everyone in the household carries the same family name.[15]

It is evident that this so-called "maternal" family of the Negro is a marked deviant from what is regarded as conventional by the white majority. Yet it must not be forgotten that the economic and social role of the man in Negro society is of the utmost significance in rounding out the picture of Negro social life. Though important from the point of view of the search for Africanisms, interest in the position of women in the family must not obscure perspective so as to preclude the incidence and role of those families wherein the common American pattern is followed. Despite the place of women in the West African family, the unit holds a prominent place for the husband and father who, as head of the polygynous group, is the final authority over its members, sharing fully in all those obligations which the family must meet if it is to survive and hold its place in the stable society of which it forms a part.

With this point in mind, certain further special characteristics of the Negro family may be considered before the causes which may best account for its place in Negro life are analyzed. Outstanding among these is the fact that an older woman frequently gives the group its unity and coherence. Frazier indicates the following sanctions in explaining the place of such elderly females in Negro families:

The Negro grandmother's importance is due to the fact not only that she has been the "oldest head" in a maternal family organization but also to her position as "granny" or midwife among a simple peasant folk. As the repository of folk wisdom concerning the inscrutable ways of nature, the grandmother has been depended upon by mothers to ease the pains of childbirth and ward off the dangers of ill luck. Children acknowledge their indebtedness to her for assuring them, during the crisis of birth, a safe entrance into the world. Even grown men and women refer to her as a second mother and sometimes show the same deference and respect for her that they accord their own mothers.[16]

The question whether or not an explanation of the importance of old women in these terms is valid may be deferred for the moment; that it is not only among the "simple peasant folk" of the countryside that she wields her power but in the city as well is to be seen from the following:

The Negro grandmother has not ceased to watch over the destiny of the Negro families as they have moved in ever increasing numbers to the cities during the present century. For example, she was present in 61 of the families of 342 junior high school students in Nashville. In 25 of these a grandfather was also present. But in 24 of the remaining 36 families, we find her in 8 families with only the mother of the children, in 7 with only the father, and in 9 she was the only adult member.[17]

How large these family groups headed by old women may be, and from how many sources their members may be drawn, is to be seen in the description of one such family given by Powdermaker:

A larger household is presided over by a woman of seventy-five. She has had two husbands, both dead now, and nine children, two of them born before she met her first husband. Her second husband had seven children by a previous marriage. She brought up three of them. Living with her now are the son and daughter of her second husband's daughter by a previous marriage. Each of these step-grand-children is married. The two young couples pay no rent, but "board" themselves. In the house also is a nine-year-old boy, the illegitimate child of a granddaughter. After this child was born, his mother left his father and went north with another man. The grandmother paid the railroad fare for the child to be sent back to Mississippi.[18]

The fact, likewise noted by Powdermaker, that "among Negroes household and family are on the whole considered synonymous" indicates how far flexibility may go; only boarderes were excluded from membership in the families studied by her.

What are the causes which, in the United States, have brought into being a type of family organization that is so distinctive when compared with the common family pattern? The preceding discussion makes it clear that no single reason will account for its establishment and persistence. Explanations based on assumptions of a theoretical nature concerning the origin of the human family may be dismissed out of hand, since the validity of such propositions has been successfully challenged many times both on methodological and on historical grounds. Thus when Puckett points out that,

It is also rather noticeable that in the Negro folk-songs, mother and child are frequently sung of, but seldom father — possibly pointing back to the African love for the mother and the uncertainty and slight consideration of fatherhood . . .[19]

the only possible comment is that his conception of African attitudes and the facts of African family life is false in the light of known facts. Similarly, when Frazier speaks of the "maternal family" as representing "in its purest and most primitive manifestation a natural family group similar to what Briffault has described as the original or earliest form of the human family,"[20] he is merely repeating poor anthropology.

One of the most popular explanations of the aberrant forms taken by the Negro family is by reference to the experience of slavery. A less extreme example of this position, conventionally phrased, is to be found in Johnson's work. Noting that the role of the mother is of "much greater importance than that in the more familiar American group," he goes on to state:

This has some explanation in the slave origins of these families. Children usually remained with the mother; the father was incidental and could very easily be sold away. The role of mother could be extended to that of "mammy" for the children of white families.[21]

Frazier has presented this point of view at greater length. One statement reads:

We have spoken of the mother as the mistress of the cabin and as the head of the family. . . . Not only did she have a more fundamental interest in her children than the father but, as a worker and a free agent, except where the master's will was concerned, she developed a spirit of independence and a keen sense of her personal rights.[22]

"In spite of the numerous separations," it is stated, "the slave mother and her children, especially those under ten, were treated as a group";[23] while, "because of the dependence of the children upon the mother it appears that the mother and smaller children were sold together."[24] To make the point, slave advertisements such as the following are cited:

A Wench, complete cook, washer and ironer, and her four children — a Boy 12, another 9, a Girl 5 that sews; and a Girl about 4 years old. Another family — a Wench, complete washer and ironer, and her Daughter, 14 years old, accustomed to the house.[25]

These citations are not made to suggest that due attention has not been paid to the place of the father in the slave family, though it is undoubtedly true that he has received less study than has the mother in research into the derivation of present-day family types among the Negroes. The fact of the matter, however, is that the roles of both parents were individually determined, varying not only from region to region and plantation to plantation, but also being affected by the reactions of individual personalities on one another. Not only was the father a significant factor during slaving, but a reading of the documents will reveal how the selling of children — even very young children — away from their mothers is stressed again and again as one of the most anguishing aspects of the slave trade. Whether in the case of newly arrived Negroes sold from the slave ships or of slaves born in this country and sold from the plantations, there was not the slightest guarantee that a mother would not be separated from her children. The impression obtained from the contemporary accounts, indeed, is that the chances were perhaps more than even that separation would occur. This means, therefore, that, though the mechanism ordinarily envisaged in establishing this "maternal" family was operative to some degeee, the role of slavery cannot be considered as having been quite as important as has been assumed.

The total economic situation of the Negro was another active force in establishing and maintaining the "maternal" family type. No considerable amount of data are available as to the inner economic organization of Negro families, but the forms of Negro family life themselves suggest that the female members of such families, and especially the elderly women, exercise appreciable control over economic resources. That the economic role of the women not only makes of them managers but also contributors whose earnings are important assets is likewise apparent. This economic aspect of their position is described by Johnson in the following terms:

The situation of economic dependence of women in cities is reversed in this community, and is reflected rather strikingly in the economic independence on the part of the Negro women in the country. Their earning power is not very much less than that of the men, and for those who do not plan independent work there is greater security in their own family organization where many hands contribute to the raising of cotton and of food than there is for them alone with a young and inexperienced husband.[26]

In Mississippi the following obtains in plantation families:

In many cases the woman is the sole breadwinner. Often there is no man in the household at all. In a number of instances, elderly women in their seventies and their middle-aged daughters, with or without children and often without husbands, form one household with the old woman as head.[27]

It is to be expected that such a situation will be reflected in property ownership:

In this town of a little more than three thousand inhabitants, . . . 202 colored people own property. The assessed value for the majority of these holdings ranges from $300 to $600. Of the 202 owners, 100 are men, owning property valued at $61,250 and 93 are women, with holdings valued at $57,460. Nine men and women own jointly property totaling $3280 in value. Among the Whites also, about half the owners are women. When White women are owners, it usually means that a man has put his property in his wife's name so that it cannot be touched if he gets into difficulty. Among the Negroes, many women bought the property themselves, with their own earnings.[28]

Of the high proportion of holdings by men in the more favored socio-economic group of Negroes, it is stated, "if more property were owned by Negroes in the lower strata, there would probably be a higher percentage of female ownership." Yet as it is, the percentage would seem to be sufficiently high in terms of current American economic patterns, especially since, as stated, Negro women actually bought and hold their property for themselves rather than for their husbands, as is the common case among the whites.

The absence of any reference to African background in the citations concerning Negro families headed by women is merely another instance of the tendency to overlook the fact that the Negro was the carrier of a preslavery tradition. It is in the writings dealing with this aspect of Negro life that we find truncated history in its most positive expression, since in this field the existence of an African past has been recognized only in terms of such denials of its vitality as were cited in the opening pages of this work. Yet the aspects of Negro family which diverge most strikingly from patterns of the white majority are seen to deviate in the direction of resemblances to West African family life.

It cannot be regarded only as coincidence that such specialized features of Negro family life in the United States as the role of women in focusing the sentiment that gives the family unit its psychological coherence, or their place in maintaining the economic stability essential to survival, correspond closely to similar facets of West African social structure. And this becomes the more apparent when we investigate the inner aspects of the family structure of Negroes in the New World outside the United States. Though everywhere the father has his place, the tradition of paternal control and the function of the father as sole or principal provider essential to the European pattern is deviated from. In the coastal region of the Guianas, for example, the mother and grandmother are essentially the mainstays of the primary relationship group. A man obtains his soul from his father, but his affections and his place in society are derived from his mother; a person's home is his mother's, and though matings often endure, a man's primary affiliation is to the maternal line. In Trinidad, Jamaica, the Virgin Islands, or elsewhere in the Caribbean, should parents separate, the children characteristically remain with their mother, visiting their father from time to time if they stay on good terms with him. The woman here is likewise an important factor in the economic scene. The open-air market is the effective agent in the retail distributive process, and business, as in West Africa, is principally in the hands of women. It is customary for them to handle the family resources, and their economic independence as traders makes for their personal independence, something which, within the family, gives them power such as is denied to women who, in accordance with the prevalent European custom, are dependent upon their husbands for support. In both West Africa and the West Indies the women, holding their economic destinies in their own hands, are fully capable of going their own ways if their husbands displease them; not being hampered by any conception of marriage as an ultimate commitment, separation is easily effected and a consequent fluidity in family personnel such as has been noted in the preceding pages of this section results. Now if to this complex is added the tradition of a sentimental attachment to the mother, derived from the situation within the polygynous households of West Africa, ample justification appears for holding that the derivations given for Negro family life by most students of the Negro family in the United States present serious gaps.

As in the case of most other aspects of Negro life, the problem becomes one of evaluating multiple forces rather than placing reliance on simpler explanations. From the point of view of the search for Africanisms, the status of the Negro family at present is thus to be regarded as the result of the play of various forces in the New World experience of the Negro, projected against a background of aboriginal tradition. Slavery did not cause the "maternal" family; but it tended to continue certain elements in the cultural endowment brought to the New World by the Negroes. The feeling between mother and children was reinforced when the father was sold away from the rest of the family; where he was not, he continued life in a way that tended to consolidate the obligations assumed by him in the integrated societies of Africa as these obligations were reshaped to fit the monogamic, paternalistic pattern of the white masters. That the plantation system did not differentiate between the sexes in exploiting slave labor tended, again, to reinforce the tradition of the part played by women in the tribal economics.

Furthermore, these African sanctions have been encouraged by the position of the Negro since freedom. As underprivileged members of society, it has been necessary for Negroes to continue calling on all the labor resources in their families if the group was to survive; and this strengthened woman's economic independence. In a society fashioned like that of the United States, economic independence for women means sexual independence, as is evidenced by the personal lives of white women from the upper socio-economic levels of society. This convention thus fed back into the tradition of the family organized about and headed by women, continuing and reinforcing it as time went on. And it is for these reasons that those aspects of Negro family life that depart from majority patterns are to be regarded as residues of African custom. Families of this kind are not African, it is true; they are, however, important as comprehending certain African survivals. For they not only illustrate the tenacity of the traditions of Africa under the changed conditions of New World life, but also in larger perspective indicate how, in the acculturative situation, elements new to aboriginal custom can reinforce old traditions, while at the same time helping to accommodate a people to a setting far different from that of their original milieu.

It will be recalled that at the outset of this section it was stated that other survivals than those to which attention has been given thus far are betokened by certain facts mentioned more or less in passing in the literature. One of these concerns the size of the relationship group. The African immediate family, consisting of a father, his wives, and their children, is but a part of a larger unit. This immediate family is generally recognized by Africanists as belonging to a local relationship group termed the "extended family," while a series of these extended families, in turn, comprise the matrilineal or patrilineal sibs, often totemic in sanction, which are the effective agents in administering the controls of the ancestral cult.

That such larger relationship groupings might actually exist in the United States was indicated during the course of a study of the physical anthropology of Mississippi Negroes, where, because of the emphasis placed on the genetic aspects of the problem being studied, entire families were measured wherever possible.[29] In the town of Amory (Monroe County) and its surrounding country, 639 persons representing 171 families were studied, the word "family" in this context signifying those standing in primary biological relationship — parents, children, and grandchildren, but not collateral relatives. How large the kinship units of wider scope are found to be in this area, however, is indicated by one group of related immediate families which comprised 141 individuals actually measured. Such matters as how many more persons this particular unit includes and its sociological implications cannot be stated, since no opportunity to probe its cultural significance has presented itself. The mere fact that a feeling of kinship as widespread as this exists among a group whose ancestors were carriers of a tradition wherein the larger relationship units are as important as in Africa does, however, give this case importance as a lead for future investigation.

Instances of similarly extensive relationship groupings are occasionally encountered in the literature. A description of one of these corresponds in almost every detail to the pattern of the extended family in West African patrilineal tribes:

The other community, composed of black families who boast of pure African ancestry, grew out of a family of five brothers, former slaves, and is known as "Blacktown," after the name of the family. Although the traditions of this community do not go back as far as those of Whitetown, the group has exhibited considerable pride in its heritage and has developed as an exclusive community under the discipline of the oldest male in the family. The founder of the community, the father of our informant, was reared in the house of his master. . . . The boundaries of the present community are practically the same as those of the old plantation, a part of which is rented. . . . But most of the land is owned by this Negro family. The oldest of the five brothers was, until his death fifteen years ago, the acknowledged head of the settlement. At present the next oldest brother is recognized as the head of the community. His two sons, one of whom was our informant, have never divided their 138 acres. He and his three brothers, with their children numbering between forty and fifty and their numerous grandchildren, are living in the settlement. Twelve of their children have left the county, and three are living in a near-by town. Our informant left the community thirty-four years ago and worked at a hotel in Boston and as a longshoreman in Philadelphia, but returned after five years away because he was needed by the old folks and longed for the association of his people. One of the sons of the five brothers who founded the settlement is both the teacher of the school and pastor of the church which serve the needs of the settlement.[30]

This passage is to be compared with the account of the formation and later constitution of the Dahomean "collectivity" and extended family.[31] In such matters as the inheritance of headship from the eldest sibling to his next in line, in the retained identity of the family land as a part of the mechanism making for retention of identity by the relationship group itself, and in the relatively small proportion of members who leave their group, immediate correspondences will be discerned.

Like the neighboring "Whitetown" — both these terms are fictitious, but the communities are presumably located in Virginia — sanctions and controls are to be seen such as mark off the African extended family group, succession from elder brother to younger being especially striking in this regard. This kind of "extended" family is also found among the racially mixed stock who, descended from freed Negroes, comprise the population of Whitetown:

At present there are in the settlement ten children and thirty grandchildren of our informant. His brother, who also lives in the settlement, has six children and one grandchild. Working under the control and direction of the head of the settlement, the children and grandchildren raise cotton, corn, peanuts, peas and tobacco. In this isolated community with its own school this family has lived for over a century. . . . These closely knit families have been kept under the rigorous discipline of the older members and still have scarcely any intercourse with the black people in the county.[32]

Botume writes of the strangeness to her, a white northerner, of this tradition of extended familial affiliation in the Sea Islands during the Civil War:

It was months before I learned their family relations. The terms "bubber" for brother, and "titty" for sister, with "nanna" for mother and "mother" for grandmother, and father for all leaders in church and society, were so generally used, I was forced to believe that they all belonged to one immense family.[33]

It is not unreasonable to suppose that this passage is indicative of survival, on the islands, of the classificatory terminology so widely employed in West Africa, though this, as well as the entire problem of the wider ramifications of kinship among Negroes in the United States, remains for future research. On the basis of such data as have been cited, however, African tradition must in the meantime be held as prominent among those forces which made for the existence of a sense of kinship among Negroes that is active over a far wider range of relationship than among whites.

What vestiges of totemic belief have persisted in the United States cannot be said. Certainly no relationship groups among Negroes claiming descent from some animal, plant, or natural phenomenon, in the classic manner of this institution, have been noted in the literature. But what may be termed the "feel" given by certain attitudes toward food may perhaps be indicative of a certain degree of retention of this African concept. Firsthand inquiry among Negroes has brought to light a surprising number of cases where a certain kind of meat — veal, pork, and lamb among others — is not eaten by a given person. Inquiry usually elicits the response, "It doesn't agree with me," and only in one or two instances did the inhibition seem to extend to relatives. Yet this fact that violation of a personal food taboo derived from the totemic animal in West Africa and in Dutch Guiana is held to bring on illness, especially skin eruptions, strikes one immediately as at least an interesting coincidence and perhaps as a hint toward a survival deriving from this element in African social organization, since it is so completely foreign to European patterns. Puckett records a statement published by Bergen in 1899 that, "Some Negroes will not eat lamb because the lamb represents Christ";[34] and this may be an instance of that syncretism which is so fundamental a mechanism in the acculturative process undergone by New World Negroes. Systematic inquiry concerning kinds of foods not eaten by given persons, the reasons or rationalizations which explain these avoidances, and particularly whether or not such taboos are held by entire families and if so, how they are transmitted, are badly needed. Such data, when available, should provide information which will tell whether or not this one aspect of an important African belief has had the strength to survive, in no matter how distorted a form, even where contact with European custom has been greatest and retention of aboriginal custom made most difficult.

Before considering other survivals of African culture, a point which touches upon certain practical implications of the materials dealt with in this section may be mentioned. At the outset of this discussion, it was noted that stress on values peculiar to Euro-American tradition has tended seriously to derogate the customary usages of Negroes which depart from the modes of life accepted by the majority. It was also pointed out that when the logical conclusions to be drawn from the position taken are accepted by Negroes themselves, this tends to destroy such sanctions as the Negroes may have developed, and injects certain added psychological difficulties into a situation that is at best difficult enough. Comment along these lines becomes especially pertinent when one encounters a passage such as the following, where the disavowal of a cultural heritage is emphasized by the assumptions mirrored in its phrases:

These settlements . . . of . . . higher economic status . . . and . . . deeply rooted patriarchal family traditions . . . represent the highest development of a moral order and a sacred society among the rural Negro population. This development has been possible because economic conditions have permitted . . . germs of culture, which have been picked up by Negro families, to take root and grow.[35]

The community referred to does not matter; it is the use of a figure which envisages a people "picking up" "germs of culture," to name but one such to be found in these lines, that gives us pause. To accept as "moral" only those values held moral by the whites, to regard as "culture" only those practices that have the sanctions of a European past, is a contributory factor in the process of devaluation, if only because to draw continually such conclusions has so cumulative an effect. A people without a past are a people who lack an anchor in the present. And recognition of this is essential if the psychological foundations of the interracial situation in this country are to be probed for their fullest significance, and proper and effective correctives for its stresses are to be achieved.

Notes

[1] Herskovits, *Life in a Haitian Valley,* pp. 107 ff., 258 ff.

[2] *Shadow of the Plantation,* p. 49.

[3] *The Negro Family in the United States,* pp. 109 f., 343 ff., 620 ff.

[4] *Negro Illegitimacy in New York City,* New York, 1926, *passim.*

[5] As indicated, for example, by Parsons, *Folk-Lore of the Sea Islands, South Carolina,* p. 206.

[6] *Shadow of the Plantation,* pp. 66 f.

[7] M. J. Herskovits, "A Note on 'Woman Marriage' in Dahomey," *Africa,* 10: 335–341, 1937.

[8] *After Freedom,* p. 149.

[9] *Ibid.,* pp. 156 ff.

[10] Frazier, *The Negro Family in the United States,* pp. 126 f.

[11] *Ibid.,* p. 326.

[12] *Ibid.,* pp. 461. f.

[13] *Shadow of the Plantation,* pp. 29, 32 f., 39 f.

[14] *Ibid.,* p. 37.

[15] *After Freedom,* pp. 146 f.

[16] *The Negro Family in the United States,* p. 153.

[17] *Ibid.,* p. 158.

[18] *After Freedom,* p. 147.

[19] *Folk Beliefs of the Southern Negro,* p. 23.

[20] "Tradition and Patterns of Negro Family Life in the United States," p. 198.

[21] *Shadow of the Plantation,* p. 29.

[22] *The Negro Family in the United States,* pp. 57 f.

[23] *Ibid.,* p. 55.

[24] "The Negro Slave Family," p. 234.

[25] *Ibid.*

[26] *Shadow of the Plantation,* pp. 48 f.

[27] Powdermaker, *After Freedom,* p. 146.

[28] *Ibid.,* p. 127.

[29] M. J. Herskovits, V. K. Cameron, and Harriet Smith, "The Physical Form of Mississippi Negroes," *American Journal of Physical Anthropology,* 16:193–201, 1931.

[30] Frazier, *The Negro Family in the United States,* pp. 258 f.

[31] Herskovits, *Dahomey,* Vol. I, pp. 139 ff.

[32] Frazier, *op. cit.,* pp. 257 f.

[33] *First Days amongst the Contrabands,* p. 48.

[34] *Folk Beliefs of the Southern Negro,* p. 559; the reference made is to Fanny D. Bergen, "Animal and Plant Lore," *Mem. Amer. Folk-Lore Society,* Vol. VII, 1899, p. 84.

[35] Frazier, *op. cit.,* p. 259.

The Frazier Thesis Applied

3

The Family in the Plantation South

Charles S. Johnson

Courtship and Marriage

Before a child reaches the age of twelve there are duties demanding, with the same insistence felt by his parents, his presence in the field. The routine of cotton cultivation has lent itself with a fatal pliancy to a division of labor capable of extension with each stage of growth from childhood to maturity. Where there are children there is always work to be done to earn the bare living they require. Where there are no children it is less possible to perform all the tasks required to earn enough to survive. Herein lies a first disorganizing factor in the family organization of the community. Immediate as well as remote survival imposes relentless demand for children's labor and the exactions of an economic system of ever increasing severity impose a forced growth upon the children from the moment of birth. Every aspect of the life urges to the earliest possible attainment of adulthood. Where there is early maturity we have come to expect early marriages, especially for women. There is, as a rule, among Negro women generally a greater tendency to early marriage than among white families, and this tendency is accentuated in cities. In southern cities it is much more pronounced than in southern rural areas, but in this special group studied the tendency is considerably less than in other southern rural areas.

The trend in this community runs in an exactly opposite direction from that of the population in general. For the general population not only are there earlier marriages in the country, but, on the whole, more marriages. Ogburn and Groves explain this by observing that women are the ones most markedly affected by urban trends. They become dissatisfied with their rural economic and social status in a monotonous environment, and move to the city where there is more life and greater economic opportunity. This independence in time results in a surplus of women at the marriageable ages in the cities. The men are more rooted in the soil.

There is a population unbalance in the rural Negro group studied but the heavier migration has been on the part of the men. The women are the stable element. There is ample support of the statistical differences observed in the large number of women heads of families, their importance to the agriculture of this area,

From Charles S. Johnson, *The Shadow of the Plantation,* pp. 47–54, 66–77, 80–90. © 1934 by the University of Chicago Press. Reprinted by permission of the publisher.

their approximation to economic equality with the men, and their present dominant role in the family.

Other factors play an even more important part in accentuating this difference. The organization of the Negro families in this area to make it the most efficient economic unit tends to discourage early marriage of either men or women. When a young person marries the original family unit is seriously disturbed. The economic returns from the period of nurturing unproductive children come only when the children, male or female, reach an age which enables them to contribute to the support and earnings of the family group. Custom and practice recognize this situation. Young people are simply not expected to marry early, and, apart from the insecurity of such a venture, when such marriages occur they encounter a pronounced disapproval. When such early marriages occur the couple is expected to live in and become a part of the household of the parents of the boy or girl.

The situation of economic independence of women in cities is reversed in this community, and is reflected rather strikingly in the economic independence on the part of the Negro women in the country. Their earning power is not very much less than that of men, and for those who do not plan independent work there is greater security in their own family organization where many hands contribute to the raising of cotton and of food than there is for them alone with a young and inexperienced husband. It is practically impossible for two young persons alone to attend to all the details of cotton cultivation on a scale sufficient for adequate support of themselves. Likewise, it is extremely unlikely that any young man will be able to accumulate sufficiently to "get on his feet" before marrying.

The condition most favorable to early marriage of a girl is that in which the girl is being sought by a widower considerably her senior, who has had years of experience with the system and who, at the same time, has already some other persons in the household; or a condition in which a young girl is sought by a younger man who is working as a plantation hand with no personal responsibilities at all. In this latter case the addition of a wife, young or old, is welcome as an additional farm hand. The experience of one of these girl-brides will make this situation more real. "I married 'fore I was fourteen years old. I run off and got married; no preacher ain't married me. The man, Mr. ———, that my husband worked for, married us. He didn't tell me to go back home, 'cause he knowed I was a good hand and then he could have me there too."

The postponement of marriage in the section which has been noted does not preclude courtship, but accentuates it, and gives rise to other social adjustments based upon this obvious economic necessity. The active passions of youth and late adolescence are present but without the usual formal social restraints. Social behavior rooted in this situation, even when its consequences are understood, is lightly censured or excused entirely. Conditions are favorable to a great amount of sex experimentation. It cannot always be determined whether this experimentation is a phase of courtship, or love-making without the immediate intention of marriage, or recreation and diversion. Whether or not sexual intercourse is accepted as a part of courtship it is certain no one is surprised when it occurs. When pregnancy follows, pressure is not strong enough to compel the father either to marry the mother or to support the child. The girl does not lose status, perceptibly, nor are her chances for marrying seriously threatened. An incidental compensation for this lack of a censuring public opinion is the freedom for children thus born from warping social condemnation. There is, in a sense, no such thing as illegitimacy in this community.

The community tends to act upon the patterns of its own social heritage. This is true of sex relations as well as of economic relations. The tradition of the plantation in relation to morals, sex relations, and marriage never has conformed to that of the world outside. Unique moral codes may develop from isolation. It has happened elsewhere. Even in America there have developed patterns of sex relations among white communities not very different. In rustic villages of Bavaria, Austria, Norway, and Switzerland the presence of illegitimate children is not a handicap to women who wish to marry, but the conditions there have been different.

In the families of this study the customary courtship period is observed, but in conformity with a tradition older than the county itself, when pregnancy follows this relationship it is not socially imperative that marriage follows. A woman may have several beaux but only one with whom she is intimate. This was more than once mentioned in the course of this study, as an approximate virtue. The character of the present concern about premarital relations is to some extent apparent in the comment of one of the women:

The first man I ever courted got me in a "family way." I uster live on P——'s place 'fore I married. My baby was ten months old when me and my husband married. I was trying to wait 'til he got on his feet and got something 'fore we married, but he never did get nothin'. . . . He knowed it was his child, 'cause he looked jest like his daddy, and after he was born we went on together jest like we was at first. I never did fool around [have sex relations] with nobody else but him, though I had other beaux and he knowed it. Then after a while me and him jest got married.

Another woman, now the mother of five children and married to a man from one of the older families in the section, remarked casually and frankly: "Our first child was born before we was married. Then he wanted to marry me, so I married him."

Younger people may court, but their affairs are not often of long duration or binding. Church meetings, church suppers, festivals and frolics, and the Saturday trip to town are the occasions on which they usually meet. At the church suppers and other more public affairs the younger men and the younger women group separately. The men entertain themselves loudly with jokes and stories, frequently ribald, and with various actions to attract the attention of the girls or to provoke laughter. The young girls when together, whether experienced or not, affect shyness but are rarely, if ever, unaware of the boys. In the course of the evening a boy may take one of the girls aside for more intimate conversation which may then lead to a less decorous intimacy.

The courtship of older couples is from the beginning a more serious adventure. When one of the older men is courting, either a young woman or one nearer to his age, a change is noted in his personal behavior. At public affairs he leaves off the familiar overalls and "dresses up." The act conspicuously alters his personality. He escorts the young woman to parties and buys ice-cream or pigs' feet or chicken or chitterlings for her. The relationship is thus noted by their friends. Where courting has gone on publicly and the sanctions thus recorded, marriage tends most often to follow the legal and approved form, whether the divorce has been legal or not.

In so general a condition of uncertainty and indifference about the legality of marriage or divorce the question is not often raised, but it is nevertheless true that for the particular ones — that is, those who have begun taking over the pattern of the new culture — the fact of legality is worth mentioning, with at least the expectation of approval.

Jealousy and the violent expressions of this passion are manifested by both men and women during the courtship period, by legally married couples and by companions in a common-law relationship. Because Ben Mason began courting Alice Harris' daughter another woman shot him five times. But Ben Mason had not himself the best reputation. A few times earlier he had accidentally killed one girl while shooting at another who had spurned his attentions. The gossip of the community for the greater part of a month centered around the murder of a young woman at one of the frolics, by a man who came in a blind rage of jealousy to kill his wife because she was "running 'round with other men." The story comes most vividly from the mother of the murdered girl:

My little gal got killed just one week ago today. She was a good chile. Never give no trouble. Yes, she was married and had a baby two years old. She and me went to one of those suppers the other night. I was sitting on the bed in one room and all of a sudden Jake Johnson run in and said, "Willa's done been killed." I run out there and there she was all heaped on the bed — limp. The house was so full, but I just screamed and run to her. I picked her up in my arms and her brains was all shot out in her hair. When I put her down I was covered with blood and I couldn't do nothing but scream. Some nigger come in there to kill his wife 'cause she was going running 'round with other men, but he missed her and put a steel bullet in my baby. This is the dress she got killed in. And I'm going to show you her wedding dress, too. The society I belongs to paid $40 for the burial. I didn't lose nothing that way. That was such a good chile; she was a good wife. Her husband said he'd get that nigger yet, but they found him. The sheriff's got him now at Tuskegee. I sure hopes they punish him good 'cause he's caused me so much pain.

In one family the wife displayed a face grotesquely twisted. Her teeth protruded through a vicious slash in her upper lip. She said:

My husband did it — jest jealous-hearted. He hit me right up there with a fence post and it wasn't bout nothing. . . . Lots of times we'd get to scrapping off of nothing. I used to could do as much wid him as he could wid me, tell he got me down, then I'd stop him. Folks used to say, "Carrie, you must be mighty bad." But I tell 'em no I ain't bad, and if they'd look at the starting of it they would see it was his fault. We hardly ever have any falling out now though. He said he didn't believe I was doing all them things he 'cused me of, but he would git in behind me for fear.

Older and more experienced men have decided that jealousy does not pay. It is a disturbing force capable of sapping the spirit of every activity.

HUSBAND: My wife and me, us been married, this coming Saturday, nigh forty years. I slapped her once since I been married. Any friends we know she meets 'em, kiss 'em, and we go right along. I ain't going to let nothing disturb me but the Lord. When you jealous you don't live long.

WIFE: You be jealous and you may be up at the church but you can't rest. The meeting won't do you a bit of good; you may be thinking about that man riding with some woman.

Sex, as such, appears to be a thing apart from marriage. A distinction is very well drawn by one unmarried middle-aged woman with several children who said: "What I wants now is a husband not a man. I wants somebody to help me take keer of these chillun." The legal relationship had little to do with her romantic life. Jealousy is manifested not so much when infidelity to the institution has been discovered as where there is evidence of a transfer of affection, whether it involves sexual intercourse or not. A woman came back from her parents' and found her husband with women in her own home. He became angry at her intrusion and began swearing. When she responded he struck her with a stick. She went home and considered herself permanently separated. The objection was not primarily to the irregularity of her husband's association with women, but to the fact that he beat her.

Tom Bright was my husband, but he fight me so I just couldn't live with him. He treat me so bad. I didn't do nothing a-tall. I uster cook his breakfast and he'd come home with a big stick and beat me. Said I didn't have breakfast done. He drank but he wa'n't drunk when he beat me. One time I went to mamma's and come back I found some women in my house. When I come in he got mad and went to cussin', so I packed up and went back home.

The comment of a woman of twenty-five who had been married twice suggests an attitude from the other side of the picture. The husband was jealous but trifling. The woman seemed to feel that he had no right to be jealous unless he was also useful.

The first man [husband] wasn't no good — just trifling. I soon got rid of him. First we kept separating and then going back. Then I met Major and my first old man started right away to getting jealous. So I left him, but I did right. I went down there to Montgomery and got my divorce. It cost me $32.50, but it was worth it, seein' it 'liminated all his 'tachment to me.

Ceremonial recognition is more often given to weddings than to any other event in the life of the family. Even though this seldom occurs now, there are sufficient traces of an old custom to allow it to be revived when it is especially desired to give formal public sanction to marriage. On these occasions the nuptials are celebrated with wine and cake and festivities, by the friends and relatives of the couple. Occasionally small tokens are exchanged. There has been a practice, tracing back several generations to slavery, of making this an occasion of festivity. Slaves, although not always encouraged to marry, and deprived of the civil sanction of a ceremony, when there was mutual desire, provided it was within the limits of the master's circumstances, were allotted a cabin, given small tokens by the master and mistress, and a ceremony, conducted by a Negro preacher and patterned after the custom of the whites. It is spoken of now by some of the older members of the community, and little change is noted in the forms of the ceremony. Speaking of slavery, one said:

The folks married then jest like they do now. They did jump over a broomstick [a custom now abandoned] but the preacher had a Bible and married them. Sometimes the sheriff married them. If you and this sister come engaged you ask Mr. —— for her and he would say, "Do you love this nigger?" and he would go and ask if she loved you. Then, whatever place you stayed on your master would have to buy whichever one would come there. . . .

Children Born out of Wedlock

The sexual unions resulting in the birth of children without the legal sanctions are of several types, and cannot properly be grouped together under the single classification of "illegitimate." Children of common-law relationships are not illegitimate, from the point of view of the community or of their stability, for many of these unions are as stable as legally sanctioned unions. They hold together for twenty and thirty years, in some cases, and lack only the sense of guilt. Again, there are competent, self-sufficient women who not only desire children but need them as later aids in the struggle for survival when their strength begins to wane, but who want neither the restriction of formal marriage nor the constant association with a husband. They get their children not so much through weakness as through their own deliberate selection of a father. Sexual unions for pleasure frequently result in children. There is a term for children born under the two latter circumstances. They are called "stolen children." "Stolen children," observed one mother, "is the best." A woman with children and who has been married though later separated from her husband may add other children to her family, without the benefit of the formal sanctions. These are "children by the way." The youthful sex experimentation, which is in part related to the late marriages, often results in children. These are normally taken into the home of the girl's parents and treated without distinction as additions to the original family. Finally, there are the children who result from the deliberate philandering of young men who "make foolments" on young girls. They are universally condemened. These children, as circumstance directs, may be placed with the parents of the mother or father of the child, an uncle, sister, or grandmother. They are accepted easily into the families on the simple basis of life and eventually are indistinguishable from any of the other children. Even if there were severe condemnation for true "illegitimates," confusion as to origin would tend both to mitigate some of the offenses and to obscure them all from specific condemnation.

The sense of guilt may be noted in some of the more advanced families, but within the community as a whole social censure is not severe, nor is there any notable loss of status because of "illegitimacy." It does not appear to be regarded as severely as, for example, the use of certain artificial forms of birth control, or "being closed out," which means having all of one's crops, stock, and tools taken over for debt.

The church recognizes illegitimacy as a "sin of the mother," and if the mother is brought into church meeting with other evidences of "sin," like card-playing or frolicking, she may be "put out of church"; but readmission is possible with a solemn promise not to do it again. Actually, there is less stress placed by the churches upon illegitimacy as a "social sin" than upon card-playing and playing ball.

The danger, from the point of view of health, is the promiscuity of relations and the passing-on of venereal infection. Some men in this section of the county have numerous children scattered about, as a result of their tireless love-making with single girls, married women with children of their own, and with widows.

The sense of shame and lowered status follows illegitimacy when the family has, for one reason or another, become compact and self-conscious; when there has been exposure to recognized standards of a higher level, as a result of children returning from boarding-school, or when the family has acquired some education. Under such circumstances families are more careful about the opinions of outsiders, and frequently force the father of the child to marry the daughter. Ownership of property tends to restrict illegitimate relations because of the economic complexities introduced, and the effect of loose domestic relations upon credit and leadership in relationships beyond the immediate community is a restraining factor.

An attempt was made to measure the extent of illegitimacy. One hundred and twenty-two women in 114 families had had 181 illegitimate children. The illegitimate children were present in all but 3 of these 114 families. It is necessary, however, to make clear, as far as possible, the condition under which illegitimacy was found in these families. In the case of 24 couples now married the wife had a child before marriage. In 14 of these 24 cases the father of these children was the present husband, and in 10 cases the woman had had the child by another man before marriage. In 2 cases the women, who had subsequently married the father of their illegitimate children, had had 4 children each. There were also 3 widowed women who had had illegitimate children since the death of their husbands. In 13 families the mother was living alone with her illegitimate children. Two of these mothers had 4 children, 2 had 3 children, and 4 had 2 children each.

One unmarried mother of thirty-three years of age had 6 children of whom 4 were living. The oldest of those living was a girl of twenty-one and the youngest a girl of ten. The father of all of them was a man legally married, with a considerable family of his own. The oldest daughter was unmarried and had 2 children. Neither of the fathers of the children had offered any support and the women have not asked for it. The mother is a one-half-share cropper, and with the children she manages her farm about as successfully as the average family with a male head. There were 8 women, separated from their husbands, who had illegitimate children. In one case the separated woman was living with her mother. Illegitimate children were also found in the case of 10 common-law couples. In 8 of these cases the children were by the men with whom the wives were living, and in some cases there were 5 or 6 illegitimate children in the family. In 31 of the families a daughter had 1 or more illegitimate children, and in 1 family 2 daughters had an illegitimate child each. Illegitimate children were also found in 9 families in which the daughter, who was the mother of the children, was dead or away. In some cases the illegitimate children in the home had been adopted. This was found to be the case in 9 families. In 6 of the families the illegitimate child belonged to relatives, as, for example, a cousin, or a sister of the mother, or a nephew's child outside of marriage. In 2 families a son's illegitimate child had been taken into the home, and in one case the father's illegitimate child had been taken in. In 5 of the families the illegitimate child belonged to a granddaughter or to a great granddaughter.

How the Children Come

I got so many chillun I don't know where they all is. I got four living and one dead that Mr. ——— is the father of. I been married once, but me and him separated. They tell me he lives some place there near Tuskegee. I ain't got no divorce. Don't know whether he left me or no; we jest 'cided to depart, and it's been a good while ago. C—— B—— was the father of two of my children. I ain't know nothing else 'bout the father of any of the rest of them, aside from them that he [pointing to Mr. ———] been the father of. I can't 'member nothing 'bout them. I got frost-bitten one time and I can't 'member so well.

The daughter emulated the mother. When asked about her daughter's child, she said:

How can I know who is the father of Corinne's baby? We done had her over there in school, and she come back and brought the baby. Whoever he is, he don't do nothing for the baby.

These is Carrie's chillun. She ain't married. She was jest sixteen when the oldest child was born. Jimmie Hall is Leonard's daddy, and Ernest Watts is Leroy's.

No, sir, they ain't all got the same father! Them three is, but these two darkest ones ain't. I ain't seen the daddy of the first ones since year 'fore last. He married and don't give no help. I love him but I don't want to marry him. We started going together when I was a girl and jest kept it up. I ain't seen these others' daddy since before this last one was born. They tell me he over the creek, but I don't know and I ain't worrying myself none about him. He ain't like Hall. I like Hall and we jest kept on going together till bad luck happened. If my mind keep on like it is, I'm going to marry a man and trust him to take care of the children.

I wasn't married to the boy's father. We was engaged to marry but he done some shooting and had to leave and he never did come back till my boy was a big boy, so I jest didn't care 'bout marrying him then. I been married to somebody else now 'bout twelve years.

On one plantation a group of Negro women were living openly with white men. Their children were mulattoes. One of the women interviewed stated that the white man for whom she had been housekeeper recently died and just left her with the house. Her job had been ringing the bell for the other Negroes to go to work, and she had been greatly disliked by the other Negro women on the plantation. In still another situation the woman and a mulatto daughter cooked for a group of white men. Said she: "They come here three times a day to eat. They provide my clothing, food, and this house." Neighbors said they were the men's "women."

Twenty-four couples among the 612 families were living together without legal sanction, in a first association. The time which these couples had been together varied from one to more than thirty years.

The frequency of children born out of wedlock and the fact that no actual disgrace attaches to irregular birth occasionally work out to the advantage of the child. Adoption has been given increased importance. There is a demand for children to adopt, and an increased social status for families which adopt children.

Adoption in turn is commonly a convenience for children without the protection of a family organization of their own. A motherly old woman said: "These chillun here, they mother in Plaza. They father somewhere 'bout near here. They all got the same mother but different fathers. The two oldest ones was born 'fore they mother married. I tuk them all soon atta they was born."

Older families, and especially old and widowed women, look upon adoption as more of a privilege than a burden: "Lord, I almost like to not be able to raise me that child; he was so sickly at first." The sentiment is sometimes carried to the point of surrounding the child with an importance which many children in normal families lack.

Separation and Divorce

The actual number of divorces is small. In the 612 families there were but 2 heads of families who could be classifeid as regularly divorced and not married again. There were other heads of families who had been regularly divorced but who had remarried. Taking account of the 8 individuals single and living alone, and the 105 who were widowed, less than half, or 231 of the 612 families, were those in which the husband and wife were married for the first time. Among the group of 105 widowed heads of families some of the mates were dead and others had gone away without declaring their intention to separate permanently. Voluntary separation in the community really amounted to divorce, for many of the parties involved remarried without regard for the legal status of their first marriage.

Divorce is one of the legal formalities introduced from the outside in regard to the meaning and purpose of which the community is profoundly confused. Some of the families thought that going from one county to another gave them the legal right to remarry. It was believed that crossing the "line" (Mason and Dixon) meant divorce. One such remarried woman exclaimed: "My husband done cross de line; don't hear nothing. He may be living or dead. Ain't dat divorce?" The simplest interpretation is that the act of separation is divorce.

Table 1: Marital Status

Single—livng alone	8
Unknown	4
Married—times unknown	1
Both married once	231
Husband married once, wife more than once	24
Husband married more than once, wife once	75
Both married more than once	74
Married but separated	52
Widowed	105
Divorced	2
Unmarried couples living together	24
Unmarried mother with children, living without father	12
	612

"They say when you separate from your husband you already 'vorced." The term "giving a strip," in common use, refers to the act of a man or woman writing or having written on a piece of paper the statement that he or she is divorced, and this stands as final.

I been married three times. My other husband's 'bout Wetumpka somewhere. We jest couldn't git along, so he revorced me, and me and the second one fought like cats and dogs. One night he fought me so I had to call for help. He left that night and the next day he got the wagon and moved, and he *asked me for a revorce;*

so I give him a strip. Marion Wood write it. If I had time I'd ramble round here and find that strip they sent me from Wetumpka.

There were other individuals who believed that the act of remarriage of their spouse, even though no divorce was secured, conferred upon them the freedom to marry again. "You see, my other husband, when we separated, got married again first, so that divorced us." A man and woman, aged forty-eight and forty-six, respectively, had been married eighteen years. It was the second marriage for both although neither had secured a divorce. Of her first husband the wife said: "My husband didn't leave me, but he got into a little trouble about some cotton situation and went away. He wanted me to go too, but I didn't want to leave my mother. He was gone a long time before I married again." The husband explained: "My wife just went away, and she's over in Cecil. I didn't have to get a divorce, because she been gone a long time."

A man who had been drafted during the World War was positive that he had been exempted by the government from any further marital responsibility: "I's an ex-soldier. They told me when I went to the army and come back that the government had done 'vorced me, and I didn't have to git naire 'vorce." The arrangement of convenience is pushed at times with an almost brutal severity. Old Amos Boyd said: "My wife she stay over in La Place. She over there for her health. She come home 'bout once a week, so I'm thinking 'bout 'vorcing her. Now a good time to 'vorce her. " When Minnie Toles was sick her husband left and went to Cecil. When he came back she told him she didn't need him and he was thereby divorced.

It would seem, again, that divorce is needed only in those cases in which there was objection of one party to the separation. "Me and him jest come here to live and she [his wife] ain't claim him, so I don't speck he need a 'vorce." The uncertainty about the meaning of divorce contributes to the uncertainty about security in marriage. One man was troubled because his wife had been gone for more than a week on a visit to her mother, and he was not sure whether or not she "had up and divorced" him. Another sent his wife away on a visit in order that he might not be embarrassed by her presence when he "made out a slip" for her divorce, which he intended to do before she got back.

There is indication that the mores are in process of change in the fact of the now serious and frequent discussion of the meaning and purpose of legal divorce. This discussion took place between a husband and wife and a visiting neighbor:

NEIGHBOR: My husband don't help me none with the child. He jest throwed me away and I was sick. I wasn't down in bed. He done married again. He didn't had to git no divorce 'cause I didn't want him no more.

WIFE: You know good and well he didn't git no divorce, 'cause you'd a knowed something 'bout it.

HUSBAND; He could a had a divorce and you not know nothing 'bout it. I had a divorce six months before my wife knowed anything 'bout it. You git a divorce through and by money. They git a pencil and figure it out for you 'thout the wife knowing nothing 'bout it.

NEIGHBOR: He jest a "run-about" man anyhow.

One reason for the small number of divorces and the curious beliefs regarding this formality has been suggested as the cultural one of introduction from without of a new device for the regulation of marital relations. Another is the actual cost of this legal procedure. Divorce, after all, is a personal matter and the introduction of a lawyer not only beclouds the issue but brings a demand for cash which few of them have. The attitude of the courts toward this omission is not severe. Rather, the disposition seems to be to ignore it as a serious offense. So long as the practice affects no one but the Negroes, and they accept it as a part of their lives, there is no necessity for insisting upon a standard which, it is assumed, they have not attained. From the point of view of the Negroes, so long as no one is seriously inconvenienced by the permanency of the separation or the fact of remarriage, it is considered an unnecessary expenditure of money to get a divorce through the courts. There is always more frequent demand for the permanent separation than there is money.

There are instances of use of the external pattern of divorce but without complete understanding of its real meaning, as, for example, when a man goes to town and "buys" a divorce for a woman he hopes to marry, even though this woman's husband may still be living in the community.

WIFE: This husband I got now bought me my divorce.

HUSBAND: I paid thirty or thirty-five dollars for it. It's different with different people. It depends on how long they been separated and what they separated for, and the lawyer too.

The influence of new ideas was evident in the family of Quarles. Both had been married before, but they had been living together about five years. The wife now thinks she should have a divorce from her first husband, and her present husband plans to go to town sometime and "buy" her one.

Causes of Separation and Divorce

Separation, like marriage, is regarded very largely as a personal matter. Desertions are frequent and almost casual, growing out of various kinds of disharmony. The woman deserts almost as frequently as the man. There are at first temporary separations following minor dissatisfactions. At any point, however, the separation may be made permanent by the remarriage of one of the parties, or some change in circumstances which places either out of reach. Couples separate six and eight times, each time returning because of the greater convenience of the existing arrangement, only to discover that the old basis of dissatisfaction had not been removed. It is more "respectable" to separate, and even to experiment further with another mate, than to tolerate certain conditions with one's legal mate.

The position of women in the community increases the rate of separation at the same time that it decreases the social consequences of this separation. A deserted woman is not entirely helpless, and occasionally her economic burden is lightened by the withdrawal of the man. The large number of women heads of families may be accounted for in part by the desertion of the men, in part by death, and in part by the withdrawal of the woman, with her children, to set up an establishment working as a tenant farmer or renter on some plantation.

An underlying provocation to separation is the lack of functional balance, with respect both to the business of earning a living and to temperamental differences. The hard and drab life of most of the families places a severe test upon this arrangement, and the weaknesses of the social restraints of the community encourage change. Separations which may be classed as desertions are, perhaps, the most numerous group and include among the underlying motives general dissatisfaction with the association, trifling or lazy husbands or wives, and such sentiments of resignation as "he jest liked some other woman better."

I divorced my first wife and I'm separated from the other one, but she ain't divorced. We didn't fuss or nothing, we just decided to quit intelligent.

Me and my wife went to Georgia, and me and her couldn't agree and she stayed in Georgia. I don't know what come of her.

My wife talking 'bout quitting me 'cause I ain't got no money. Good time to quit now when I ain't got nothing.

My ole lady jest walked off; say she goin' to be her own boss.

My wife jest left. She didn't ask for no 'vorce — just told me to quit writin' to her in her name 'cause she was married. Dey didn't git no 'vorce. After she married I didn't have no 'vorce. I didn't know she'd quit me till her father told me.

An old man, calm and deliberate as he smoked his pipe, recounted this series of disturbances in his domestic life:

In all I been married four times. The first wife, somebody poisoned her with Paris green. An old woman poisoned her 'cause she couldn't whip her. She lived nine months and died on the Jordan place near Downs. The second wife, Mary Ann, I quit her. She over there in Bullock County. The third wife caught fire and died. The next one been gone since March, 1929. I didn't quit her; I was gwine ter quit but she didn't gimme time; she quit me. She wouldn't listen to me. If I say "don't go" then it's best for her not to go.

In a situation in which separation is so lightly regarded there is little occasion to make specific the causes.

Me and my fust wife separated. Don't know where she is — me and her jest parted.

My husband lives in Bullock. Don't know why he leave me. Jest picked up and left. He don't give me nothing. I don't know whether we separated or no. He jest lives over there and I lives over here. He got three of the children over there with him.

Of the specific causes of separation, cruelty is perhaps the most frequently mentioned. Here, again, the women are not always at a disadvantage, for they know how to fight back. Where this resistance is effective there follows a mutually respectful truce, or a separation based upon incompatibility.

Tom Kerns was my husband, but he fight so I jest couldn't live with him. He treat me so bad.

I have been married two years. We went to the courthouse in Tuskegee. I have been back home to mother's more than ten times since we been married. Sometimes I stays two days and sometimes two weeks. My husband don't go away and leave me. He jest likes to fight and do's lots of things when I go home. My mother tells me to go back home.

I been married but my husband been too mean. Dis man ain't like him.

He was jest too mean. He was too old, too.

Me and my husband been parted three years. He was mean and lazy. . . .

What Is Respectable?

The families of the community do not act upon a single standard of propriety or of morals. Ideals and life-conceptions vary strikingly, not only with respect to content, but with respect to definition and emphasis. There is, moreover, an extraordinary overlapping and fusing of traits and heritages in a community which holds its members with varying degrees of cohesion. Notions of respectability rest upon the social customs which have grown up with the group, upon an adaptation of the early social patterns to which they were exposed, and upon the newer patterns which are being slowly introduced.

It is possible to trace roughly some of these standards by reference to degrees of isolation. Geographical remoteness from the centers of sophistication and cultural change is important but not the only determining factor in isolation. The old traditions persist virtually unchanged in some families, whether they live near the highway or far in the back country. The present picture, however, is one of confusion, arising from the conflict of different ideals and ways of life. A family will reflect one set of moral ideals regarding marriage and another regarding divorce, or one regarding legitimacy and another regarding extra-marital sex relations. Generally

speaking, home-ownership and education tend to mark these differences in standards.

It is important to point out first what seems to be a conformity to the conventions of the group itself without reference to outside standards and ideals. One
family with two unmarried daughters, both of whom had several children, had very
positive notions about what was respectable and what was not. The father stressed
the responsibility of his family to the children of his daughters, discounting the value
of marriage as such. He was satisfied to keep out of contact with the law. In personal
relations his attitude was that of the frontier, relying upon his ability to effect a
personal settlement of differences which ordinarily are handled in the courts.

Ain't none of my daughters got married but dey is my chillun, and I take care
of all of dem. The fathers of dey chillun don't come here less dey come right. I tell
'em all to stay way from my house. I don't git into no trouble with nobody. I am
dis old and never been to jail, never been handcuffed or had a fight. My brothers
git into trouble, but I ain't never had a fight. I keep my gun near 'cause if anyone
tries to bother me, gonna shoot 'em shore. Gonna shoot 'em shore.

It is not regarded as the proper thing to demand or even to ask the father of
an unmarried woman's child to support the child. "No, these babies don't git no
help from dey daddies. Help, nothing! I wouldn't let them beg them to do it for
nothing in the world. I wouldn't bother them for a pocket handkerchief. They don't
git no help atall from dey daddies' side." Another woman with children "by the
way" explained: "Sherman Biggers is the daddy of two of dem. Sherman gives
Bertha a dress now and den, but he don't give her no money. I don't worry him
for it 'cause I don't see him have it."

On the other hand, there is the suggestion of approval if the responsibility of
the father is assumed without prompting. "This here baby is my daughter's baby.
She is jest fifteen years old herself. The father paid the doctor bills and give it
clothes."

Community gossip exercises restraint, but in certain cases in which the question
of "illegitimacy" was an issue, the direction of this control was away from marriage.
The mother of a young girl who had a child by the son of a neighbor refused to
let her daughter marry the boy, in spite of mutual desires, because the mother of
the boy had made uncomplimentary remarks about the girl. "My oldest daughter
ain't married and she has a baby seven days old. The baby's father, why he's up
the road there 'bout two miles from here. His mamma jest talked 'bout her so I
wouldn't let her marry him. She tried to 'scandalize' her name." It would be a
mistake to assume from the practices current that there is indifference to standards.
Indeed, there is a rather rigid conformity to those standards of the group which
are distilled from personal experience rather than from the abstractions of moral
philosophy.

There are limits to the sexual freedom tolerated, and when these limits are reached violators are treated with unmistakable group disapproval. The community, for example, has its gay Lotharios, who exploit existing conventions to their advantage. A young man, illiterate but loose and boastful, was discussing marriage. He said if he married and could not get along, "then I quits and marries again. I got six more [wives] coming." Someone remarked that his father had been married to the same woman forty years, and he replied: "De Bible say go 'round and see about the ofren [orphan] chillun." This last was intended as a ribald paraphrase of the Bible to give swagger to his sexual promiscuity. Community disapproval was certain and severe on the man who violated local usages by refusing to assume any responsibility. "He's a yaller boy who ain't done nothing but go 'round and fool all these girls. That was the second time he done make foolments on her, too, 'cause she lost the other one." The community also has its "fast women," but they are not the familiar "prostitute" type. Rather, they are women who flaunt, with their sex, the dominant economic concern and interest of the group. They are the ones who maliciously, and to no useful end, steal other women's men and through the men the earnings to which another woman has made an important contribution. One woman in commenting about such a character said: "She go 'round braggin' she don't spend no money. She got 'em workin' for her. You be workin' and she goin' 'round dressed up like 'Miss Ann' while you go naked." The usual connotation of "fastness" in women had less relationship to sex morals than to age of sexual maturity. "I was a fast little thing; up and married at thirteen. (That man jest kept goin' and comin' back, till finally he jest didn't come back at all.)" There are women who give their favors freely, but seldom on a purely commercial basis.

On the other hand, there is a strong current of approval of alliances, whether legal or not, which offer the highest chances of survival in the environment. A mother who had never been married said: "I ain't want no husband myself, and I don't care if Alder [her daughter] marries or no. Willis [father of Alder's child] is a smart man. Alder's father asked me to marry him, but I tole him I don' want no husband."

A common-sense view of marriage in this setting classifies it as a serious hazard. There is no more steady, hard-working woman in the community than Della Promise. She knows how to keep herself and her house clean, belongs to church and to several societies, manages her children with notable success, and in other respects is regular and reliable. She has never been married, and has no apologies to make about it. Seriously and with conviction she said: "Everybody don't git married, and if I can't git the one I want I don't want to git married. I never seen but one boy I thought I could marry, and me and him had ways too much alike, and I knowed we couldn't git along, so I jest has my chillun and raises 'em myself." Married life imposes certain obligations which are, in the feeling of this element of the community, more binding than necessary or practicable. It gives license to mistreatment; it imposes the risk of unprofitable husbands; and it places an impossible tax upon freedom in the form of a divorce. For example: "Men jest git you a house full of chillun and leave you." Or again: "I been married but my husband been too mean.

He beated me too much. Dis man I'm livin' wid now ain't like him. He's nice. I like him. I been thinkin' 'bout marrying, but I don't want to marry now."

It is, in a very practical sense, less respectable to be beaten by one's husband than to be living with a man peacefully and happily, though not married to him. The lack of legal obligation acts as a restraint upon mistreatment, for the services of the woman are of very real importance to the man. As Artie Joe McDaniel, who has been living with Robert Jackson for several years, said with some pride in her independence: "He's nice all right, but I ain't thinking 'bout marrying. Soon as you marry a man he starts mistreating you, and I'm not going to be mistreated no more." Experience dictates numerous expressions of caution on the part of the older women.

If you ain't married don't you eber go git yourself no *rainbow*. First thing you know you'll be sick of it.

Ain't nobody got nothing to give me but God, and if I don't trust Him I'm lost.

Men ain't nothin' but overalls.

Better git a good holt 'fore you git into this marryin' business, 'cause there'll be some tight times if you don't.

Gambling is condemned. This is no doubt a result of the influence of the church with its prohibition of indulgence in certain forms of worldliness. Any form of life-activity which does not involve obvious and direct manual labor may be said to be under suspicion and disapproval. A possible exception is the religious ministry, and most of the preachers who reside in the community are also farmers.

Likewise, the influence of the prohibition of the church is seen, somewhat unfortunately, in the ban on baseball, but with profound wisdom in the disapproval of the secular "frolics." "I don't go to them frolics. People git drunk and comes back and tries to show everybody who dey is." Frolics are not respectable. One woman, expressing her disapproval of them, based this disapproval on the fact that "they don't show the right respect for women." She explained the meaning of "respect" by saying that they had "splashed a woman's brains out last Saturday night." The following account by the mother of a boy who had killed a woman at another of these affairs both characterizes the "frolics" and helps to define the proper sphere of women.

My son John was a good boy. They tell me that the woman what he killed was dancing on the floor that night. She hadn't been long settin' down. It was jest awful. John didn't give up till yesterday, and when he did give up they got the boy what lent him the pistol too. See how kin folks git one 'nother in trouble? I guess, though, they can't do nothing but make him pay for loaning John that pistol. He wasn't after that chile he killed. He jest couldn't rest, I reckon, till he give hisself up. If John hadn't had that pistol he wouldn't a shot it, and if that woman had stayed at home she wouldn't a got killed. I don't believe in women goin' to suppers. They ought to stay at home where they belong.

Quite apart from the question of sex, respectability has other concerns in this level of the culture of the group. One of the most frequent assertions in evidence of respectability is the fact that no one of the family has been in jail. The Boyd family is one of the oldest in the community. There are 26 children in the family, of whom 11 are still living — 5 girls and 6 boys — all born since slavery. Said one of these: "Papa rents from the man what set him free. We have never been nowhere else but right here. Papa died right over there; all of us live on this plantation. None of us ever been in prison or in suits or nothing. We are always in hopes of getting something." An old man who had several grown sons in the neighborhood gave this formula of success: "I works hard to keep out of lawsuits and trouble. Nobody don't bother me, and I don't bother nobody."

A practice which has the disapproval of the group is begging. The sentiment is well expressed by one of the older members of the community in her comment when she heard that a neighbor had asked a stranger for some money for food and snuff. She was caustic in her criticism: "I don't 'cept charity from nobody. I don't tote a bucket 'round under my dress beggin'. Work is honorable and good. I believe in it. 'Tain't livin' right to go beggin'." Work is a virtue even though there are lazy members in the group. Women are justified in leaving husbands who are lazy and trifling. More than this, the values attached to work transcend those attached to legitimacy. "Me and my husband been parted three years. We couldn't git along. He was so mean. He ain't helped me none. He was jest so lazy, he didn't wanna work. He ain't none of my child's father. The daddy is dead. I never was married to my child's daddy." The community standing of this woman and her own self-respect were such that she felt completely free to censure the behavior of the young school-teacher who came from the outside. "She was pretty good, but last year she wasn't nothing but a little courtin' girl. The big boys wouldn't go to school. She was so young they didn't want her to teach them."

Begging is, however, different from mutual assistance between neighbors. This is probably the root of that same mutualism which is reflected in the case of newly arrived southern immigrants to the North. They are at first most reticent about applying to the public agencies for relief, despite their poverty. There is a common disposition to help one another with food and shelter. When they become more sophisticated they discover in these agencies a mysterious means of getting something for nothing, which holds dangers both to working habits and to self-respect.

The families in the community, clinging to their own standards of respectability, found it difficult at first to adjust themselves to the policies of the Red Cross, although these services are now widely used. One of the families, although poor, was outraged and humiliated by the organization's method of determining the need for assistance. Said the wife:

My husband went to the Red Cross to get the money they owed him, 'cause his son died in the army. The Red Cross ain't never give us nothing. When my husband gone down there they was so pikus and close, and ain't give us nothing. There was an old man down there wid a lot of chilluns, and they ain't give him nothing neither. They jest lecture and act indifferent. They make you feel so shame over the way you have to git it, you don't want it.

When Fannie Ford, who had worked all her life and lived hard, reached the point of being unable to purchase either food or clothing, she still maintained her pride. "Folks say, 'Sister Fannie, you go on down to the Red Cross.' I said, 'Jesus don't send me there,' but they ain't done nothing anyhow. No, I don't ask 'em. I don't like to be a charitable person. I jest went 'long and made out somehow." Thus, an enlightened piece of human engineering which provides a device for necessary relief may arouse a conflict of ideals of respectability no less significant than in the clash of two cultures.

Clearly enough, a transition from the imperatives of one cultural level to that of another is taking place, and this change is being manifested in other ways more advantageous to the group. There is a reaching-out for the new standards, although these standards are not as yet always adequately conceived. Definitions of the situation are frequently mixed and confused. Illegitimacy, for example, though regarded by some families as something not entirely to be countenanced, is considered by others a lesser social evil and affront to decency than desertion following a forced marriage. Mary Blyden was conscious of a certain personal superiority over her neighbors. She attributes this advancement, of which she is pardonably proud, to the fact that she likes to associate with "cultured people."

I don't get into no trouble 'cause I love to be with cultural people. They always trying to have something. Them others they always trying to git something for nothing. The Bible say "seek and ye shall find," and they got more time to seek then we have, 'cause while we out there in the field they 'round seeking. This is my daughter's child [illegitimate] here. His father's name Asbestos Key. He Maggie Key's son. He ain't do nothing for the child. You know these young people has a peculiar way of doing things now. They go from house to house dropping chillun just like an old house cat. I don't believe in forcing 'em to marry, though. I had a cousin once and her father forced the man to marry her and after the marriage was all over he walked out one door and she the other, and they ain't seed one another since. This 'suading and coaxing and begging 'em to marry jest ain't get you no place. It's my child so I take it as my 'sponsibility.

A shade removed from this attitude is that represented by a family in which the mother showed no sensitiveness about her daughter's illegitimate children, but the daughter, on the other hand, withdrew in embarrassment when the subject came up. The younger generation is slowly picking up new notions although they cannot always escape the current of the old life to make the shift to the new.

The female head of another family, with four children in school, felt warranted in setting her own notions to the conventions of the community. She said with pride: "I don't believe much in these stolen children. Me, I married in my mother's house before I broke my virtue."

Freedom from the economic compulsions of the life of the community carries with it almost unvaryingly a corresponding freedom from many of the social customs. The family of Cox's have lived in the community over eighteen years, own eighty acres of land for which they paid twenty-two dollars an acre, and have sent their children to school. One daughter, who teaches a four-month-term school in Russell County, has attended a summer session at Alabama State College. When the mother was asked about the marital status of her children, she said none of her girls was married, and added emphatically, "Neither of them has had any children either." The remark, as well as the emphasis, was offered without prompting and reflected a new consciousness to the changing mores. The father in this family raised cotton but also did public work and hauling. By this means, and aided by his sons, he accumulated enough cash for a part payment of one thousand dollars on his house and farm. The family wore very good clothing but adhered to the custom of going barefoot. The family organization follows roughly the essential pattern of the community with respect to the family economic unit, but this has been modified in such a manner as to avoid the ordinary stresses of the system. The sons live in the household but cultivate plots which they rent from their father, paying him back in cotton.

Thomas Germany has lived in the county twenty-seven years. He owns his farm of one hundred and twenty-nine acres for which he paid twenty-eight hundred dollars in 1904. He can "read a little," although his wife is illiterate, but all of the five grandchildren whom they are rearing are in school. They made a point of stressing that they had never "been in trouble." The mother still uses the community midwife instead of a doctor, although she has now lost respect for this practice. She is convinced that she lost her last baby through the ignorance and carelessness of the midwife, but the pressure of the group impels her to continue using a midwife rather than get talked about. Although the house is in poor repair it is enclosed with a fence — something very unusual in the section. There are blinds at the windows and a lightning rod on the roof. They have planted a fruit orchard. These were indices to the family. It happened that the wife had been married before, and she was asked where she secured her divorce. The answer was a retort with considerable feeling: "Where else do you suppose I got the divorce if not at the courthouse?" The family had few friends in the community and wanted but few. They get along now by "tending to their own business." One of the grandchildren is illegitimate and the family is miserably conscious of the sin of the daughter.

Edgar Hill is one of the few mulatto men observed to be married to a woman of perceptibly darker complexion. They have a pleasant home life, and although they are not home-owners they have well-defined notions about marriage and family relations. There was an expression of indignation when the question was asked if the woman was the mother of all the children in the family. "She is my wife; who else would be the mother?" Similarly, the man raised his eyebrows in shocked surprise when asked if they had ever been separated and shouted "No." To still another regarding sleeping with the windows open (a practice extremely uncommon in the community) he answered, "Yes, we sleep with the windows open and doors too."

A further indication of the changing mores appears in the experience of Sherman Riggs, who has thirteen children — eleven by his wife and two by a woman neighbor. He regards himself as an upright man, trying to do what is best. He was an officer in the church and is in good standing in the societies. Conflict in his mind arose over the question of marrying the woman by whom he had had several children, to satisfy new notions about legitimacy and respectability.

I get lonesome lots of times but a man is crazy to see something won't do and then walk in it. I done tried it [referring to his period of common-law association with his woman neighbor]. I mean by that just like you have a pencil, if you saw it wouldn't write you wouldn't bother with it. A new broom sweeps clean, and when I marries I wants to marry for pleasure. The fellow pecking the rock can see more than the fellow not pecking the rock. I like Minty all right, but now a fellow's got to use common sense. *The world is so critical now a fellow is scared to do anything.* I left off most of my frolics when I was young. But common sense got to come in. You tak' a cow and tie it out before a lot of grass — the cow will bite first one bunch of grass then another, trying to see which one he likes the best; so that the way with a man.

Despite the unevenness of life, the amount of sexual freedom, the frequency of separation and realignment of families, the number of children born out of formal wedlock and the customary provisions for them, codes and conventions consistent with the essential routine of their lives do arise which represent a form of organization adapted to the total environment. Where social processes such as these proceed largely unconsciously, the surviving folkways may reasonably be presumed to have a foundation in the fundamental needs of community and human nature. The marriage relation under slavery, despite its lack of the sanctions by the dominant society, had some seriousness of purpose for the slaves and was forced to accommodate itself to the convenience of the institution of slavery with respect to continuity, fertility, selection of mates, change of mates, the quasi-eugenic demands of the institution with respect to breeding, and similar circumstances.

It is scarcely conceivable that the isolation of this group at any point could be so complete as to prevent the introduction of a different body of sentiments and practices in accord with a more advanced conception of life and social relations. The total situation, thus, would be expected to represent different stages of cultural evolution, from the almost complete acceptance of the original sanctions of the group under slave tradition to the fullest acceptance of the new codes introduced, whether thoroughly comprehended or not. Disorganization is most acute where these sanctions are in conflict and the individuals are firmly rooted in neither of the patterns of life-organization.

Crucible of Identity: The Negro Lower-Class Family

Lee Rainwater

As long as Negroes have been in America, their marital and family patterns have been subjects of curiosity and amusement, moral indignation and self-congratulation, puzzlement and frustration, concern and guilt, on the part of white Americans.[1] As some Negroes have moved into middle-class status, or acquired standards of American common-man respectability, they too have shared these attitudes toward the private behavior of their fellows, sometimes with a moral punitiveness to rival that of whites, but at other times with a hard-headed interest in causes and remedies rather than moral evaluation. Moralism permeated the subject of Negro sexual, marital, and family behavior in the polemics of slavery apologists and abolitionists as much as in the Northern and Southern civil rights controversies of today. Yet, as long as the dialectic of good or bad, guilty or innocent, overshadows a concern with who, why, and what can be, it is unlikely that realistic and effective social planning to correct the clearly desperate situation of poor Negro families can begin.

This paper is concerned with a description and analysis of slum Negro family patterns as these reflect and sustain Negroes' adaptations to the economic, social, and personal situation into which they are born and in which they must live. As such it deals with facts of lower-class life that are usually forgotten or ignored in polite discussion. We have chosen not to ignore these facts in the belief that to do so can lead only to assumptions which would frustrate efforts at social reconstruction, to strategies that are unrealistic in the light of the actual day-to-day reality of slum Negro life. Further, this analysis will deal with family patterns which interfere with the efforts slum Negroes make to attain a stable way of life as working- or middle-class individuals and with the effects such failure in turn has on family life. To be sure, many Negro families live *in* the slum ghetto, but are not *of* its culture

Lee Rainwater, "Crucible of Identity: The Negro Lower-Class Family," *Daedalus,* XCV (Winter, 1966), 172–216. Reprinted by permission of *Daedalus,* Journal of the American Academy of Arts and Sciences, Boston, Massachusetts.

(though even they, and particularly their children, can be deeply affected by what happens there). However, it is the individuals who succumb to the distinctive family life style of the slum who experience the greatest weight of deprivation and who have the greatest difficulty responding to the few self-improvement resources that make their way into the ghetto. In short, we propose to explore in depth the family's role in the "tangle of pathology" which characterizes the ghetto.

The social reality in which Negroes have had to make their lives during the 450 years of their existence in the western hemisphere has been one of victimization "in the sense that a system of social relations operates in such a way as to deprive them of a chance to share in the more desirable material and non-material products of a society which is dependent, in part, upon their labor and loyalty." In making this observation, St. Clair Drake goes on to note that Negroes are victimized also because "they do not have the same degree of access which others have to the attributes needed for rising in the general class system — money, education, 'contacts,' and 'know-how.' "[2] The victimization process started with slavery; for 350 years thereafter Negroes worked out as best they could adaptations to the slave status. After emancipation, the cultural mechanisms which Negroes had developed for living the life of victim continued to be serviceable as the victimization process was maintained first under the myths of white supremacy and black inferiority, later by the doctrines of gradualism which covered the fact of no improvement in position, and finally by the modern Northern system of ghettoization and indifference.

When lower-class Negroes use the expression, "Tell it like it is," they signal their intention to strip away pretense, to describe a situation or its participants as they really are, rather than in a polite or euphemistic way. "Telling it like it is" can be used as a harsh, aggressive device, or it can be a healthy attempt to face reality rather than retreat into fantasy. In any case, as he goes about his field work, the participant observer studying a ghetto community learns to listen carefully to any exchange preceded by such an announcement because he knows the speaker is about to express his understanding of how his world operates, of what motivates its members, of how they actually behave.

The first responsibility of the social scientist can be phrased in much the same way: "Tell it like it is." His second responsibility is to try to understand why "it" is that way, and to explore the implications of what and why for more constructive solutions to human problems. Social research on the situation of the Negro American has been informed by four main goals: (1) to describe the disadvantaged position of Negroes, (2) to disprove the racist ideology which sustains the caste system, (3) to demonstrate that responsibility for the disadvantages Negroes suffer lies squarely upon the white caste which derives economic, prestige, and psychic benefits from the operation of the system, and (4) to suggest that in reality whites would be better rather than worse off if the whole jerry-built caste structure were to be dismantled. The successful accomplishment of these *intellectual* goals has been a towering achievement, in which the social scientists of the 1920's, '30's, and '40's can take great pride; that white society has proved so recalcitrant to utilizing this intellectual accomplishment is one of the great tragedies of our time, and provides the stimulus for further social research on "the white problem."

Yet the implicit paradigm of much of the research on Negro Americans has been an overly simplistic one concentrating on two terms of an argument:

White cupidity————————→Negro suffering.

As an intellectual shorthand, and even more as a civil rights slogan, this simple model is both justified and essential. But, as a guide to greater understanding of the Negro situation as human adaptation to human situations, the paradigm is totally inadequate because it fails to specify fully enough the *process* by which Negroes adapt to their situations as they do, and the limitations one kind of adaptation places on possibilities for subsequent adaptations. A reassessment of previous social research, combined with examination of current social research on Negro ghetto communities, suggests a more complex, but hopefully more vertical, model:

White cupidity
creates
Structural conditions highly inimical to basic social adaptation (low-income availability, poor education, poor services, stigmatization)
to which Negroes adapt
by
Social and personal responses which serve to sustain the individual in his punishing world but also generate aggressiveness toward the self and others
which results in
Suffering directly inflicted by Negroes on themselves and on others.

In short, whites, by their greater power, create situations in which Negroes do the dirty work of caste victimization for them.

The white caste maintains a cadre of whites whose special responsibility is to enforce the system in brutal or refined ways (the Klan, the rural sheriff, the metropolitan police, the businessman who specializes in a Negro clientele, the Board of Education). Increasingly, whites recruit to this cadre middle-class Negroes who can soften awareness of victimization by their protective coloration. These special cadres, white and/or Negro, serve the very important function of enforcing caste standards by whatever means seems required, while at the same time concealing from an increasingly "unprejudiced" public the unpleasant facts they would prefer to ignore. The system is quite homologous to the Gestapo and concentration camps of Nazi Germany, though less fatal to its victims.

For their part, Negroes creatively adapt to the system in ways that keep them alive and extract what gratification they can find, but in the process of adaptation they are constrained to behave in ways that inflict a great deal of suffering on those with whom they make their lives, and on themselves. The ghetto Negro is constantly confronted by the immediate necessity to suffer in order to get what he wants of those few things he can have, or to make others suffer, or both — for example, he suffers as exploited student and employee, as drug user, as loser in the competitive game of his peer-group society; he inflicts suffering as disloyal spouse, petty thief, knife- or gun-wielder, petty con man.

It is the central thesis of this paper that the caste-facilitated infliction of suffering by Negroes on other Negroes and on themselves appears most poignantly within the confines of the family, and that the victimization process as it operates in families prepares and toughens its members to function in the ghetto world, at the same time that it seriously interferes with their ability to operate in any other world. This, however, is very different from arguing that "the family is to blame" for the deprived situation ghetto Negroes suffer; rather we are looking at the logical outcome of the operation of the widely ramified and interconnecting caste system. In the end we will argue that only palliative results can be expected from attempts to treat directly the disordered family patterns to be described. Only a change in the original "inputs" of the caste system, the structural conditions inimical to basic social adaptation, can change family forms.

Almost thirty years ago, E. Franklin Frazier foresaw that the fate of the Negro family in the city would be a highly destructive one. His readers would have little reason to be surprised at observations of slum ghetto life today:

. . . As long as the bankrupt system of southern agriculture exists, Negro families will continue to seek a living in the towns and cities. . . . They will crowd the slum areas of southern cities or make their way to northern cities where their families will become disrupted and their poverty will force them to depend upon charity.[3]

The Autonomy of the Slum Ghetto

Just as the deprivations and depredations practiced by white socity have had their effect on the personalities and social life of Negroes, so also has the separation from the ongoing social life of the white community had its effect. In a curious way, Negroes have had considerable freedom to fashion their own adaptations within their separate world. The larger society provides them with few resources but also with minimal interference in the Negro community on matters which did not seem to affect white interests. Because Negroes learned early that there were a great many things they could not depend upon whites to provide they developed their own solutions to recurrent human issues. These solutions can often be seen to combine, along with the predominance of elements from white culture, elements that are distinctive to the Negro group. Even more distinctive is the *configuration* which emerges from those elements Negroes share with whites and those which are different.

It is in this sense that we may speak of a Negro subculture, a distinctive *patterning* of existential perspectives, techniques for coping with the problems of social life, views about what is desirable and undesirable in particular situations. This subculture, and particularly that of the lower-class, the slum, Negro, can be seen as his own creation out of the elements available to him in response to (1) the conditions of life set by white society and (2) the selective freedom which that society allows (or must put up with, given the pattern of separateness on which it insists).

Out of this kind of "freedom" slum Negroes have built a culture which has some elements of intrinsic value and many more elements that are highly destructive to the people who must live in it. The elements that whites can value they constantly borrow. Negro arts and language have proved so popular that such commentators on American culture as Norman Mailer and Leslie Fiedler have noted processes of Negro-ization of white Americans as a minor theme of the past thirty years.[4] A fairly large proportion of Negroes with national reputations are engaged in the occupation of diffusing to the larger culture these elementts of intrinsic value.

On the negative side, this freedom has meant, as social scientists who have studied Negro communities have long commented, that many of the protections offered by white institutions stop at the edge of the Negro ghetto: there are poor police protection and enforcement of civil equities, inadequate schooling and medical service, and more informal indulgences which whites allow Negroes as a small price for feeling superior.

For our purposes, however, the most important thing about the freedom whites have allowed Negroes within their own world is that it has required them to work out their own ways of making it from day to day, from birth to death. The subculture that Negroes have created may be imperfect but it has been viable for centuries; it behooves both white and Negro leaders and intellectuals to seek to understand it even as they hope to change it.[5]

Negroes have created, again particularly within the lower-class slum group, a range of institutions to structure the tasks of living a victimized life and to minimize the pain it inevitably produces. In the slum ghetto these institutions include prominently those of the social network — the extended kinship system and the "street system" of buddies and broads which tie (although tenuously and unpredictably) the "members" to each other — and the institutions of entertainment (music, dance, folk tales) by which they instruct, explain, and accept themselves. Other institutions function to provide escape from the society of the victimized: the church (Hereafter!) and the civil rights movement (Now!).

The Functional Autonomy of the Negro Family

At the center of the matrix of Negro institutional life lies the family. It is in the family that individuals are trained for participation in the culture and find personal and group identity and continuity. The "freedom" allowed by white society is greatest here, and this freedom has been used to create an institutional variant more distinctive perhaps to the Negro subculture than any other. (Much of the content of Negro art and entertainment derives exactly from the distinctive characteristics of Negro family life.) At each stage in the Negro's experience of American life — slavery, segregation, de facto ghettoization — whites have found it less necessary to interfere in the relations between the sexes and between parents and children than in other areas of the Negro's existence. His adaptations in this area, therefore, have been less constrained by whites than in many other areas.

Now that the larger society is becoming increasingly committed to integrating Negroes into the main stream of American life, however, we can expect increasing constraint (benevolent as it may be) to be placed on the autonomy of the Negro family system.[6] These constraints will be designed to pull Negroes into meaningful integration with the larger society, to give up ways which are inimical to successful performance in the larger society, and to adopt new ways that are functional in that society. The strategic questions of the civil rights movement and of the war on poverty are ones that have to do with how one provides functional equivalents for the existing subculture before the capacity to make a life within its confines is destroyed.

The history of the Negro family has been ably documented by historians and sociologists.[7] In slavery, conjugal and family ties were reluctantly and ambivalently recognized by the slave holders, were often violated by them, but proved necessary to the slave system. This necessity stemmed both from the profitable offspring of slave sexual unions and the necessity for their nurture, and from the fact that the slaves' efforts to sustain patterns of sexual and parental relations mollified the men and women whose labor could not simply be commanded. From nature's promptings, the thinning memories of African heritage, and the example and guilt-ridden permission of the slave holders, slaves constructed a partial family system and sets of relations that generated conjugal and familial sentiments. The slave holder's recognition in advertisements for runaway slaves of marital and family sentiments as motivations for absconding provides one indication that strong family ties were possible, though perhaps not common, in the slave quarter. The mother-centered family with its emphasis on the primacy of the mother-child relation and only tenuous ties to a man, then, is the legacy of adaptations worked out by Negroes during slavery.

After emancipation this family design often also served well to cope with the social disorganization of Negro life in the late nineteenth century. Matrifocal families, ambivalence about the desirability of marriage, ready acceptance of illegitimacy, all sustained some kind of family life in situations which often made it difficult to maintain a full nuclear family. Yet in the hundred years since emancipation, Negroes in rural areas have been able to maintain full nuclear families almost as well as similarly situated whites. As we will see, it is the move to the city that results in the very high proportion of mother-headed households. In the rural system the man continues to have important functions; it is difficult for a woman to make a crop by herself, or even with the help of other women. In the city, however, the woman can earn wages just as a man can, and she can receive welfare payments more easily than he can. In rural areas, although there may be high illegitimacy rates and high rates of marital disruption, men and women have an interest in getting together; families are headed by a husband-wife pair much more often than in the city. That pair may be much less stable than in the more prosperous segments of Negro and white communities but it is more likely to exist among rural Negroes than among urban ones.

The matrifocal character of the Negro lower-class family in the United States has much in common with Caribbean Negro family patterns; research in both areas has done a great deal to increase our understanding of the Negro situation. However, there are important differences in the family forms of the two areas.[8] The impact of white European family models has been much greater in the United States than in the Caribbean both because of the relative population proportions of white and colored peoples and because equalitarian values in the United States have had a great impact on Negroes even when they have not on whites. The typical Caribbean mating pattern is that women go through several visiting and common-law unions but eventually marry; that is, they marry legally only relatively late in their sexual lives. The Caribbean marriage is the crowning of a sexual and procreative career; it is considered a serious and difficult step.

In the United States, in contrast, Negroes marry at only a slightly lower rate and slightly higher age than whites.[9] Most Negro women marry relatively early in their careers; marriage is not regarded as the same kind of crowning choice and achievement that it is in the Caribbean. For lower-class Negroes in the United States marriage ceremonies are rather informal affairs. In the Caribbean, marriage is regarded as quite costly because of the feasting which goes along with it; ideally it is performed in church.

In the United States, unlike the Caribbean, early marriage confers a kind of permanent respectable status upon a woman which she can use to deny any subsequent accusations of immorality or promiscuity once the marriage is broken and she becomes sexually involved in visiting or common-law relations. The relevant effective status for many Negro women is that of "having been married" rather than "being married"; having the right to be called "Mrs." rather than currently being Mrs. Someone-in-Particular.

For Negro lower-class women, then, first marriage has the same kind of importance as having a first child. Both indicate that the girl has become a woman but neither one that this is the last such activity in which she will engage. It seems very likely that only a minority of Negro women in the urban slum go through their child-rearing years with only one man around the house.

Among the Negro urban poor, then, a great many women have the experience of heading a family for part of their mature lives, and a great many children spend some part of their formative years in a household without a father-mother pair. From Table 1 we see that in 1960, forty-seven per cent of the Negro poor urban families with children had a female head. Unfortunately, cumulative statistics are hard to come by; but, given this very high level for a cross-sectional sample (and taking into account the fact that the median age of the children in these families is about six years), it seems very likely that as many as two-thirds of Negro urban poor children will not live in families headed by a man and a woman throughout the first eighteen years of their lives.

Table 1: Proportion of Female Heads for Families with Children by Race, Income, and Urban-Rural Categories

Negroes	Rural	Urban	Total
under $3000	18%	47%	36%
$3000 and over	5	8	7
Total	14	23	21
Whites			
under $3000	12%	38%	22%
$3000 and over	2	4	3
Total	4	7	6

Source: U.S. Census: 1960, PC (1) D. U. S. Volume, Table 225; State Volume, Table 140.

One of the other distinctive characteristics of Negro families, both poor and not so poor, is the fact that Negro households have a much higher proportion of relatives outside the mother-father-children triangle than is the case with whites. For example, in St. Louis Negro families average 0.8 other relatives per household compared to only 0.4 for white families. In the case of the more prosperous Negro families this is likely to mean that an older relative lives in the home providing baby-sitting services while both the husband and wife work and thus further their climb toward stable working- or middle-class status. In the poor Negro families it is much more likely that the household is headed by an older relative who brings under her wings a daughter and that daughter's children. It is important to note that the three-generation household with the grandmother at the head exists only when there is no husband present. Thus, despite the high proportion of female-headed households in this group and despite the high proportion of households that contain other relatives, we find that almost all married couples in the St. Louis Negro slum community have their own household. In other words, when a couple marries it establishes its own household; when that couple breaks up the mother either maintains that household or moves back to her parents or grand-parents.

Finally we should note that Negro slum families have more children than do either white slum families or stable working- and middle-class Negro families. Mobile Negro families limit their fertility sharply in the interest of bringing the advantages of mobility more fully to the few children that they do have. Since the Negro slum family is both more likely to have the father absent and more likely to have more children in the family, the mother has a more demanding task with fewer resources at her disposal. When we examine the patterns of life of the stem family we shall see that even the presence of several mothers does not necessarily lighten the work load for the principal mother in charge.

The Formation and Maintenance of Families

We will outline below the several stages and forms of Negro lower-class family life. At many points these family forms and the interpersonal relations that exist within them will be seen to have characteristics in common with the life styles of white lower-class families.[10] At other points there are differences, or the Negro pattern will be seen to be more sharply divergent from the family life of stable working- and middle-class couples.

It is important to recognize that lower-class Negroes know that their particular family forms are different from those of the rest of the society and that, though they often see these forms as representing the only ways of behaving given their circumstances, they also think of the more stable family forms of the working class as more desirable. That is, lower-class Negroes know what the "normal American family" is supposed to be like, and they consider a stable family-centered way of life superior to the conjugal and familial situations in which they often find themselves. Their conceptions of the good American life include the notion of a father-husband who functions as an adequate provider and interested member of the family, a hard-working home-bound mother who is concerned about her children's welfare and her husband's needs, and children who look up to their parents and perform well in school and other outside places to reflect credit on their families. This image of what family life can be like is very real from time to time as lower-class men and women grow up and move through adulthood. Many of them make efforts to establish such families but find it impossible to do so either because of the direct impact of economic disabilities or because they are not able to sustain in their day-to-day lives the ideals which they hold.[11] While these ideals do serve as a meaningful guide to lower-class couples who are mobile out of the group, for a great many others the existence of such ideas about normal family life represents a recurrent source of stress within families as individuals become aware that they are failing to measure up to the ideals, or as others within the family and outside it use the ideals as an aggressive weapon for criticizing each other's performance. It is not at all uncommon for husbands or wives or children to try to hold others in the family to the norms of stable family life while they themselves engage in behaviors which violate these norms. The effect of such criticism in the end is to deepen commitment to the deviant sexual and parental norms of a slum subculture. Unless they are careful, social workers and other professionals exacerbate the tendency to use the norms of "American family life" as weapons by supporting these norms in situations where they are in reality unsupportable, thus aggravating the sense of failing and being failed by others which is chronic for lower-class people.

Going Together

The initial steps toward mating and family formation in the Negro slum take place in a context of highly developed boys' and girls' peer groups. Adolescents tend to become deeply involved in their peer-group societies beginning as early as the age of twelve or thirteen and continue to be involved after first pregnancies and first marriages. Boys and girls are heavily committed both to their same sex peer groups and to the activities that those groups carry out. While classical gang activity does not necessarily characterize Negro slum communities everywhere, loosely-knit peer groups do.

The world of the Negro slum is wide open to exploration by adolescent boys and girls: "Negro communities provide a flow of common experience in which young people and their elders share, and out of which delinquent behavior emerges almost imperceptibly."[12] More than is possible in white slum communities, Negro adolescents have an opportunity to interact with adults in various "high life" activities; their behavior more often represents an identification with the behavior of adults than an attempt to set up group standards and activities that differ from those of adults.

Boys and young men participating in the street system of peer-group activity are much caught up in games of furthering and enhancing their status as significant persons. These games are played out in small and large gatherings through various kinds of verbal contests that go under the names of "sounding," "signifying," and "working game." Very much a part of a boy's or man's status in this group is his ability to win women. The man who has several women "up tight," who is successful in "pimping off" women for sexual favors and material benefits, is much admired. In sharp contrast to white lower-class groups, there is little tendency for males to separate girls into "good" and "bad" categories.[13] Observations of groups of Negro youths suggest that girls and women are much more readily referred to as "that bitch" or "that whore" than they are by their names, and this seems to be a universal tendency carrying no connotation that "that bitch" is morally inferior to or different from other women. Thus, all women are essentially the same, all women are legitimate targets, and no girl or woman is expected to be virginal except for reason of lack of opportunity or immaturity. From their participation in the peer group and according to standards legitimated by the total Negro slum culture, Negro boys and young men are propelled in the direction of girls to test their "strength" as seducers. They are mercilessly rated by both their peers and the opposite sex in their ability to "talk" to girls; a young man will go to great lengths to avoid the reputation of having a "weak" line.[14]

The girls share these definitions of the nature of heterosexual relations; they take for granted that almost any male they deal with will try to seduce them and that given sufficient inducement (social not monetary) they may wish to go along with his line. Although girls have a great deal of ambivalence about participating in sexual relations, this ambivalence is minimally moral and has much more to do with a desire not to be taken advantage of or get in trouble. Girls develop defenses against the exploitative orientations of men by devaluing the significance of sexual relations ("he really didn't do anything bad to me"), and as time goes on by developing their own appreciation of the intrinsic rewards of sexual intercourse.

The informal social relations of slum Negroes begin in adolescence to be highly sexualized. Although parents have many qualms about boys and, particularly, girls entering into this system, they seldom feel there is much they can do to prevent their children's sexual involvement. They usually confine themselves to counseling somewhat hopelessly against girls becoming pregnant or boys being forced into situations where they might have to marry a girl they do not want to marry.

Girls are propelled toward boys and men in order to demonstrate their maturity and attractiveness; in the process they are constantly exposed to pressures for seduction, to boys "rapping" to them. An active girl will "go with" quite a number of boys, but she will generally try to restrict the number with whom she has intercourse to the few to whom she is attracted or (as happens not infrequently) to those whose threats of physical violence she cannot avoid. For their part, the boys move rapidly from girl to girl seeking to have intercourse with as many as they can and thus build up their "reps." The activity of seduction is itself highly cathected; there is gratification in simply "talking to" a girl as long as the boy can feel that he has acquitted himself well.

At sixteen Joan Bemias enjoys spending time with three or four very close girl friends. She tells us they follow this routine when the girls want to go out and none of the boys they have been seeing lately is available: "Every time we get ready to go someplace we look through all the telephone numbers of boys we'd have and we call them and talk so sweet to them that they'd come on around. All of them had cars, you see. (I: What do you do to keep all these fellows interested?) Well nothing. We don't have to make love with all of them. Let's see, Joe, J. B., Albert, and Paul, out of all of them I've been going out with I've only had sex with four boys, that's all." She goes on to say that she and her girl friends resist boys by being unresponsive to their lines and by breaking off relations with them on the ground that they're going out with other girls. It is also clear from her comments that the girl friends support each other in resisting the boys when they are out together in groups.

Joan has had a relationship with a boy which has lasted six months, but she has managed to hold the frequency of intercourse down to four times. Initially she managed to hold this particular boy off for a month but eventually gave in.

Becoming Pregnant

It is clear that the contest elements in relationships between men and women continue even in relationships that become quite steady. Despite the girls' ambivalence about sexual relations and their manifold efforts to reduce its frequency, the operation of chance often eventuates in their becoming pregnant.[15] This was the case with Joan. With this we reach the second stage in the formation of families, that of premarital pregnancy. (We are outlining an ideal-typical sequence and not, of course, implying that all girls in the Negro slum culture become pregnant before they marry, but only that a great many of them do.)

Joan was caught despite the fact that she was considerably more sophisticated about contraception than most girls or young women in the group (her mother had both instructed her in contraceptive techniques and constantly warned her to take precautions). No one was particularly surprised at her pregnancy although she, her boy friend, her mother, and others regarded it as unfortunate. For girls in the Negro slum, pregnancy before marriage is expected in much the same way that parents expect their children to catch mumps or chicken pox; if they are lucky it will not happen but if it happens people are not too surprised and everyone knows what to do about it. It was quickly decided that Joan and the baby would stay at home. It seems clear from the preparations that Joan's mother is making that she expects to have the main responsibility for caring for the infant. Joan seems quite indifferent to the baby; she shows little interest in mothering the child although she is not particularly adverse to the idea so long as the baby does not interfere too much with her continued participation in her peer group.

Establishing who the father is under these circumstances seems to be important and confers a kind of legitimacy on the birth; not to know who one's father is, on the other hand, seems the ultimate in illegitimacy. Actually Joan had a choice in the imputation of fatherhood; she chose J. B. because he is older than she, and because she may marry him if he can get a divorce from his wife. She could have chosen Paul (with whom she had also had intercourse at about the time she became pregnant), but she would have done this reluctantly since Paul is a year younger than she and somehow this does not seem fitting.

In general, when a girl becomes pregnant while still living at home it seems taken for granted that she will continue to live there and that her parents will take a major responsibility for rearing the children. Since there are usually siblings who can help out and even siblings who will be playmates for the child, the addition of a third generation to the household does not seem to place a great stress on relationships within the family. It seems common for the first pregnancy to have a liberating influence on the mother once the child is born in that she becomes socially and sexually more active than she was before. She no longer has to be concerned with preserving her status as a single girl. Since her mother is usually willing to take care of the child for a few years, the unwed mother has an opportunity to go out with girl friends and with men and thus become more deeply involved in the peer-group society of her culture. As she has more children and perhaps marries she will find it necessary to settle down and spend more time around the house fulfilling the functions of a mother herself.

It would seem that for girls pregnancy is the real measure of maturity, the dividing line between adolescence and womanhood. Perhaps because of this, as well as because of the ready resources for child care, girls in the Negro slum community show much less concern about pregnancy than do girls in the white lower-class community and are less motivated to marry the fathers of their children. When a girl becomes pregnant the question of marriage certainly arises and is considered, but the girl often decides that she would rather not marry the man either because she does not want to settle down yet or because she does not think he would make a good husband.

It is in the easy attitudes toward premarital pregnancy that the matrifocal character of the Negro lower-class family appears most clearly. In order to have and raise a family it is simply not necessary, though it may be desirable, to have a man around the house. While the AFDC program may make it easier to maintain such attitudes in the urban situation, this pattern existed long before the program was initiated and continues in families where support comes from other sources.

Finally it should be noted that fathering a child similarly confers maturity on boys and young men although perhaps it is less salient for them. If the boy has any interest in the girl he will tend to feel that the fact that he has impregnated her gives him an additional claim on her. He will be stricter in seeking to enforce his exclusive rights over her (though not exclusive loyalty to her). This exclusive right does not mean that he expects to marry her but only that there is a new and special bond between them. If the girl is not willing to accept such claims she may find it necessary to break off the relationship rather than tolerate the man's jealousy. Since others in the peer group have a vested interest in not allowing a couple to be too loyal to each other they go out of their way to question and challenge each partner abut the loyalty of the other, thus contributing to the deterioration of the relationship. This same kind of questioning and challenging continues if the couple marries and represents one source of the instability of the marital relationship.

Getting Married

As noted earlier, despite the high degree of premarital sexual activity and the rather high proportion of premarital pregnancies, most lower-class Negro men and women eventually do marry and stay together for a shorter or longer period of time. Marriage is an intimidating prospect and is approached ambivalently by both parties. For the girl it means giving up a familiar and comfortable home that, unlike some other lower-class subcultures, places few real restrictions on her behavior. (While marriage can appear to be an escape from interpersonal difficulties at home, these difficulties seldom seem to revolve around effective restrictions placed on her behavior by her parents.) The girl also has good reason to be suspicious of the likelihood that men will be able to perform stably in the role of husband and provider; she is reluctant to be tied down by a man who will not prove to be worth it.

From the man's point of view the fickleness of women makes marriage problematic. It is one thing to have a girl friend step out on you, but it is quite another to have a wife do so. Whereas premarital sexual relations and fatherhood carry almost no connotation of responsibility for the welfare of the partner, marriage is supposed to mean that a man behaves more responsibly, becoming a provider for his wife and children even though he may not be expected to give up all the gratifications of participation in the street system.

For all of these reasons both boys and girls tend to have rather negative views of marriage as well as a low expectation that marriage will prove a stable and gratifying existence. When marriage does take place it tends to represent a tentative commitment on the part of both parties with a strong tendency to seek greater commitment on the part of the partner than on one's own part. Marriage is regarded as a fragile arrangement held together primarily by affectional ties rather than instrumental concerns.

In general, as in white lower-class groups, the decision to marry seems to be taken rather impulsively.[16] Since everyone knows that sooner or later he will get married, in spite of the fact that he may not be sanguine about the prospect, Negro lower-class men and women are alert for clues that the time has arrived. The time may arrive because of a pregnancy in a steady relationship that seems gratifying to both partners, or as a way of getting out of what seems to be an awkward situation, or as a self-indulgence during periods when a boy and a girl are feeling very sorry for themselves. Thus, one girl tells us that when she marries her husband will cook all of her meals for her and she will not have any housework; another girl says that when she marries it will be to a man who has plenty of money and will have to take her out often and really show her a good time.

Boys see in marriage the possibility of regular sexual intercourse without having to fight for it, or a girl safe from venereal disease, or a relationship to a nurturant figure who will fulfill the functions of a mother. For boys, marriage can also be a way of asserting their independence from the peer group if its demands become burdensome. In this case the young man seeks to have the best of both worlds.[17]

Marriage as a way out of an unpleasant situation can be seen in the case of one of our informants, Janet Cowan:

Janet has been going with two men, one of them married and the other single. The married man's wife took exception to their relationship and killed her husband. Within a week Janet and her single boy friend, Howard, were married. One way out of the turmoil the murder of her married boy friend stimulated (they lived in the same building) was to choose marriage as a way of "settling down." However, after marrying the new couple seemed to have little idea how to set themselves up as a family. Janet was reluctant to leave her parents' home because her parents cared for her two illegitimate children. Howard was unemployed and therefore unacceptable in his parent-in-laws' home, nor were his own parents willing to have his wife move in with them. Howard was also reluctant to give up another girl friend in another part of town. Although both he and his wife maintained that it was all right for a couple to step out on each other so long as the other partner did not know about it, they were both jealous if they suspected anything of this kind. In the end they gave up on the idea of marriage and went their separate ways.

In general, then, the movement toward marriage is an uncertain and tentative one. Once the couple does settle down together in a household of their own, they have the problem of working out a mutually acceptable organization of rights and duties, expectations and performances, that will meet their needs.

Husband-Wife Relations

Characteristic of both the Negro and white lower class is a high degree of conjugal role segregation.[18] That is, husbands and wives tend to think of themselves as having very separate kinds of functioning in the instrumental organization of family life, and also as pursuing recreational and outside interests separately. The husband is expected to be a provider; he resists assuming functions around the home so long as he feels he is doing his proper job of bringing home a pay check. He feels he has the right to indulge himself in little ways if he is successful at this task. The wife is expected to care for the home and children and make her husband feel welcome and comfortable. Much that is distinctive to Negro family life stems from the fact that husbands often are not stable providers. Even when a particular man is, his wife's conception of men in general is such that she is pessimistic about the likelihood that he will continue to do well in this area. A great many Negro wives work to supplement the family income. When this is so the separate incomes earned by husband and wife tend to be treated not as "family" income but as the individual property of the two persons involved. If their wives work, husbands are likely to feel that they are entitled to retain a larger share of the income they provide; the wives, in turn, feel that the husbands have no right to benefit from the purchases they make out of their own money. There is, then, "my money" and "your money." In this situation the husband may come to feel that the wife should support the children out of her income and that he can retain all of his income for himself.

While white lower-class wives often are very much intimidated by their husbands, Negro lower-class wives come to feel that they have a right to give as good as they get. If the husband indulges himself, they have the right to indulge themselves. If the husband steps out on his wife, she has the right to step out on him. The commitment of husbands and wives to each other seems often a highly instrumental one after the "honeymoon" period. Many wives feel they owe the husband nothing once he fails to perform his provider role. If the husband is unemployed the wife increasingly refuses to perform her usual duties for him. For example one woman, after mentioning that her husband had cooked four eggs for himself, commented, "I cook for him when he's working but right now he's unemployed; he can cook for himself." It is important, however, to understand that the man's status in the home depends not so much on whether he is working as on whether he brings money into the home. Thus, in several of the families we have studied in which the husband receives disability payments his status is as well-recognized as in families in which the husband is working.[19]

Because of the high degree of conjugal role segregation, both white and Negro lower-class families tend to be matrifocal in comparison to middle-class families. They are matrifocal in the sense that the wife makes most of the decisions that keep the family going and has the greatest sense of responsibility to the family. In white as well as in Negro lower-class families women tend to look to their female relatives for support and counsel, and to treat their husbands as essentially uninterested in the day-to-day problems of family living.[20] In the Negro lower-class family these tendencies are all considerably exaggerated so that the matrifocality is much clearer than in white lower-class families.

The fact that both sexes in the Negro slum culture have equal right to the various satisfactions of life (earning an income, sex, drinking, and peer-group activity which conflicts with family responsibilities) means that there is less pretense to patriarchal authority in the Negro than in the white lower class. Since men find the overt debasement of their status very threatening, the Negro family is much more vulnerable to disruption when men are temporarily unable to perform their provider roles. Also, when men are unemployed the temptations for them to engage in street adventures which repercuss on the marital relationship are much greater. This fact is well-recognized by Negro lower-class wives; they often seem as concerned about what their unemployed husbands will do instead of working as they are about the fact that the husband is no longer bringing money into the home.

It is tempting to cope with the likelihood of disloyalty by denying the usual norms of fidelity, by maintaining instead that extra-marital affairs are acceptable as long as they do not interfere with family functioning. Quite a few informants tell us this, but we have yet to observe a situation in which a couple maintains a stable relationship under these circumstances without a great deal of conflict. Thus one woman in her forties who has been married for many years and has four children first outlined this deviant norm and then illustrated how it did not work out:

My husband and I, we go out alone and sometimes stay all night. But when I get back my husband doesn't ask me a thing and I don't ask him anything. . . . A couple of years ago I suspected he was going out on me. One day I came home and my daughter was here. I told her to tell me when he left the house. I went into the bedroom and got into bed and then I heard him come in. He left in about ten minutes and my daughter came in and told me he was gone. I got out of bed and put on my clothes and started following him. Soon I saw him walking with a young girl and I began walking after them. They were just laughing and joking right out loud right on the sidewalk. He was carrying a large package of hers. I walked up behind them until I was about a yard from them. I had a large dirk which I opened and had decided to take one long slash across the both of them. Just when I decided to swing at them I lost my balance — I have a bad hip. Anyway, I didn't cut them because I lost my balance. Then I called his name and he turned around and stared at me. He didn't move at all. He was shaking all over. That girl just ran away from us. He still had her package so the next day she called on the telephone and said she wanted to come pick it up. My husband washed his face, brushed his teeth, took out his false tooth and started scrubbing it and put on a clean shirt and everything, just for her. We went downstairs together and gave her the package and she left.

So you see my husband does run around on me and it seems like he does it a lot. The thing about it is he's just getting too old to be pulling that kind of stuff. If a young man does it then that's not so bad — but an old man, he just looks foolish. One of these days he'll catch me but I'll just tell him, "Buddy, you owe me one," and that'll be all there is to it. He hasn't caught me yet though.

In this case, as in others, the wife is not able to leave well enough alone; but jealousy forces her to a confrontation. Actually seeing her husband with another woman stimulates her to violence.

With couples who have managed to stay married for a good many years, these peccadillos are tolerable although they generate a great deal of conflict in the marital relationship. At earlier ages the partners are likely to be both prouder and less inured to the hopelessness of maintaining stable relationships; outside involvements are therefore much more likely to be disruptive of the marriage.

Marital Breakup

The precipitating causes of marital disruption seem to fall mainly into economic or sexual categories. As noted, the husband has little credit with his wife to tide him over periods of unemployment. Wives seem very willing to withdraw commitment from husbands who are not bringing money into the house. They take the point of view that he has no right to take up space around the house, to use its facilities, or to demand loyalty from her. Even where the wife is not inclined to press these claims, the husband tends to be touchy because he knows that such definitions are usual in his group, and he may, therefore, prove difficult for even a well-meaning wife to deal with. As noted above, if husbands do not work they tend to play around. Since they continue to maintain some contact with their peer groups, whenever they have time on their hands they move back into the world of the street system and are likely to get involved in activities which pose a threat to their family relationships.

Drink is a great enemy of the lower-class housewife, both white and Negro. Lower-class wives fear their husband's drinking because it costs money, because the husband may become violent and take out his frustrations on his wife, and because drinking may lead to sexual involvements with other women.[21]

The combination of economic problems and sexual difficulties can be seen in the case of the following couple in their early twenties:

When the field worker first came to know them, the Wilsons seemed to be working hard to establish a stable family life. The couple had been married about three years and had a two-year-old son. Their apartment was very sparsely furnished but also very clean. Within six weeks the couple had acquired several rooms of inexpensive furniture and obviously had gone to a great deal of effort to make a liveable home. Husband and wife worked on different shifts so that the husband could take care of the child while the wife worked. They looked forward to saving enough money to move out of the housing project into a more desirable neighborhood. Six weeks later, however, the husband had lost his job. He and his wife were in great conflict. She made him feel unwelcome at home and he strongly suspected her of going out with other men. A short time later they had separated. It is impossible to disentangle the various factors involved in this separation into a sequence of cause and effect, but we can see something of the impact of the total complex.

First Mr. Wilson loses his job: "I went to work one day and the man told me that I would have to work until 1:00. I asked him if there would be any extra pay for working overtime and he said no. I asked him why and he said, 'If you don't like it you can kiss my ass.' He said that to me. I said, 'Why do I have to do all that?' He said, 'Because I said so.' I wanted to jam (fight) him but I said to myself I don't want to be that ignorant, I don't want to be as ignorant as he is, so I just cut out and left. Later his father called me (it was a family firm) and asked why I left and I told him. He said, 'If you don't want to go along with my son then you're fired.' I said O.K. They had another Negro man come in to help me part time before they fired me. I think they were trying to have him work full time because he worked for them before. He has seven kids and he takes their shit."

The field worker observed that things were not as hard as they could be because his wife had a job, to which he replied, "Yeah, I know, that's just where the trouble is. My wife has become independent since she began working. If I don't get a job pretty soon I'll go crazy. We have a lot of little arguments about nothing since she got so independent." He went on to say that his wife had become a completely different person recently; she was hard to talk to because she felt that now that she was working and he was not there was nothing that he could tell her. On her last pay day his wife did not return home for three days; when she did she had only seven cents left from her pay check. He said that he loved his wife very much and had begged her to quit fooling around. He is pretty sure that she is having an affair with the man with whom she rides to work. To make matters worse his wife's sister counsels her that she does not have to stay home with him as long as he is out of work. Finally the wife moved most of their furniture out of the apartment so that he came home to find an empty apartment. He moved back to his parents' home (also in the housing project).

One interesting effect of this experience was the radical change in the husband's attitudes toward race relations. When he and his wife were doing well together and had hopes of moving up in the world he was quite critical of Negroes; "Our people are not ready for integration in many cases because they really don't know how to act. You figure if our people don't want to be bothered with whites then why in hell should the white man want to be bothered with them. There are some of us who are ready; there are others who aren't quite ready yet so I don't see why they're doing all this hollering." A scarce eight months later he addressed white people as he spoke for two hours into a tape recorder, "If we're willing to be with you, why aren't you willing to be with us? Do our color make us look dirty and low-down and cheap? Or do you know the real meaning of 'nigger'? Anyone can be a nigger, white, colored, orange or any other color. It's something that you labeled us with. You put us away like you put a can away on the shelf with a label on it. The can is marked 'Poison: stay away from it.' You want us to help build your country but you don't want us to live in it. . . . You give me respect; I'll give you respect. If you threaten to take my life, I'll take yours and believe me I know how to take a life. We do believe that man was put here to live together as human beings; not one that's superior and the one that's a dog, but as human beings. And if you don't want to live this way then you become the dog and we'll become the human beings. There's too much corruption, too much hate, too much one in- dividual trying to step on another. If we don't get together in a hurry we will destroy each other." It was clear from what the respondent said that he had been much influenced by Black Muslim philosophy, yet again and again in his comments one can see the displacement into a public, race relations dialogue of the sense of rage, frustration and victimization that he had experienced in his ill-fated marriage.[22]

Finally, it should be noted that migration plays a part in marital disruption. Sometimes marriages do not break up in the dramatic way described above but rather simply become increasingly unsatisfactory to one or both partners. In such a situation the temptation to move to another city, from South to North, or North to West, is great. Several wives told us that their first marriages were broken when they moved with their children to the North and their husbands stayed behind.

"After we couldn't get along I left the farm and came here and stayed away three or four days. I didn't come here to stay. I came to visit but I liked it and so I said, 'I'm gonna leave!' He said, 'I'll be glad if you do.' Well, maybe he didn't mean it but I thought he did. . . . I miss him sometimes, you know. I think about him, I guess. But just in a small way. That's what I can't understand about life sometimes; you know — how people can go on like that and still break up and meet somebody else. Why couldn't — oh, I don't know!"

The gains and losses in marriage and in the post-marital state often seem quite comparable. Once they have had the experience of marriage, many women in the Negro slum culture see little to recommend it in the future, important as the first marriage may have been in establishing their maturity and respectability.

The House of Mothers

As we have seen, perhaps a majority of mothers in the Negro slum community spend at least part of their mature life as mothers heading a family. The Negro mother may be a working mother or she may be an AFDC mother, but in either case she has the problems of maintaining a household, socializing her children, and achieving for herself some sense of membership in relations with other women and with men. As is apparent from the earlier discussion, she often receives her training in how to run such a household by observing her own mother manage without a husband. Similarly she often learns how to run a three-generation household because she herself brought a third generation into her home with her first, premarital, pregnancy.

Because men are not expected to be much help around the house, having to be head of the household is not particularly intimidating to the Negro mother if she can feel some security about income. She knows it is a hard, hopeless, and often thankless task, but she also knows that it is possible. The maternal household in the slum is generally run with a minimum of organization. The children quickly learn to fend for themselves, to go to the store, to make small purchases, to bring change home, to watch after themselves when the mother has to be out of the home, to amuse themselves, to set their own schedules of sleeping, eating, and going to school. Housekeeping practices may be poor, furniture takes a terrific beating from the children, and emergencies constantly arise. The Negro mother in this situation copes by not setting too high standards for herself, by letting things take their course. Life is most difficult when there are babies and preschool children around because then the mother is confined to the home. If she is a grandmother and the children are her daughter's, she is often confined since it is taken as a matter of course that the mother has the right to continue her outside activities and that the grandmother has the duty to be responsible for the child.

In this culture there is little of the sense of the awesome responsibility of caring for children that is characteristic of the working and middle class. There is not the deep psychological involvement with babies which has been observed with the working-class mother.[23] The baby's needs are cared for on a catch-as-catch-can basis. If there are other children around and they happen to like babies, the baby can be over-stimulated; if this is not the case, the baby is left alone a good deal of the time. As quickly as he can move around he learns to fend for himself.

The three-generation maternal household is a busy place. In contrast to working- and middle-class homes it tends to be open to the world, with many non-family members coming in and out at all times as the children are visited by friends, the teenagers by their boy friends and girl friends, the mother by her friends and perhaps an occasional boy friend, and the grandmother by fewer friends but still by an occasional boy friend.

The openness of the household is, among other things, a reflection of the mother's sense of impotence in the face of the street system. Negro lower-class mothers often indicate that they try very hard to keep their young children at home and away from the streets; they often seem to make the children virtual prisoners in the home. As the children grow and go to school they inevitably do become involved in peer-group activities. The mother gradually gives up, feeling that once the child is lost to this pernicious outside world there is little she can do to continue to control him and direct his development. She will try to limit the types of activities that go on in the home and to restrict the kinds of friends that her children can bring into the home, but even this she must give up as time goes on, as the children become older and less attentive to her direction.

The grandmothers in their late forties, fifties, and sixties tend increasingly to stay at home. The home becomes a kind of court at which other family members gather and to which they bring their friends for sociability, and as a by-product provide amusement and entertainment for the mother. A grandmother may provide a home for her daughters, their children, and sometimes their children's children, and yet receive very little in a material way from them; but one of the things she does receive is a sense of human involvement, a sense that although life may have passed her by she is not completely isolated from it.

The lack of control that mothers have over much that goes on in their households is most dramatically apparent in the fact that their older children seem to have the right to come home at any time once they have moved and to stay in the home without contributing to its maintenance. Though the mother may be resentful about being taken advantage of, she does not feel she can turn her children away. For example, sixty-five-year-old Mrs. Washington plays hostess for weeks or months at a time to her forty-year-old daughter and her small children, and to her twenty-three-year-old granddaughter and her children. When these daughters come home with their families the grandmother is expected to take care of the young children and must argue with her daughter and granddaughter to receive contributions to the daily household ration of food and liquor. Or, a twenty-year-old son comes home from the Air Force and feels he has the right to live at home without working and to run up an eighty-dollar long-distance telephone bill.

Even aged parents living alone in small apartments sometimes acknowledge such obligations to their children or grandchildren. Again, the only clear return they receive for their hospitality is the reduction of isolation that comes from having people around and interesting activity going on. When in the Washington home the daughter and granddaughter and their children move in with the grandmother, or when they come to visit for shorter periods of time, the occasion has a party atmosphere. The women sit around talking and reminiscing. Though boy friends may be present, they take little part; instead they sit passively, enjoying the stories and drinking along with the women. It would seem that in this kind of party activity the women are defined as the stars. Grandmother, daughter, and granddaughter in turn take the center of the stage telling a story from the family's past, talking about a particularly interesting night out on the town or just making some general observation about life. In the course of these events a good deal of liquor is consumed. In such a household as this little attention is paid to the children since the competition by adults for attention is stiff.

Boy Friends, Not Husbands

It is with an understanding of the problems of isolation which older mothers have that we can obtain the best insight into the role and function of boy friends in the maternal household. The older mothers, surrounded by their own children and grandchildren, are not able to move freely in the outside world, to participate in the high life which they enjoyed when younger and more foot-loose. They are disillusioned with marriage as providing any more secure economic base than they can achieve on their own. They see marriage as involving just another responsibility without a concomitant reward — "It's the greatest thing in the world to come home in the afternoon and not have some curly-headed twot in the house yellin' at me and askin' me where supper is, where I've been, what I've been doin', and who I've been seein'." In this situation the woman is tempted to form relationships with men that are not so demanding as marriage but still provide companionship and an opportunity for occasional sexual gratification.

There seem to be two kinds of boy friends. Some boy friends "pimp" off mothers; they extract payment in food or money for their companionship. This leads to the custom sometimes called "Mother's Day," the tenth of the month when the AFDC checks come.[24] On this day one can observe an influx of men into the neighborhood, and much partying. But there is another kind of boy friend, perhaps more numerous than the first, who instead of being paid for his services pays for the right to be a pseudo family member. He may be the father of one of the woman's children and for this reason makes a steady contribution to the family's support, or he may simply be a man whose company the mother enjoys and who makes reasonable gifts to the family for the time he spends with them (and perhaps implicitly for the sexual favors he receives). While the boy friend does not assume fatherly authority within the family, he often is known and liked by the children. The older children appreciate the meaningfulness of their mother's relationship with him — one girl said of her mother's boy friend:

"We don't none of us (the children) want her to marry again. It's all right if she wants to live by herself and have a boy friend. It's not because we're afraid we're going to have some more sisters and brothers, which it wouldn't make us much difference, but I think she be too old."

Even when the boy friend contributes ten or twenty dollars a month to the family he is in a certain sense getting a bargain. If he is a well-accepted boy friend he spends considerable time around the house, has a chance to relax in an atmosphere less competitive than that of his peer group, is fed and cared for by the woman, yet has no responsibilities which he cannot renounce when he wishes. When women have stable relationships of this kind with boy friends they often consider marrying them but are reluctant to take such a step. Even the well-liked boy friend has some shortcomings — one woman said of her boy friend:

"Well, he works; I know that. He seems to be a nice person, kind hearted. He believes in survival for me and my family. He don't much mind sharing with my youngsters. If I ask him for a helping hand he don't seem to mind that. The only part I dislike is his drinking."

The woman in this situation has worked out a reasonably stable adaptation to the problems of her life; she is fearful of upsetting this adaptation by marrying again. It seems easier to take the "sweet" part of the relationship with a man without the complexities that marriage might involve.

It is in the light of this pattern of women living in families and men living by themselves in rooming houses, odd rooms, here and there, that we can understand Daniel Patrick Moynihan's observation that during their mature years men simply disappear; that is, that census data show a very high sex ratio of women to men.[25] In St. Louis, starting at the age range twenty to twenty-four there are only seventy-two men for every one hundred women. This ratio does not climb to ninety until the age range fifty to fifty-four. Men often do not have real homes; they move about from one household where they have kinship or sexual ties to another; they live in flop houses and rooming houses; they spend time in institutions. They are not household members in the only "homes" that they have — the homes of their mothers and of their girl friends.

It is in this kind of world that boys and girls in the Negro slum community learn their sex roles. It is not just, or even mainly, that fathers are often absent but that the male role models around boys are ones which emphasize expressive, affectional techniques for making one's way in the world. The female role models available to girls emphasize an exaggerated self-sufficiency (from the point of view of the middle class) and the danger of allowing oneself to be dependent on men for anything that is crucial. By the time she is mature, the woman learns that she is most secure when she herself manages the family affairs and when she dominates her men. The man learns that he exposes himself to the least risk of failure when he does not assume a husband's and father's responsibilities but instead counts on his ability to court women and to ingratiate himself with them.

Identity Processes in the Family

Up to this point we have been examining the sequential development of family stages in the Negro slum community, paying only incidental attention to the psychological responses family members make to these social forms and not concerning ourselves with the effect the family forms have on the psychosocial development of the children who grow up in them. Now we want to examine the effect that growing up in this kind of a system has in terms of socialization and personality development.

Household groups function for cultures in carrying out the initial phases of socialization and personality formation. It is in the family that the child learns the most primitive categories of existence and experience, and that he develops his most deeply held beliefs about the world and about himself.[26] From the child's point of view, the household *is* the world; his experiences as he moves out of it into the larger world are always interpreted in terms of his particular experience within the home. The painful experiences which a child in the Negro slum culture has are, therefore, interpreted as in some sense a reflection of this family world. The impact of the system of victimization is transmitted through the family; the child cannot be expected to have the sophistication an outside observer has for seeing exactly where the villains are. From the child's point of view, if he is hungry it is his parents' fault; if he experiences frustrations in the streets or in the school it is his parents' fault; if that world seems incomprehensible to him it is his parents' fault; if people are aggressive or destructive toward each other it is his parents' fault, not that of a system of race relations. In another culture this might not be the case; if a subculture could exist which provided comfort and security within its limited world and the individual experienced frustration only when he moved out into the larger society, the family might not be thought so much to blame. The effect of the caste system, however, is to bring home through a chain of cause and effect all of the victimization processes, and to bring them home in such a way that it is often very difficult even for adults in the system to see the connection between the pain they feel at the moment and the structured patterns of the caste system.

Let us take as a central question that of identity formation within the Negro slum family. We are concerned with the question of who the individual believes himself to be and to be becoming. For Erikson, identity means a sense of continuity and social sameness which bridges what the individual *"was* as a child and what he is *about to become* and also reconciles his *conception of himself* and his community's recognition of him." Thus identity is a "self-realization coupled with a mutual recognition."[27] In the early childhood years identity is family-bound since the child's identity is his identity *vis-à-vis* other members of the family. Later he incorporates into his sense of who he is and is becoming his experiences outside the family, but always influenced by the interpretations and evaluations of those experiences that the family gives. As the child tries on identities, *announces* them, the family sits as judge of his pretensions. Family members are both the most important judges and the most critical ones, since who he is allowed to become affects them in their own identity strivings more crucially than it affects anyone else. The child seeks a sense of valid identity, a sense of being a particular person with a satisfactory degree of congruence between who he feels he is, who he announces himself to be, and where he feels his society places him.[28] He is uncomfortable when he experiences disjunction between his own needs and the kinds of needs legitimated by those around him, or when he feels a disjunction between his sense of himself and the image of himself that others play back to him.[29]

"Tell It Like It Is"

When families become involved in important quarrels the psychosocial underpinnings of family life are laid bare. One such quarrel in a family we have been studying brings together in one place many of the themes that seem to dominate identity problems in Negro slum culture. The incident illustrates in a particularly forceful and dramatic way family processes which our field work, and some other contemporary studies of slum family life, suggests unfold more subtly in a great many families at the lower-class level. The family involved, the Johnsons, is certainly not the most disorganized one we have studied; in some respects their way of life represents a realistic adaptation to the hard living of a family nineteen years on AFDC with a monthly income of $202 for nine people. The two oldest daughters, Mary Jane (eighteen years old) and Esther (sixteen) are pregnant; Mary Jane has one illegitimate child. The adolescent sons, Bob and Richard, are much involved in the social and sexual activities of their peer group. The three other children, ranging in age from twelve to fourteen, are apparently also moving into this kind of peer-group society.

When the argument started Bob and Esther were alone in the apartment with Mary Jane's baby. Esther took exception to Bob's playing with the baby because she had been left in charge; the argument quickly progressed to a fight in which Bob cuffed Esther around, and she tried to cut him with a knife. The police were called and subdued Bob with their nightsticks. At this point the rest of the family and the field worker arrived. As the argument continued, these themes relevant to the analysis which follows appeared:

1. The sisters said that Bob was not their brother (he is a half-brother to Esther, and Mary Jane's full brother). Indeed, they said their mother "didn't have no husband. These kids don't even know who their daddies are." The mother defended herself by saying that she had one legal husband, and one common-law husband, no more.

2. The sisters said that their fathers had never done anything for them, nor had their mother. She retorted that she had raised them "to the age of womanhood" and now would care for their babies.

3. Esther continued to threaten to cut Bob if she got a chance (a month later they fought again, and she did cut Bob, who required twenty-one stitches).

4. The sisters accused their mother of favoring their lazy brothers and asked her to put them out of the house. She retorted that the girls were as lazy, that they made no contribution to maintaining the household, could not

get their boy friends to marry them or support their children, that all the support came from her AFDC check. Mary Jane retorted that "the baby has a check of her own."

5. The girls threatened to leave the house if their mother refused to put their brothers out. They said they could force their boy friends to support them by taking them to court, and Esther threatened to cut her boy friend's throat if he did not co-operate.

6. Mrs. Johnson said the girls could leave if they wished but that she would keep their babies; "I'll not have it, not knowing who's taking care of them."

7. When her thirteen-year-old sister laughed at all of this, Esther told her not to laugh because she, too, would be pregnant within a year.

8. When Bob laughed, Esther attacked him and his brother by saying that both were not man enough to make babies, as she and her sister had been able to do.

9. As the field worker left, Mrs. Johnson sought his sympathy. "You see, Joe, how hard it is for me to bring up a family. . . . They sit around and talk to me like I'm some kind of a dog and not their mother."

10. Finally, it is important to note for the analysis which follows that the following labels — "black-assed," "black bastard," "bitch," and other profane terms — were liberally used by Esther and Mary Jane, and rather less liberally by their mother, to refer to each other, to the girls' boy friends, to Bob, and to the thirteen-year-old daughter.

Several of the themes outlined previously appear forcefully in the course of this argument. In the last year and a half the mother has become a grandmother and expects shortly to add two more grandchildren to her household. She takes it for granted that it is her responsibility to care for the grandchildren and that she has the right to decide what will be done with the children since her own daughters are not fully responsible. She makes this very clear to them when they threaten to move out, a threat which they do not really wish to make good nor could they if they wished to.

However, only as an act of will is Mrs. Johnson able to make this a family. She must constantly cope with the tendency of her adolescent children to disrupt the family group and to deny that they are in fact a family — "He ain't no brother of mine"; "The baby has a check of her own." Though we do not know exactly what processes communicate these facts to the children it is clear that in growing up they have learned to regard themselves as not fully part of a solidary collectivity. During the quarrel this message was reinforced for the twelve-, thirteen-, and fourteen-year-old daughters by the four-way argument among their older sisters, older brother, and their mother.

The argument represents vicious unmasking of the individual members' pretenses to being competent individuals.[30] The efforts of the two girls to present themselves as masters of their own fate are unmasked by the mother. The girls in turn unmask the pretensions of the mother and of their two brothers. When the thirteen-year-old daughter expresses some amusement they turn on her, telling her that it won't be long before she too becomes pregnant. Each member of the family in turn is told that he can expect to be no more than a victim of his world, but that this is somehow inevitably his own fault.

In this argument masculinity is consistently demeaned. Bob has no right to play with his niece, the boys are not really masculine because at fifteen and sixteen years they have yet to father children, their own fathers were no-goods who failed to do anything for their family. These notions probably come originally from the mother, who enjoys recounting the story of having her common-law husband imprisoned for nonsupport, but this comes back to haunt her as her daughters accuse her of being no better than they in ability to force support and nurturance from a man. In contrast, the girls came off somewhat better than the boys, although they must accept the label of stupid girls because they have similarly failed and inconveniently become pregnant in the first place. At least they can and have had children and therefore have some meaningful connection with the ongoing substance of life. There is something important and dramatic in which they participate, while the boys, despite their sexual activity, "can't get no babies."

In most societies, as children grow and are formed by their elders into suitable members of the society they gain increasingly a sense of competence and ability to master the behavioral environment their particular world presents. But in Negro slum culture growing up involves an ever-increasing appreciation of one's shortcomings, of the impossibility of finding a self-sufficient and gratifying way of living.[31] It is in the family first and most devastatingly that one learns these lessons. As the child's sense of frustration builds he too can strike out and unmask the pretensions of others. The result is a peculiar strength and a pervasive weakness. The strength involves the ability to tolerate and defend against degrading verbal and physical aggressions from others and not to give up completely. The weakness involves the inability to embark hopefully on any course of action that might make things better, particularly action which involves cooperating and trusting attitudes toward others. Family members become potential enemies to each other, as the frequency of observing the police being called in to settle family quarrels brings home all too dramatically.

The conceptions parents have of their children are such that they are constantly alert as the child matures to evidence that he is as bad as everyone else. That is, in lower-class culture human nature is conceived of as essentially bad, destructive, immoral.[32] This is the nature of things. Therefore any one child must be inherently bad unless his parents are very lucky indeed. If the mother can keep the child insulated from the outside world, she feels she may be able to prevent his inherent badness from coming out. She feels that once he is let out into the larger world the badness will come to the fore since that is his nature. This means that in the identity development of the child he is constantly exposed to identity labeling by his parents as a bad person. Since as he grows up he does not experience his world as particularly gratifying, it is very easy for him to conclude that this lack of gratification is due to the fact that something is wrong with him. This, in turn, can readily be assimilated to the definitions of being a bad person offered him by those with whom he lives.[33] In this way the Negro slum child learns his culture's conception of being-in-the-world, a conception that emphasizes inherent evil in a chaotic, hostile, destructive world.

Blackness

To a certain extent these same processes operate in white lower-class groups, but added for the Negro is the reality of blackness. "Black-assed" is not an empty pejorative adjective. In the Negro slum culture several distinctive appellations are used to refer to oneself and others. One involves the terms "black" or "nigger." Black is generally a negative way of naming, but nigger can be either negative or positive, depending upon the context. It is important to note that, at least in the urban North, the initial development of racial identity in these terms has very little directly to do with relations with whites. A child experiences these identity placements in the context of the family and in the neighborhood peer group; he probably very seldom hears the same terms used by whites (unlike the situation in the South). In this way, one of the effects of ghettoization is to mask the ultimate enemy so that the understanding of the fact of victimization by a caste system comes as a late acquisition laid over conceptions of self and of other Negroes derived from intimate, and to the child often traumatic, experience within the ghetto community. If, in addition, the child attends a ghetto school where his Negro teachers either overtly or by implication reinforce his community's negative conceptions of what it means to be black, then the child has little opportunity to develop a more realistic image of himself and other Negroes as being damaged by whites and not by themselves. In such a situation, an intelligent man like Mr. Wilson (quoted on pages 93–94) can say with all sincerity that he does not feel most Negroes are ready for integration — only under the experience of certain kinds of intense personal threat coupled with exposure to an ideology that places the responsibility on whites did he begin to see through the direct evidence of his daily experience.

To those living in the heart of a ghetto, black comes to mean not just "stay back," but also membership in a community of persons who think poorly of each other, who attack and manipulate each other, who give each other small comfort in a desperate world. Black comes to stand for a sense of identity as no better than these destructive others. The individual feels that he must embrace an unattractive self in order to function at all.

We can hypothesize that in those families that manage to avoid the destructive identity imputations of "black" and that manage to maintain solidarity against such assaults from the world around, it is possible for children to grow up with a sense of both Negro and personal identity that allows them to socialize themselves in an anticipatory way for participation in the larger society.[34] This broader sense of identity, however, will remain a brittle one as long as the individual is vulnerable to attack from within the Negro community as "nothing but a nigger like everybody else" or from the white community as "just a nigger." We can hypothesize further that the vicious unmasking of essential identity as black described above is least likely to occur within families where the parents have some stable sense of security, and where they therefore have less need to protect themselves by disavowing responsibility for their children's behavior and denying the children their patrimony as products of a particular family rather than of an immoral nature and an evil community.

In sum, we are suggesting that Negro slum children as they grow up in their families and in their neighborhoods are exposed to a set of experiences — and a rhetoric which conceptualizes them — that brings home to the child an understanding of his essence as a weak and debased person who can expect only partial gratification of his needs, and who must seek even this level of gratification by less than straightforward means.

Strategies for Living

In every society complex processes of socialization inculcate in their members strategies for gratifying the needs with which they are born and those which the society itself generates. Inextricably linked to these strategies, both cause and effect of them, are the existential propositions which members of a culture entertain about the nature of their world and of effective action within the world as it is defined for them. In most of American society two grand strategies seem to attract the allegiance of its members and guide their day-to-day actions. I have called these strategies those of *the good life* and of *career success.*[35] A good life strategy involves efforts to get along with others and not to rock the boat, a comfortable familism grounded on a stable work career for husbands in which they perform adequately at the modest jobs that enable them to be good providers. The strategy of career success is the choice of ambitious men and women who see life as providing opportunities to move from a lower to a higher status, to "accomplish something," to achieve greater than ordinary material well-being, prestige, and social recognition. Both of these strategies are predicated on the assumption that the world is inherently rewarding if one behaves properly and does his part. The rewards of the world may come easily or only at the cost of great effort, but at least they are there.

In the white and particularly in the Negro slum worlds little in the experience that individuals have as they grow up sustains a belief in a rewarding world. The strategies that seem appropriate are not those of a good, family-based life or of a career, but rather *strategies for survival.*

Much of what has been said above can be summarized as encouraging three kinds of survival strategies. One is the strategy of the *expressive life style* which I have described elsewhere as an effort to make yourself interesting and attractive to others so that you are better able to manipulate their behavior along lines that will provide some immediate gratification.[36] Negro slum culture provides many examples of techniques for seduction, of persuading others to give you what you want in situations where you have very little that is tangible to offer in return. In order to get what you want you learn to "work game," a strategy which requires a high development of a certain kind of verbal facility, a sophisticated manipulation of promise and interim reward. When the expressive strategy fails or when it is unavailable there is, of course, the great temptation to adopt a *violent strategy* in which you force others to give you what you need once you fail to win it by verbal and other symbolic means.[37] Finally, and increasingly as members of the Negro slum culture grow older, there is the *depressive strategy* in which goals are increasingly constricted to the bare necessities for survival (not as a social being but simply as an organism).[38] This is the strategy of "I don't bother anybody and I hope nobody's gonna bother me; I'm simply going through the motions to keep body (but not soul) together." Most lower-class people follow mixed strategies, as Walter Miller has observed, alternating among the excitement of the expressive style, the desperation of the violent style, and the deadness of the depressed style.[39] Some members of the Negro slum world experiment from time to time with mixed strategies that also incorporate the stable working-class model of the good American life, but this latter strategy is exceedingly vulnerable to the threats of unemployment or a less than adequate pay check, on the one hand, and the seduction and violence of the slum world around them, on the other.

Remedies

Finally, it is clear that we, no less than the inhabitants of the ghetto, are not masters of their fate because we are not masters of our own total society. Despite the battles with poverty on many fronts we can find little evidence to sustain our hope of winning the war, given current programs and strategies.

The question of strategy is particularly crucial when one moves from an examination of destructive cultural and interaction patterns in Negro families to the question of how these families might achieve a more stable and gratifying life. It is tempting to see the family as the main villain of the piece, and to seek to develop programs which attack directly this family pathology. Should we not have extensive programs of family therapy, family counseling, family-life education, and the like? Is this not the prerequisite to enabling slum Negro families to take advantage of other opportunities? Yet, how pale such efforts seem compared to the deep-seated problems of self-image and family process described above. Can an army of social workers undo the damage of three hundred years by talking and listening without massive changes in the social and economic situations of the families with whom they are to deal? And, if such changes take place, will the social-worker army be needed?

If we are right that present Negro family patterns have been created as adaptations to a particular socioeconomic situation, it would make more sense to change that socioeconomic situation and then depend upon the people involved to make new adaptations as time goes on. If Negro providers have steady jobs and decent incomes, if Negro children have some realistic expectation of moving toward such a goal, if slum Negroes come to feel that they have the chance to affect their own futures and to receive respect from those around them, then (and only then) the destructive patterns described are likely to change. The change, though slow and uneven from individual to individual, will in a certain sense be automatic because it will represent an adaptation to changed socioeconomic circumstances which have direct and highly valued implications for the person.

It is possible to think of three kinds of extra-family change that are required if family patterns are to change; these are outlined below as pairs of current deprivations and needed remedies:

Deprivation Effect of Caste Victimization	Needed Remedy
I. Poverty	Employment income for men; income maintenance for mothers
II. Trained incapacity to function in a bureaucratized and industrialized world	Meaningful education of the next generation
III. Powerlessness and stigmatization	Organizational participation for aggressive pursuit of Negroes' self-interest
	Strong sanctions against callous or indifferent service to slum Negroes
	Pride in group identity, Negro *and* American

Unless the major effort is to provide these kinds of remedies, there is a very real danger that programs to "better the structure of the Negro family" by direct intervention will serve the unintended functions of distracting the country from the pressing needs for socioeconomic reform and providing an alibi for the failure to embark on the basic institutional changes that are needed to do anything about abolishing both white and Negro poverty. It would be sad, indeed, if, after the Negro revolt brought to national prominence the continuing problem of poverty, our expertise about Negro slum culture served to deflect the national impulse into symptom-treatment rather than basic reform. If that happens, social scientists will have served those they study poorly indeed.

Let us consider each of the needed remedies in terms of its probable impact on the family. First, the problem of poverty: employed men are less likely to leave their families than are unemployed men, and when they do stay they are more likely to have the respect of their wives and children. A program whose sole effect would be to employ at reasonable wages slum men for work using the skills they now have would do more than any other possible program to stabilize slum family life. But the wages must be high enough to enable the man to maintain his self-respect as a provider, and stable enough to make it worthwhile to change the nature of his adaptation to his world (no one-year emergency programs will do). Once men learn that work pays off it would be possible to recruit men for part-time retraining for more highly skilled jobs, but the initial emphasis must be on the provision of full-time, permanent unskilled jobs. Obviously it will be easier to do this in the context of full employment and a tight labor market.[40]

For at least a generation, however, there will continue to be a large number of female-headed households. Given the demands of socializing a new generation for non-slum living, it is probably uneconomical to encourage mothers to work. Rather, income maintenance programs must be increased to realistic levels, and mothers must be recognized as doing socially useful work for which they are paid rather than as "feeding at the public trough." The bureaucratic morass which currently hampers flexible strategies of combining employment income and welfare payments to make ends meet must also be modified if young workers are not to be pushed prematurely out of the home.

Education has the second priority. (It is second only because without stable family income arrangements the school system must work against the tremendous resistance of competing life-style adaptations to poverty and economic insecurity.) As Kenneth Clark has argued so effectively, slum schools now function more to stultify and discourage slum children than to stimulate and train them. The capacity of educators to alibi their lack of commitment to their charges is protean. The making of a different kind of generation must be taken by educators as a stimulating and worthwhile challenge. Once the goal has been accepted they must be given the resources with which to achieve it and the flexibility necessary to experiment with different approaches to accomplish the goal. Education must be broadly conceived to include much more than classroom work, and probably more than a nine-months schedule.[41]

If slum children can come to see the schools as representing a really likely avenue of escape from their difficult situation (even before adolescence they know it is the only *possible* escape), then their commitment to school activities will feed back into their families in a positive way. The parents will feel proud rather than ashamed, and they will feel less need to damn the child as a way to avoid blaming themselves for his failure. The sense of positive family identity will be enriched as the child becomes an attractive object, an ego resource, to his parents. Because he himself feels more competent, he will see them as less depriving and weak. If children's greater commitment to school begins to reduce their involvement in destructive or aimless peer-group activities this too will repercuss positively on the family situation since parents will worry less about their children's involvement in an immoral outside world, and be less inclined to deal with them in harsh, rejecting, or indifferent ways.

Cross-cutting the deprivations of poverty and trained incapacity is the fact of powerlessness and stigmatization. Slum people know that they have little ability to protect themselves and to force recognition of their abstract rights. They know that they are looked down on and scape-goated. They are always vulnerable to the slights, insults, and indifference of the white and Negro functionaries with whom they deal — policemen, social workers, school teachers, landlords, employers, retailers, janitors. To come into contact with others carries the constant danger of moral attack and insult.[42] If processes of status degradation within families are to be interrupted, then they must be interrupted on the outside first.

One way out of the situation of impotence and dammed-up in-group aggression is the organization of meaningful protest against the larger society. Such protest can and will take many forms, not always so neat and rational as the outsider might hope. But, coupled with, and supporting, current programs of economic and educational change, involvement of slum Negroes in organizational activity can do a great deal to build a sense of pride and potency. While only a very small minority of slum Negroes can be expected to participate personally in such movements, the vicarious involvement of the majority can have important effects on their sense of self-respect and worth.

Some of the needed changes probably can be made from the top, by decision in Washington, with minimal effective organization within the slum; but others can come only in response to aggressive pressure on the part of the victims themselves. This is probably particularly true of the entrenched tendency of service personnel to enhance their own sense of self and to indulge their middle-class *ressentiment* by stigmatizing and exploiting those they serve. Only effective protest can change endemic patterns of police harassment and brutality, or teachers' indifference and insults, or butchers' heavy thumbs, or indifferent street cleaning and garbage disposal. And the goal of the protest must be to make this kind of insult to the humanity of the slum-dweller too expensive for the perpetrator to afford; it must cost him election defeats, suspensions without pay, job dismissals, license revocations, fines, and the like.

To the extent that the slum dweller avoids stigmatization in the outside world, he will feel more fully a person within the family and better able to function constructively within it since he will not be tempted to make up deficits in self-esteem in ways that are destructive of family solidarity. The "me" of personal identity and the multiple "we" of family, Negro, and American identity are all inextricably linked; a healthier experience of identity in any one sector will repercuss on all the others.

Notes

[1] This paper is based in part on research supported by a grant from the National Institutes of Mental Health, Grant No. MH-09189, "Social and Community Problems in Public Housing Areas." Many of the ideas presented stem from discussion with the senior members of the Pruitt-Igoe research staff — Alvin W. Gouldner, David J. Pittman, and Jules Henry — and with the research associates and assistants on the project. I have made particular use of ideas developed in discussions with Boone Hammond, Joyce Ladner, Robert Simpson, David Schulz, and William Yancey. I also wish to acknowledge helpful suggestions and criticisms by Catherine Chilman, Gerald Handel, and Marc J. Swartz. Although this paper is not a

formal report of the Pruitt-Igoe research, all of the illustrations of family behavior given in the text are drawn from interviews and observations that are part of that study. The study deals with the residents of the Pruitt-Igoe housing projects in St. Louis. Some 10,000 people live in these projects which comprise forty-three eleven-story buildings near the downtown area of St. Louis. Over half of the households have female heads, and for over half of the households the principal income comes from public assistance of one kind or another. The research has been in the field for a little over two years. It is a broad community study which thus far has relied principally on methods of participant observation and open-ended interviewing. Data on families come from repeated interviews and observations with a small group of families. The field workers are identified as graduate students at Washington University who have no connection with the housing authority or other officials, but are simply interested in learning about how families in the project live. This very intensive study of families yields a wealth of information (over 10,000 pages of interview and observation reports) which obviously cannot be analyzed within the limits of one article. In this article I have limited myself to outlining a typical family stage sequence and discussing some of the psychosocial implications of growing up in families characterized by this sequence. In addition, I have tried to limit myself to findings which other literature on Negro family life suggests are not limited to the residents of the housing projects we are studying.

² St. Clair Drake, "The Social and Economic Status of the Negro in the United States," *Daedalus* (Fall 1965), p. 772.

³ E. Franklin Frazier, *The Negro Family in the United States* (Chicago, 1939), p. 487.

⁴ Norman Mailer, "The White Negro" (City Lights Books, San Francisco, Calif., 1957); and Leslie Fiedler, *Waiting for the End* (New York, 1964), pp. 118–137.

⁵ See Alvin W. Gouldner, "Reciprocity and Autonomy in Functional Theory," in Llewellyn Gross (ed.), *Symposium of Sociological Theory* (Evanston, Ill., 1958), for a discussion of functional autonomy and dependence of structural elements in social systems. We are suggesting here that lower-class groups have a relatively high degree of functional autonomy *vis-à-vis* the total social system because that system does little to meet their needs. In general the fewer the rewards a society offers members of a particular group in the society, the more autonomous will that group prove to be with reference to the norms of the society. Only by constructing an elaborate repressive machinery, as in concentration camps, can the effect be otherwise.

⁶ For example, the lead sentence in a *St. Louis Post Dispatch* article of July 20, 1965, begins "A White House study group is laying the groundwork for an attempt to better the structure of the Negro family."

⁷ See Kenneth Stampp, *The Peculiar Institution* (New York, 1956); John Hope Franklin, *From Slavery to Freedom* (New York, 1956); Frank Tannenbaum, *Slave and Citizen* (New York, 1946); E. Franklin Frazier, *op. cit.;* and Melville J. Herskovits, *The Myth of the Negro Past* (New York, 1941).

⁸ See Raymond T. Smith, *The Negro Family in British Guiana* (New York, 1956); J. Mayone Stycos and Kurt W. Back, *The Control of Human Fertility in Jamaica* (Ithaca, N.Y., 1964); F. M. Henriques, *Family and Colour in Jamaica* (London, 1953); Judith Blake, *Family Structure in Jamaica* (Glencoe, Ill., 1961); and Raymond T. Smith, "Culture and Social Structure in The Caribbean," *Comparative Studies in Society and History,* Vol. VI (The Hague, The Netherlands, October 1963), pp. 24–46. For a broader comparative discussion of the matrifocal family see Peter Kunstadter, "A Survey of the Consanguine or Matrifocal Family," *American Anthropologist,* Vol. 65, No. 1 (February 1963), pp. 56–66; and Ruth M. Boyer, "The Matrifocal Family Among the Mescalero: Additional Data," *American Anthropologist,* Vol. 66, No. 3 (June 1964), pp. 593–602.

⁹ Paul C. Glick, *American Families* (New York, 1957), pp. 133 ff.

¹⁰ For discussions of white lower-class families, see Lee Rainwater, Richard P. Coleman, and Gerald Handel, *Workingman's Wife* (New York, 1959); Lee Rainwater, *Family Design* (Chicago, 1964); Herbert Gans, *The Urban Villagers* (New York, 1962); Albert K. Cohen and Harold M. Hodges, "Characteristics of the Lower-Blue-Collar-Class," *Social Problems,* Vol. 10, No. 4 (Spring 1963), pp. 303–334; S. M. Miller, "The American Lower Classes: A Typological Approach," in Arthur B. Shostak and William Gomberg, *Blue Collar World* (Englewood Cliffs, N.J., 1964); and Mirra Komarovsky, *Blue Collar Marriage* (New York,

1964). Discussions of Negro slum life can be found in St. Clair Drake and Horace R. Cayton, *Black Metropolis* (New York, 1962), and Kenneth B. Clark, *Dark Ghetto* (New York, 1965); and of Negro community life in small-town and rural settings in Allison Davis, Burleigh B. Gardner, and Mary Gardner, *Deep South* (Chicago, 1944), and Hylan Lewis, *Blackways of Kent* (Chapel Hill, N.C., 1955).

[11] For general discussions of the extent to which lower-class people hold the values of the larger society, see Albert K. Cohen, *Delinquent Boys* (New York, 1955); Hyman Rodman, "The Lower Class Value Stretch," *Social Forces*, Vol. 42, No. 2 (December 1963), pp. 205 ff.; and William L. Yancey, "The Culture of Poverty: Not So Much Parsimony," unpublished manuscript, Social Science Institute, Washington University.

[12] James F. Short, Jr., and Fred L. Strodtbeck, *Group Process and Gang Delinquency* (Chicago, 1965), p. 114. Chapter V (pages 102–115) of this book contains a very useful discussion of differences between white and Negro lower-class communities.

[13] Discussions of white lower-class attitudes toward sex may be found in Arnold W. Green, "The Cult of Personality and Sexual Relations," *Psychiatry*, Vol. 4 (1941), pp. 343–348; William F. Whyte, "A Slum Sex Code," *American Journal of Sociology*, Vol. 49, No. 1 (July 1943), pp. 24–31; and Lee Rainwater, "Marital Sexuality in Four Cultures of Poverty," *Journal of Marriage and the Family*, Vol. 26, No. 4 (November 1964), pp. 457–466.

[14] See Boone Hammond, "The Contest System: A Survival Technique," Master's Honors paper, Washington University, 1965. See also Ira L. Reiss, "Premarital Sexual Permissiveness Among Negroes and Whites," *American Sociological Review*, Vol. 29, No. 5 (October 1964), pp. 688–698.

[15] See the discussion of aleatory processes leading to premarital fatherhood in Short and Strodtbeck, *op. cit.*, pp. 44–45.

[16] Rainwater, *And the Poor Get Children, op. cit.*, pp. 61–63. See also, Carlfred B. Broderick, "Social Heterosexual Development Among Urban Negroes and Whites," *Journal of Marriage and the Family*, Vol. 27 (May 1965), pp. 200–212. Broderick finds that although white boys and girls, and Negro girls, become more interested in marriage as they get older, Negro boys become less interested in late adolescence than they were as preadolescents.

[17] Walter Miller, "The Corner Gang Boys Get Married," *Trans-action*, Vol. 1, No. 1 (November 1963), pp. 10–12.

[18] Rainwater, *Family Design, op. cit.*, pp. 28–60.

[19] Yancey, *op. cit.* The effects of unemployment on the family have been discussed by E. Wright Bakke, *Citizens Without Work* (New Haven, Conn., 1940); Mirra Komarovsky, *The Unemployed Man and His Family* (New York, 1960); and Earl L. Koos, *Families in Trouble* (New York, 1946). What seems distinctive to the Negro slum culture is the short time lapse between the husband's loss of a job and his wife's considering him superfluous.

[20] See particularly Komarovsky's discussion of "barriers to marital communications" (Chapter 7) and "confidants outside of marriage" (Chapter 9), in *Blue Collar Marriage, op. cit.*

[21] Rainwater, *Family Design, op. cit.*, pp. 305–308.

[22] For a discussion of the relationship between Black Nationalist ideology and the Negro struggle to achieve a sense of valid personal identity, see Howard Brotz, *The Black Jews of Harlem* (New York, 1963), and E. U. Essien-Udom, *Black Nationalism: A Search for Identity in America* (Chicago, 1962).

[23] Rainwater, Coleman, and Handel, *op. cit.*, pp. 88–102.

[24] Cf. Michael Schwartz and George Henderson, "The Culture of Unemployment: Some Notes on Negro Children," in Shostak and Gomberg, *op. cit.*

[25] Daniel Patrick Moynihan, "Employment, Income, and the Ordeal of the Negro Family," *Daedalus* (Fall 1965), pp. 760–61.

[26] Talcott Parsons concludes his discussion of child socialization, the development of an "internalized family system," and internalized role differentiation by observing, "The internalization of the family collectivity as an object and its values should not be lost sight of. This

is crucial with respect to . . . the assumption of representative roles outside the family on behalf of it. Here it is the child's family membership which is decisive, and thus his acting in a role in terms of its values for 'such as he.' " Talcott Parsons and Robert F. Bales, *Family, Socialization and Interaction Process* (Glencoe, Ill., 1955), p. 113.

[27] Erik H. Erikson, "Identity and the Life Cycle," *Psychological Issues,* Vol. 1, No. 1 (1959).

[28] For discussion of the dynamics of the individual's *announcements* and the society's *placements* in the formation of identity, see Gregory Stone, "Appearance and the Self," in Arnold Rose, *Human Behavior in Social Process* (Boston, 1962), pp. 86–118.

[29] The importance of identity for social behavior is discussed in detail in Ward Goodenough, *Cooperation and Change* (New York, 1963), pp. 176–251, and in Lee Rainwater, "Work and Identity in the Lower Class," in Sam H. Warner, Jr., *Planning for the Quality of Urban Life* (Cambridge, Mass., forthcoming). The images of self and of other family members is a crucial variable in Hess and Handel's psychosocial analysis of family life; see Robert D. Hess and Gerald Handel, *Family Worlds* (Chicago, 1959), especially pp. 6–11.

[30] See the discussion of "masking" and "unmasking" in relation to disorganization and re-equilibration in families by John P. Spiegel, "The Resolution of Role Conflict within the Family," in Norman W. Bell and Ezra F. Vogel, *A Modern Introduction to the Family* (Glencoe, Ill., 1960), pp. 375–377.

[31] See the discussion of self-identity and self-esteem in Thomas F. Pettigrew, *A Profile of the Negro American* (Princeton, N.J., 1964), pp. 6–11.

[32] Rainwater, Coleman, and Handel, *op. cit.,* pp. 44–51. See also the discussion of the greater level of "anomie" and mistrust among lower-class people in Ephraim Mizruchi, *Success and Opportunity* (New York, 1954). Unpublished research by the author indicates that for one urban lower-class sample (Chicago) Negroes scored about 50 per cent higher on Srole's anomie scale than did comparable whites.

[33] For a discussion of the child's propensity from a very early age for speculation and developing explanations, see William V. Silverberg, *Childhood Experience and Personal Destiny* (New York, 1964), pp. 81 ff.

[34] See Ralph Ellison's autobiographical descriptions of growing up in Oklahoma City in his *Shadow and Act* (New York, 1964).

[35] Rainwater, "Work and Identity in the Lower Class," *op. cit.*

[36] *Ibid.*

[37] Short and Strodtbeck see violent behavior in juvenile gangs as a kind of last resort strategy in situations where the actor feels he has no other choice. See Short and Strodtbeck, *op. cit.,* pp. 248–264.

[38] Wiltse speaks of a "pseudo depression syndrome" as characteristic of many AFDC mothers. Kermit T. Wiltse, "Orthopsychiatric Programs for Socially Deprived Groups," *American Journal of Orthopsychiatry,* Vol. 33, No. 5 (October 1963), pp. 806–813.

[39] Walter B. Miller, "Lower Class Culture as a Generating Milieu of Gang Delinquency," *Journal of Social Issues,* Vol. 14, No. 3 (1958), pp. 5–19.

[40] This line of argument concerning the employment problems of Negroes, and poverty war strategy more generally, is developed with great cogency by James Tobin, "On Improving the Economic Status of the Negro," *Daedalus* (Fall 1965), and previously by Gunnar Myrdal, in his *Challenge to Affluence* (New York, 1963), and Orville R. Gursslin and Jack L. Roach, in their "Some Issues in Training the Employed," *Social Problems,* Vol. 12, No. 1 (Summer 1964), pp. 68–77.

[41] See Chapter 6 (pages 111–153) of Kenneth Clark, *op. cit.,* for a discussion of the destructive effects of ghetto schools on their students.

[42] See the discussion of "moral danger" in Lee Rainwater, "Fear and the House-as-Haven in the Lower Class," *Journal of the American Institute of Planners,* February 1966.

Fathers without Children

Elliot Liebow

In the springtime, on a Sunday afternoon, Richard's four-year-old son lay seriously ill in Ward E of Children's Hospital. He and the other twelve children in the ward, almost all from low-income Negro families, were being visited by some twenty-five relatives and friends. Not a single man was among the visitors.

The men had their reasons. Some had separated from their wives and children and did not know their children were hospitalized. Others knew but couldn't or wouldn't make it. Richard had intended going but something came up, he would probably go tomorrow, and anyway, he never did like being in a hospital, not even to visit someone else.

But whether the fathers were living with their children or not, the result was the same: there were no men visiting the children in Ward E. This absence of the father is one of the chief characteristics of the father-child relationship.

The father-child relationship, however, is not the same for all streetcorner fathers, nor does a given relationship necessarily remain constant over time. Some fathers are not always "absent" and some are less "absent" than others. Moreover, the same father may have relationships of different intensity with his different children at the same time. The spectrum of father-child relationships is a broad one, ranging from complete ignorance of the child's existence to continuous, day-by-day contact between father and child. The emotional content of the relationships ranges from what, to the outside observer, may seem on the father's part callous indifference or worse, all the way to hinted private intimacies whose intensity can only be guessed at.

Leaving aside, for the present, the emotional and affective content, father-child relationships can be grossly sorted out and located along a spectrum based upon the father's willingness to acknowledge paternity, his willingness to acknowledge responsibility for and to provide financial support, and the frequency and duration of contact. At the low end of the spectrum are those relationships in which the children are born of casual, short-term, even single-encounter unions; at the high end are legitimate children of married parents, all of whom live in the same household. Since the majority of streetcorner men do not live in the same households as their children, the majority of father-child relationships appear at

From Elliot Liebow, *Tally's Corner: A Study of Negro Street Corner Men*, 72–102. Copyright © 1967 by Little, Brown and Co. Reprinted by permission of Little, Brown, and Co.

the low and low-middle bands of the spectrum. The number falls off quickly as one approaches the other end.

At the low end of the spectrum there may be no father-child relationship at all. In some cases, the father may not know he is the father of the child; in others, even the mother may not know who the father is. Here, too, at the low end, are those fathers who acknowledge possible or actual paternity but who have had no subsequent contact with mother or child. Such seems to be the case with many of the men who, while still in their teens, had a baby "back home." Thus, Richard recalls that, before his marriage to Shirley, a girl told him he was the father of her child. He did nothing about it and neither did she "because there was nothing she could do."[1] Richard subsequently saw the mother and child on the street during a visit back home but did not speak to them. His sheepish laugh seemed a mixture of masculine pride and guilty embarrassment as he admitted that the child looked startlingly like himself.

Somewhat further along the spectrum are the relationships of Wesley and Earl with their children. Each has a child "back home" in the Carolinas and each acknowledges his paternity. Wesley has visited his hometown and has seen the mother of his child once or twice since the birth of the baby. Wesley and the child's mother are on friendly terms but Wesley gives her nothing and she asks for nothing. Earl's child also lives with its mother but Earl and the mother have remained fond of one another. Earl sees her regularly and sometimes sees the child, too, on those two or three times a year he goes back home. If he has spare cash, he leaves it with her for the baby.

In the middle range of the spectrum are the father-child relationships of those once-married men who, though separated from their wives and children, remain accessible to them. These men admit to a financial responsibility for their children, provide emergency and sometimes routine financial support, and are more or less informed about their children's general well-being. Contacts between the men and their separated families are almost always initiated by the mothers, usually for the purpose of getting money for the children. Sea Cat's wife calls him on the telephone in his rooming house to tell him when she is coming. Sometimes she brings one or both of their children, sometimes not. Stoopy's wife does not usually call. She comes on Saturday mornings, brings the two children along and stays for an hour or two.

Relationships in this middle range are by no means limited to legitimate children. Tally is the father of Bess's eighteen-month-old son. For a time, at least, their relationship was indistinguishable from Sea Cat's and Stoopy's relationships with their wives and children. On Tally's pay day, Bess would sometimes call the Carryout shop and ask that Tally be told she would be there that evening. Tally would meet her on the corner, pay her taxicab fare, then give her five or ten dollars for a doctor, a pair of shoes, or other extra expenses for the child.

In those few cases where the child is cared for by the father's mother or other members of his family, the father-child relationship seems to be closer than when the child is with the mother or member of her family. Such a child regularly carries the father's family name. The father provides at least partial financial support. He is often informed of the child's special needs and general well-being and, even where they are separated by great distances, father and child see each other one or more times during the year. Sweets, for example, has a child "back home." The child is being raised by Sweets's mother. Occasional letters are exchanged during the course of the year, and there are birthday cards and gifts for the child. Sweets manages to get down there for one or two weekends a year and, during the summer, his mother and his child come to spend a week or two with him in Washington. Tonk's relationship with his seven-year-old daughter, also "back home" where she is raised by Tonk's mother, is an even stronger one. They exchange letters and gifts and, at school's end, she comes to spend the whole summer with him. Stanton's daughter lives with his "sister"[2] only two blocks from where Stanton lives. The daughter remains his financial responsibility and, depending on circumstance or need, she moves in with him occasionally for short periods of time.

At the high end of the spectrum are those relationships where father and child are regular members of the same household. In such cases, even when the father and mother are not formally married to one another, there is no question but that the child carries the father's family name. Whether his wife is working or not, and unlike the men who are separated from their children, the father who is living with his children is, in his own eyes and in the eyes of those around him, charged with the day-to-day support of his wife and children. Father and child, as members of the same household, are in more or less continuous contact.

Looking at the spectrum as a whole, the modal father-child relationship for these streetcorner men seems to be one in which the father is separated from the child, acknowledges his paternity, admits to financial responsibility but provides financial support irregularly, if at all, and then only on demand or request. His contacts with the child are infrequent, irregular, and of short (minutes or hours) duration.

When we look away from these more formal aspects of father-child relationships and turn to their quality and texture, a seeming paradox emerges. The men who do not live with their own children seem to express more affection for their children and treat them more tenderly than those who do live with them. Moreover, the men are frequently more affectionate toward other men's children than toward their own.

Fathers who live with their children, for example, seem to take no pleasure in their children and give them little of their time and attention. They seldom mention their children in casual conversation and are never seen sitting or playing with them on the steps or in the street. The fathers do not take their children to tag along while they lounge on the streetcorner or in the Carry-out, nor do they, as they see other fathers in the neighborhood do, promenade with them on Easter Sunday or take them for walks on any other Sunday or holiday. When the father walks into the home, the child may not even look up from what he is doing and the father, for his part, takes no more notice than he receives. If their eyes happen to catch one another's glances, father and child seem to look without seeing until one or the other looks elsewhere.

Perhaps this routine absence of warmth and affection accounts for the way in which an offhand gesture by the father can suddenly deepen the relationship for the child, for however brief a time. John casually distributed some change among his six children. His wife Lorena describes what happened:

He give Buddy and the others a dime. You'd think Jesus had laid something on them. They went all around the neighborhood bragging their daddy give them a dime. I give them nickels and dimes all day long and they don't think anything about it. But John, he can give them a dime and they act like he gave them the whole world.

Since father and child are seldom together outside the home, it is in the home that casual gestures bespeaking paternal warmth and tenderness are most likely to occur. Leroy and two friends are in Leroy's house passing the time. Leroy sits on the bed and absentmindedly strokes the head of his small son lying next to him. In Richard's house, Richard distractedly rolls a ball or marble back and forth across the floor to his four-year-old son, at the same time going on with his drinking and talking; or he casually beckons to his son to come stand between his knees and, with one hand around the child's waist, the other around a can of beer, he goes on talking.

The easy manner with which the fathers manage these intimacies suggests that they have occurred before. But the child does not manage them casually. He is excited by these intimacies, and the clear delight he takes from them suggests that he assigns to them a special quality and that they are by no means routine. Indeed, physical contact between father and son seems generally to be infrequent. When it does take place, it is just as likely to be a slap as a caress.

Compared with fathers who live with their children, separated fathers who remain in touch with their children speak about them more often and show them more warmth when father and child are together. For separated fathers, the short, intermittent contacts with their children are occasions for public display of parental tenderness and affection. When Bess brought the baby along on her money-collecting visits to the Carry-out, she and Tally would sometimes remain on the corner with Tally holding the baby in his arms, cooing at or nuzzling the baby as he and Bess talked. On a Saturday morning, after a visit from his wife, Stoopy stands on the corner with three other men, watching his wife disappear down the street with their two school-age children on either side of her. "There goes my heart," says Stoopy, "those two kids, they're my heart." The other men nod understandingly. They would have felt and said the same thing had they been in his place.

These are fathers whose children are raised by the mothers. Even closer to his child is the father whose child is raised by the father's mother or members of his family. For him, too, the child is "my heart," "my life," or "the apple of my eye."

Parental pride and affection are even more in public evidence when father and child are together. When Tonk's daughter arrives for her summer stay, Tonk walks around holding her hand, almost parading, stopping here and there to let bystanders testify that they didn't know Tonk had such a pretty girl, such a smart girl, or a girl who has grown so much so quickly. No, Sweets won't be at the Carry-out tomorrow afternoon, he has to take his daughter shopping for some clothes. He swears he didn't recognize her when his mother first walked up with her. It hadn't even been a year and he almost didn't know his own kid. If she hadn't called him "Daddy" he would still not have known, that's how big she got. And (with pride), she wants to be with him all the time she's here, go everywhere he goes.

But after the brief visit is over, each goes back to his own life, his own world, in which the other plays so small a part that he may be forgotten for long stretches of time. "Out of sight, out of mind" is not far off the mark at all for any of these separated father-child relationships.

There are many ways to explain this paradox in which fathers who live with their children appear to be less warm, tender and affectionate in their face-to-face relationships with their children than separated fathers.[3] The most obvious, perhaps, is that the separated father, like the proverbial doting grandfather or favorite uncle, not charged with the day-to-day responsibility for the child, with the routine rearing and disciplining and support of this child, can afford to be attentive and effusive. Since his meetings with the child are widely spaced, he comes to them fresh and rested; since the meetings are brief, he can give freely of himself, secure in the knowledge he will soon go back to his own child-free routine.

No doubt, factors such as these are at work here and do account, in part, for the differences between fathers living with and those not living with their children. But one of the most striking things about the relationship between the streetcorner men and children is that the closest of all relationships are those where the men do live with the children, where they have accepted day-to-day responsibility for the children, but where they have done so on a voluntary basis, that is, where the children are not their own.

Not all streetcorner men who took on the role of stepfather or adoptive father were able or even attempted to establish a warm personal relationship with the children they were living with, but some of them were better able to achieve and sustain such relationships than any of the biological fathers. Thus, Robert, who had been living with Siserene and her four children for a year and a half, had become, in that time, a primary source of aid and comfort to the children. When they fell or were hit or had an object of value taken from them, they ran to Robert if he was there. He comforted them, laughed with them, and arbitrated their disputes. He painted pictures for them, made plywood cutouts of the Seven Dwarfs for them, and brought home storybooks.

Before and after Leroy and Charlene had their own child, Leroy looked after Charlene's little sisters and brother to such an extent that both their mother and the children themselves came to rely on him. Together with Calvin, a frail and ailing forty-year-old alcoholic and homosexual who looked after the children in exchange for a place to live, Leroy bathed the children, braided the girls' hair, washed their clothes at "the Bendix" (laundromat), played with them, and on their birthdays went shoplifting to get them gifts. Even more than to Leroy, the children were attached to Calvin. When he could summon the courage, Calvin often interceded on their behalf when their mother was dealing out punishment. There was little that Calvin did not do for the children. He played with them during the day when they were well and stayed up with them at night when they were sick. During one period, when he had resolved to stop his homosexual practices (he had been married and a father), he resumed them only on those occasions when there was no food or money in the house and only long enough to "turn a trick" and get food for the children. When this did not work he raided the Safeway, despite his terror of still another jail sentence. He was proud of the part he played in their lives and he played it so well that the children took his love and support for granted.

It would seem, then, that differences in father-child relationships do not depend so much on whether the man is in continuous as against intermittent or occasional contact with the child but on whether the man voluntarily assumes the role of father or has it thrust upon him.

The man who lives with his wife and children is under legal and social constraints to provide for them, to be a husband to his wife and a father to his children. The chances are, however, that he is failing to provide for them, and failure in this primary function contaminates his performance as father in other respects as well. The more demonstrative and accepting he is of his children, the greater is his public and private commitment to the duties and responsibilities of fatherhood; and the greater his commitment, the greater and sharper his failure as the provider and head of the family. To soften this failure, and to lessen the damage to his public and self-esteem, he pushes the children away from him, saying, in effect, "I'm not even trying to be your father so now I can't be blamed for failing to accomplish what I'm not trying to do."

For the father separated from his children, there is no longer the social obligation to be their chief support. His performance as father is no longer an issue. His failure is an accomplished fact. But now that he is relatively free of the obligations of fatherhood, he can, in his intermittent contacts with his children, by giving money for their support and by being solicitous and affectionate with them, enjoy a modest success as father in precisely those same areas in which he is an established failure.

This is even more clearly seen in the man who lives with a woman who has had children by another man. For these men, obligations to the children are minor in comparison with those of fathers living with their children. Where the father lives with his own children, his occasional touch or other tender gesture is dwarfed by his unmet obligations. No matter how much he does, it is not enough. But where the man lives with children not his own, every gentleness and show of concern and affection redounds to his public and private credit; everything is profit. For him, living with children is not, as it is for the father, charged with failure and guilt.

Since his own and others' expectations of him as father are minimal, he is free to enter into a close relationship with the children without fear of failure and uninhibited by guilt. It is as if living with your own children is to live with your failure, but to live with another man's children is, so far as children are concerned, to be in a fail-proof situation: you can win a little or a lot but, however small your effort or weak your performance, you can almost never lose.[4]

In addition to the very gross factors so far considered in father-child relationships, any one of a number of other factors may pull father and child closer together or push them further apart.[5] Looking only at separated fathers, for example, who are in the majority on the streetcorner, it seems as if their relationships with their children depend to a striking degree on the father's relationships with the adult who is taking care of the child. Thus, as has been suggested earlier, fathers (e.g., Tonk and Sweets) whose children are living with the father's mother or other members of his family seem to be closer to their children than those (e.g., Sea Cat, Stoopy) whose children are living with the mother or members of her family. And when the child is with its mother, as in the great majority of cases, the frequency of contact between father and child clearly depends more on the father's relationship with the mother than on his relationship with the child himself. It is almost as if the men have no direct relationship with their children independent of their relationship with the mother. Whether in different states or in different sections of the same city, these children are never sent to spend a weekend, a Sunday, or even a few hours alone with their fathers. If, like Earl, the father does visit the child's household, it is primarily to see the mother rather than the child. As a rule, children born of short-term unions see their fathers only if and when the father and mother maintain or reestablish a personal relationship.

The dependence of the father-child on the father-mother relationship is clearly evident in the follow-up of Tally's relationship with Bess and their son. We have here, too, a picture of the way in which the father-child relationship can change over time.

After the birth of their baby, and after she and Tally had stopped going out together, Bess came to the corner only on Tally's pay day (Wednesdays), sometimes bringing the child along, sometimes not. But as Bess and Tally rediscovered their attraction for each other, she began to bring the baby regularly, coming now on Friday or Saturday evenings and sleeping over with the baby in Tally's room until Sunday night or Monday morning. On these weekends, Tally sometimes took the boy into the Carry-out shop for a soda or, on one occasion, marched up the street with the child on his shoulder, proudly announcing that Bess had "sent the men to get a loaf of bread." But after a few weeks, Tally and Bess had a fight. Bess stayed away from the neighborhood, and Tally's contacts with his son — dependent as they were on his relationship with Bess — ended abruptly.

The incidental, derivative character of the father-child relationship is not something which arises only after the birth of the child and the separation of the parents. It is rooted in values which, even before conception, boldly and explicitly assert the primacy of the man-woman relationship over a possible father-child relationship, and this primacy continues in effect over the actual father-child relationship when a child is born.

Although the relationship with children is secondary to the man-woman relationship, streetcorner men do want children quite apart from the generalized desire to have a family and be the head of it. A man who has no children may want a child to confirm his masculinity; another may want his girl or wife to conceive in order to reduce the chances of her "cheating" or "cutting out"; and still another man may want a particular woman to have his baby because this may guarantee a continuing relationship with this woman.

Fathers and nonfathers alike also see children as liabilities. The principal liability is the financial one. On the one hand, everyone agrees that a man ought to support his children; on the other hand, money is chronically in short supply. To the men, including those who do not, in fact, contribute to their children's support, children are real, imagined, or pretended economic liabilities. Having to buy food, shoes, clothes or medicine for a child, or having to make a support payment, serve equally well as reason or excuse for asking to borrow money or refusing to lend any. Everywhere one turns, the consensus is that "Children, they'll snatch a lot of biscuits off the table [children are expensive]." So and so had a baby? "Children, they'll snatch a lot of biscuits off the table." So and so is shacking up with a woman with three kids? "Children, they'll snatch a lot of biscuits off the table."

The more the children, of course, the greater the liability. Sweets says he met a girl he likes so much that he is thinking of moving in with her "even though she's got two kids." Bernard doesn't want his girl to have any more children because "I got more than I can stand [economically] right now."

Children — one's own as well as someone else's — are also seen as liabilities in the all-important world of man-woman relationships. Where eating, sleeping, child rearing and lovemaking are frequently confined to a single room, children render privacy a scarce commodity. Not only do they constitute a standing deterrent to secrecy (so essential to the maintenance of clandestine relationships) but they may severely limit the man's freedom of action in other ways as well.

Tonk, for example, made no secret of the fact that having his seven-year-old daughter with him for the summer was not an unmixed blessing. Tonk and his wife Pearl had no children. Pearl wanted the child to remain with them permanently but Tonk insisted on her returning to his mother in the fall, complaining that he has to take care of his daughter when Pearl is not home (she worked nights), and that to do this on a year-round basis would seriously compromise his freedom.

Tonk knew whereof he spoke. A few days later, on a Saturday night while Pearl was at work, Tonk went for a ride with William and two women, taking his daughter with him. The next day, serious trouble arose when the little girl pointed to one of the women and told Pearl, "She's the one who was in my daddy's arms."

Children threaten not only exposure of illicit relationships but also active interference. Indeed, when Tonk and Earlene were kissing in the car, his daughter kept trying to pull them apart, screaming at Earlene "You're not my mother! You're not my mother!"[6]

Older children, in this respect, are bigger nuisances. Clarence lived with his wife and children but saw a great deal of Nancy. Their relationship was a stormy one. Once, when Nancy and Clarence were fighting, Nancy's twelve-year-old son hit Clarence with a baseball bat. This occasioned no surprise to the men on the street and little sympathy for Clarence. The slapstick aspects of it aside, most of the men merely shrugged their shoulders. After all, it was common knowledge that a liaison with a woman who has a half-grown son is a dangerous one. Clarence had gone into it with his eyes open.

Women are painfully aware that men see children as liabilities and that a women who has children may find it difficult to establish a satisfactory relationship with a man. Richard and Shirley are having a fight and Richard has told Shirley she is free to take the children and leave. Shirley is crying hard:

Where can I go? To my mother's grave? To the D.C. morgue where they burned [cremated] my sister last month? You know I'm all alone, so where can I go? Nobody wants a woman with three babies.[7]

Lorena voices a sentiment widespread among women in her contemptuous assessment of men as fathers. In a kitchen discussion with Shirley and Charlene, she dismisses men's protests of love and concern for their children by citing their failure to follow through in action and concludes that, in fact, men regard children as liabilities.

They [men] say they love them. Shit. If they love them, would they let them go hungry? In raggedy-ass clothes? They don't love them. Children are just a tie to a man.

Women are especially resentful of men's instrumental use of children, their use of children as tools for punishment or control in the man-woman relationship.[8] The mother-child relationship, generally conceded to be far closer than the bond between father and children, renders the mother especially vulnerable to such tactics. One woman dreads a fight with her husband because the children will suffer for it. She knows and he knows that he can "get" her by slapping the children around. Another woman, separated from her husband, gets only occasional financial support from him but she is afraid to take him to court for fear that, in order to get back at her, he would go to jail rather than send her money for the children. Leroy regularly uses his small son Donald as a sword of Damocles to control Charlene. Sometimes, during the course of a fight, he denies that Donald is his son and, secure in the knowledge that she has no place to go, he throws Charlene and the child, together with their belongings, out of the apartment (room). When the initiative lies with

Charlene and she, in turn, threatens to leave him, Leroy forces her to remain by refusing to let her take the child. At other times he simply threatens to take Donald "back home" and give him to his grandmother to raise.

The widespread acknowledgment that the mother's attachment for the child is greater than the father's also provides the logical justification for assigning to the father (in theory) the role of principal disciplinarian. Responsibility for meting out physical punishment theoretically falls to the man because mothers are inhibited from punishing their children by virtue of being mothers.

"The man is way more important in bringing up a child," one man said, explaining that the father can discourage wrongdoing with a slap or a beating. Not so the woman. "The woman — well, she birthed him and she can't bring herself to hurt her baby, no matter what he does."

Men's assertions that their wives are "too easy" on the children are commonplace. "She's too easy, always kissing him and picking him up. She doesn't care if he keeps shittin' and pissin' on the floor." Tally, separated from his wife and children, continues to complain that his wife never whips them. "She's always hugging them and talking to them but sometimes they ain't going to learn [unless they are given a whipping]."

Women sometimes contend that a mother alone can raise children properly but they concede that, other things being equal, the children are better off when there's a man around to provide or threaten punishment. "I raised my three that way [alone], but it's better if there's a man. Children fear a man but they don't fear their mother. My son don't fear me at all."

Men see physical punishment as a necessary and proper part of child rearing. "A child, he needs it hard else he ain't going to learn" or "It's important [to hit children] to help them know right from wrong" are sentiments that all men subscribe to. But everyone agrees, too, that punishment ought to be meted out at the appropriate time. "You can't let them keep on doing bad things and then whip them for things they did a long time ago. You got to whip them when they done it, so they'll know what it's for." Society is seen as positively sanctioning physical punishment by specifying the way in which it is to be meted out. "You can hurt a child hitting him with a stick or in the eyes or his head. That's why it's against the law to do it like that. You're supposed to hit him on his thighs or something like that."

When one looks at the same men as sons rather than as fathers, the father-child relationship appears to be a far more distant one. In part, this may be due to the deterioration of the father-child relationship over time and to the different assessments that father and son make of their relationship, each from his own perspective. When the child is very young, the father may still be living with the family or, in any event, making an attempt to help out in some way. But after the father has left, as he usually does, the growing distance in time and space between father and family makes it increasingly difficult to sustain even a semblance of family ties between the man, on one hand, and his wife and children on the other. Just as Tally, or Stoopy, or any of the others do now, their own fathers probably spoke warmly of their children to their friends, admitted that they should be doing more for their children, and considered that, under the circumstances, they were "doing what I can." But from the child's point of view — and he sees even more from the vantage point of adulthood — the father is the man who ran out on his mother, his brothers and sisters and himself; who had, perhaps, to be taken to court to force him to pay a few dollars toward the support of his wife and children; and who, even when he was home, is perhaps best remembered with a switch or belt in his hand.

The men seldom refer to their fathers spontaneously. A group of men can reminisce for hours without the word being mentioned. Many men seem never to have known their fathers: "I don't remember him"; "He left [or died] before I was born," or simply, "Shit."

Sea Cat, who was born and raised in the neighborhood, and whose mother continued to live there, never mentioned his father at all. Leroy was raised by his grandparents. His mother and father lived in the same city, but Leroy, who remained close to his mother, mentions his father only to fix relationships or to set a scene.

Richard's father left the family while Richard was still a small child. His family operates a beer joint in Carolina and Richard has seen him on occasion, while passing through the town. His father has never seen Richard's wife or children. Richard and his father never did get along. "We just don't see eye to eye."

Tally's father also left his wife and children when Tally was a small child. "He was a racketeer, a gambler. He never worked a day in his life." When Tally was about nine or ten he was sent to stay with his father and stepmother in Birmingham. He doesn't remember why he was sent there or how long he remained. All he remembers is that his father once gave him a terrible beating.

Sometimes a brief encounter may throw light on both sides of the father-child relationship. In the episode reported below, we catch a glimpse of the man as son, husband and father. The contrast between the mother-son and father-son relationship is almost too sharp and clear, each terrifying in its own way.[9] Preston is in his middle thirties. Dressed in old army khakis, with his hands thrust in his pockets as he leans against a lamppost or the storefront, he is a regular fixture at the Downtown Cafe. Sometimes when the cafe is short of help, Preston is called to fill in. Such was the case this day when I took a seat at the bar. Preston brought me a beer and started the conversation.

"You know, I had a lot of trouble since I seen you last."

"What kind of trouble?"

"My mother died."

"I'm sorry to hear that."

"Yes, she died three weeks ago. I've been drinking myself to death ever since. Last week I drank up every cent I made before I got it. I don't know what to do. I've been thinking of killing myself."

"You just need a little more time. Three weeks isn't very long for something like this. You'll straighten out."

"Maybe I will, maybe I won't. My mother was all I had. I been thinking I'll go to the pet shop and get a cat."

"How about your father?"

"F — k that mother. I don't even want to think about him."

"Do you have any kids?"

"What good are they? They're in Germany and Japan. I've been thinking I'll get married. But that's no good unless you get a girl who understands you."

He took a box from beneath the counter and asked me to open it. Inside was a flimsy nightgown decorated with bright-colored flowers. With tears in his eyes, he explained that he had bought this for his mother for her stay in the hospital but never got to give it to her. On the night of the day he bought it, he got a call from the Washington Hospital Center to come immediately. He ran all the way but his mother was already dead. Preston did not remember the subsequent events very clearly. He said he began drinking very heavily that night and either that same night or the next morning he had to go to the D.C. morgue to identify his mother's body. When the morgue attendant pulled the sheet back from his mother's face, Preston smashed the attendant in the mouth. He held up the scabby knuckles of his right fist as evidence.

"Why'd you hit him?"

"Because he showed me my dead mother."

Notes

[1] He explained that "back home" a (Negro) woman in such a predicament has no legal recourse. If she files a paternity suit, the judge asks her if the putative father forced himself on her. When she admits he did not, the judge dismisses the case.

[2] Stanton and this (unrelated) woman "go for brother and sister."

[3] Since the attempt here is to sort out the different streetcorner father-child relationships rather than to judge them, it is not relevant that the father's willingness to remain with his children and support them, day in, day out, may be a better measure of the man as father than his expressive behavior in his face-to-face contacts with his children.

[4] Unless, of course, the man violates the ordinary decencies of everyday life and goes out of his way to abuse the child.

[5] For example, the child's sex, age or skin color; whether or not he is legitimate; number, sex and relative age and skin color of siblings; age and marital status of the father; literacy of father, child or other concerned adults (for written communications); accessibility or physical distance of separation, personality variables and so forth. The data generally are too thin to permit an assignment of relative weight to these but the evidence does suggest that no one of them is an overriding or controlling factor in the relationship. Among these factors, however, skin color appears to be one of the most important, the light-skinned child being

preferred to the child with dark skin. There is also a clear preference for the legitimate child but, by itself, illegitimacy is no bar to a close father-child relationship. Sex of the child is important to some men but some seem to prefer boys, others girls. Most of the closest father-child relationships I have observed were with daughters but the total numbers are too few and the number of other variables too many to warrant even a tentative generalization. For a discussion of skin color in parent-child relationships, see St. Clair Drake and Horace Cayton, *Black Metropolis*, pp. 498 ff, esp. p. 503. Morris Rosenberg's study of New York State school children offers strong evidence that lower-class fathers tend to be closer to their daughters than to their sons (*Society and the Adolescent Self-Image*, p. 42 ff).

⁶ Of course, Pearl was not her mother either. I assume that the child was using "mother" here to mean father's wife or stepmother. My notes do not say whether the child called Pearl "Mama." I would guess not since they were together only during the summer.

⁷ Other things being equal, children also compromise the market value of the working- or middle-class widow or divorcee.

⁸ A practice which tends to support the argument of the primacy of the man-woman over the father-child relationship.

⁹ "Even among some of the poorest families, the mother's affectional life may be centered upon a son or daughter. . . . Her attitude often presents a *striking contrast to that of the father.*" (Emphasis added.) E. Franklin Frazier, *The Negro Family in the United States,* p. 468.

The Moynihan Report

4

The Negro Family: The Case for National Action

Daniel P. Moynihan

The Negro American Family

At the heart of the deterioration of the fabric of Negro society is the deterioration of the Negro family.

It is the fundamental source of the weakness of the Negro community at the present time.

There is probably no single fact of Negro American life so little understood by whites. The Negro situation is commonly perceived by whites in terms of the visible manifestations of discrimination and poverty, in part because Negro protest is directed against such obstacles, and in part, no doubt, because these are facts which involve the actions and attitudes of the white community as well. It is more difficult, however, for whites to perceive the effect that three centuries of exploitation have had on the fabric of Negro society itself. Here the consequences of the historic injustices done to Negro Americans are silent and hidden from view. But here is where the true injury has occurred: unless this damage is repaired, all the effort to end discrimination and poverty and injustice will come to little.

The role of the family in shaping character and ability is so pervasive as to be easily overlooked. The family is the basic social unit of American life; it is the basic socializing unit. By and large, adult conduct in society is learned as a child.

A fundamental insight of psychoanalytic theory, for example, is that the child learns a way of looking at life in his early years through which all later experience is viewed and which profoundly shapes his adult concuct.

It may be hazarded that the reason family structure does not loom larger in public discussion of social issues is that people tend to assume that the nature of family life is about the same throughout American society. The mass media and the development of suburbia have created an image of the American family as a highly standardized phenomenon. It is therefore easy to assume that whatever it is that makes for differences among individuals or groups of individuals, it is not a different family structure.

From Daniel P. Moynihan, *The Negro Family: The Case for National Action* (U.S. Government Printing Office, 1965).

There is much truth to this; as with any other nation, Americans are producing a recognizable family system. But that process is not completed by any means. There are still, for example, important differences in family patterns surviving from the age of the great European migration to the United States, and these variations account for notable differences in the progress and assimilation of various ethnic and religious groups. A number of immigrant groups were characterized by unusually strong family bonds; these groups have characteristically progressed more rapidly than others.

But there is one truly great discontinuity in family structure in the United States at the present time: that between the white world in general and that of the Negro American.

The white family has achieved a high degree of stability and is maintaining that stability. By contrast, the family structure of lower-class Negroes is highly unstable, and in many urban centers is approaching complete breakdown.

N.b. There is considerable evidence that the Negro community is in fact dividing between a stable middle-class group that is steadily growing stronger and more successful, and an increasingly disorganized and disadvantaged lower-class group. There are indications, for example, that the middle-class Negro family puts a higher premium on family stability and the conserving of family resources than does the white middle-class family. The discussion of this paper is not, obviously, directed to the first group excepting as it is affected by the experiences of the second — an important exception.

There are two points to be noted in this context.

First, the emergence and increasing visibility of a Negro middle class may beguile the nation into supposing that the circumstances of the remainder of the Negro community are equally prosperous, whereas just the opposite is true at present, and is likely to continue so.

Second, the lumping of all Negroes together in one statistical measurement very probably conceals the extent of the disorganization among the lower-class group. If conditions are improving for one and deteriorating for the other, the resultant statistical averages might show no change. Further, the statistics on the Negro family and most other subjects treated in this paper refer only to a specific point in time. They are a vertical measure of the situation at a given moment. They do not measure the experience of individuals over time. Thus the average monthly unemployment rate for Negro males for 1964 is recorded as 9 percent. But *during* 1964, some 29 percent of Negro males were unemployed at one time or another. Similarly, for example, if 36 percent of Negro children are living in broken homes *at any specific moment,* it is likely that a far higher proportion of Negro children find themselves in that situation *at one time or another* in their lives.

Nearly a quarter of Negro women living in cities who have ever married are divorced, separated, or are living apart from their husbands.

The rates are highest in the urban Northeast where 26 percent of Negro women ever married are either divorced, separated, or have their husbands absent.

Percent Distribution of Ever-Married Females with Husbands Absent or Divorced, Rural-Urban, 1960

	Urban		Rural nonfarm		Rural farm	
	Nonwhite	White	Nonwhite	White	Nonwhite	White
Total, husbands absent or divorced	22.9	7.9	14.7	5.7	9.6	3.0
Total, husbands absent	17.3	3.9	12.6	3.6	8.6	2.0
Separated	12.7	1.8	7.8	1.2	5.6	0.5
Husbands absent for other reasons	4.6	2.1	4.8	2.4	3.0	1.5
Total, divorced	5.6	4.0	2.1	2.1	1.0	1.0

Source: *U.S. Census of Population, 1960, Nonwhite Population by Race*, PC (2) 1c, table 9, pp. 9–10.

On the urban frontier, the proportion of husbands absent is even higher. In New York City in 1960, it was 30.2 percent, *not* including divorces.

Among ever-married nonwhite women in the nation, the proportion with husbands present *declined* in *every* age group over the decade 1950–60, as follows:

Age	Percent with Husbands Present	
	1950	1960
15–19 years	77.8	72.5
20–24 years	76.7	74.2
25–29 years	76.1	73.4
30–34 years	74.9	72.0
35–39 years	73.1	70.7
40–44 years	68.9	68.2

Although similar declines occurred among white females, the proportion of white husbands present never dropped below 90 percent except for the first and last age group.

Both white and Negro illegitimacy rates have been increasing, although from dramatically different bases. The white rate was 2 percent in 1940; it was 3.07 percent in 1963. In that period, the Negro rate went from 16.8 percent to 23.6 percent.

The number of illegitimate children per 1,000 live births increased by 11 among whites in the period 1940–63, but by 68 among non-whites. There are, of course, limits to the dependability of these statistics. There are almost certainly a considerable number of Negro children who, although technically illegitimate, are in fact the offspring of stable unions. On the other hand, it may be assumed that many births that are in fact illegitimate are recorded otherwise. Probably the two opposite effects cancel each other out.

Percent Distribution of Ever-Married Negro Females with Husbands
Absent or Divorced, in Urban Areas, by Region, 1960

	Northeast	North Central	South	West
Total, husbands absent or divorced	25.6	22.6	21.5	24.7
Divorced	3.9	7.3	4.8	9.9
Separated	16.0	11.7	11.9	10.7
Husbands absent for other reasons	5.7	3.6	4.8	4.1

Source: *U.S. Census of Population, 1960, Nonwhite Population by Race,* PC (2) 1c, table 9, pp. 9–10.

A 1960 study of Aid to Dependent Children in Cook County, Ill., stated:

The 'typical' ADC mother in Cook County was married and had children by her husband, who deserted; his whereabouts are unknown, and he does not contribute to the support of his children. She is not free to remarry and has had an illegitimate child since her husband left. (Almost 90 percent of the ADC families are Negro.)

The steady expansion of this welfare program, as of public assistance programs in general, can be taken as a measure of the steady disintegration of the Negro family structure over the past generation in the United States.

The Roots of the Problem

Slavery

The most perplexing question about American slavery, which has never been altogether explained, and which indeed most Americans hardly know exists, has been stated by Nathan Glazer as follows: "Why was American slavery the most awful the world has ever known?" The only thing that can be said with certainty is that this is true: it was.

American slavery was profoundly different from, and in its lasting effects on individuals and their children, indescribably worse than, any recorded servitude, ancient or modern. The peculiar nature of American slavery was noted by Alexis de Tocqueville and others, but it was not until 1948 that Frank Tannenbaum, a South American specialist, pointed to the striking differences between Brazilian and American slavery. The feudal, Catholic society of Brazil had a legal and religious tradition which accorded the slave a place as a human being in the hierarchy of society — a luckless, miserable place, to be sure, but a place withal. In contrast, there was nothing in the tradition of English law or Protestant theology which could accommodate to the fact of human bondage — the slaves were therefore reduced to the status of chattels — often, no doubt, well cared for, even privileged chattels, but chattels nevertheless.

Glazer, also focusing on the Brazil-United States comparison, continues.

In Brazil, the slave had many more rights than in the United States: he could legally marry, he could, indeed had to, be baptized and become a member of the Catholic Church, his family could not be broken up for sale, and he had many days on which he could either rest or earn money to buy his freedom. The Government encouraged manumission, and the freedom of infants could often be purchased for a small sum at the baptismal font. In short: the Brazilian slave knew he was a man, and that he differed in degree, not in kind, from his master.

[In the United States,] the slave was totally removed from the protection of organized society (compare the elaborate provisions for the protection of slaves in the Bible), his existence as a human being was given no recognition by any religious or secular agency, he was totally ignorant of and completely cut off from his past, and he was offered absolutely no hope for the future. His children could be sold, his marriage was not recognized, his wife could be violated or sold (there was something comic about calling the woman with whom the master permitted him to live a "wife"), and he could also be subject, without redress, to frightful barbarities — there were presumably as many sadists among slaveowners, men and women, as there are in other groups. The slave could not, by law, be taught to read or write; he could not practice any religion without the permission of his master, and could never meet with his fellows, for religious or any other purposes, except in the presence of a white; and finally, if a master wished to free him, every legal obstacle was used to thwart such action. This was not what slavery meant in the ancient world, in medieval and early modern Europe, or in Brazil and the West Indies.

More important, American slavery was also awful in its effects. If we compared the present situation of the American Negro with that of, let us say, Brazilian Negroes (who were slaves 20 years longer), we begin to suspect that the differences are the result of very different patterns of slavery. Today the Brazilian Negroes are Brazilians; though most are poor and do the hard and dirty work of the country, as Negroes do in the United States, they are not cut off from society. They reach into its highest strata, merging there — in smaller and smaller numbers, it is true, but with complete acceptance — with other Brazilians of all kinds. The relations between Negroes and whites in Brazil show nothing of the mass irrationality that prevails in this country.

Stanley M. Elkins, drawing on the aberrant behavior of the prisoners in Nazi concentration camps, drew an elaborate parallel between the two institutions. This thesis has been summarized as follows by Thomas F. Pettigrew:

Both were closed systems, with little chance of manumission, emphasis on survival, and a single, omnipresent authority. The profound personality change created by Nazi internment, as independently reported by a number of psychologists and psychiatrists who survived, was toward childishness and total acceptance of the SS guards as father-figures — a syndrome strikingly similar to the "Sambo" caricature of the Southern slave. Nineteenth-century racists readily believed that the "Sambo" personality was simply an inborn racial type. Yet no African anthropological data have ever shown any personality type resembling Sambo; and the concentration camps molded the equivalent personality pattern in a wide variety of Caucasian prisoners. Nor was Sambo merely a product of "slavery" in the abstract, for the less devastating Latin American system never developed such a type.

Extending this line of reasoning, psychologists point out that slavery in all its forms sharply lowered the need for achievement in slaves. . . . Negroes in bondage, stripped of their African heritage, were placed in a completely dependent role. All of their rewards came, not from individual initiative and enterprise, but from absolute obedience — a situation that severely depresses the need for achievement among all peoples. Most important of all, slavery vitiated family life. . . . Since many slaveowners neither fostered Christian marriage among their slave couples nor hesitated to separate them on the auction block, the slave household often developed a fatherless matrifocal (mother-centered) pattern.

The Reconstruction

With the emancipation of the slaves, the Negro American family began to form in the United States on a widespread scale. But it did so in an atmosphere markedly different from that which has produced the white American family.

The Negro was given liberty, but not equality. Life remained hazardous and marginal. Of the greatest importance, the Negro male, particularly in the South, became an object of intense hostility, an attitude unquestionably based in some measure on fear.

When Jim Crow made its appearance towards the end of the 19th century, it may be speculated that it was the Negro male who was most humiliated thereby; the male was more likely to use public facilities, which rapidly became segregated once the process began, and just as important, segregation, and the submissiveness it exacts, is surely more destructive to the male than to the female personality. Keeping the Negro "in his place" can be translated as keeping the Negro male in his place: the female was not a threat to anyone.

Unquestionably, these events worked against the emergence of a strong father figure. The very essence of the male animal, from the bantam rooster to the four-star general, is to strut. Indeed, in 19th century America, a particular type of exaggerated male boastfulness became almost a national style. Not for the Negro male. The "sassy nigger" was lynched.

In this situation, the Negro family made but little progress toward the middle-class pattern of the present time. Margaret Mead has pointed out that "In every known human society, everywhere in the world, the young male learns that when he grows up one of the things which he must do in order to be a full member of society is to provide food for some female and her young." This pattern is not immutable, however: it can be broken, even though it has always eventually reasserted itself.

Within the family, each new generation of young males learn the appropriate nurturing behavior and superimpose upon their biologically given maleness this learned parental role. When the family breaks down — as it does under slavery, under certain forms of indentured labor and serfdom, in periods of extreme social unrest during wars, revolutions, famines, and epidemics, or in periods of abrupt transition from one type of economy to another — this delicate line of transmission is broken. Men may flounder badly in these periods, during which the primary unit may again become mother and child, the biologically given, and the special conditions under which man has held his social traditions in trust are violated and distorted.

E. Franklin Frazier makes clear that at the time of emancipation Negro women were already "accustomed to playing the dominant role in family and marriage relations" and that this role persisted in the decades of rural life that followed.

Urbanization

Country life and city life are profoundly different. The gradual shift of American society from a rural to an urban basis over the past century and a half has caused abundant strains, many of which are still much in evidence. When this shift occurs suddenly, drastically, in one or two generations, the effect is immensely disruptive of traditional social patterns.

It was this abrupt transition that produced the wild Irish slums of the 19th century Northeast. Drunkenness, crime, corruption, discrimination, family disorganization, juvenile delinquency were the routine of that era. In our own time, the same sudden transition has produced the Negro slum — different from, but hardly better than its predecessors, and fundamentally the result of the same process.

Negroes are now more urbanized than whites.

Negro families in the cities are more frequently headed by a woman than those in the country. The difference between the white and Negro proportions of families headed by a woman is greater in the city than in the country.

The promise of the city has so far been denied the majority of the Negro migrants, and most particularly the Negro family.

In 1939, E. Franklin Frazier described its plight movingly in that part of *The Negro Family* entitled "In the City of Destruction":

The impact of hundreds of thousands of rural southern Negroes upon northern metropolitan communities presents a bewildering spectacle. Striking contrasts in levels of civilization and economic well-being among these newcomers to modern

Urban Population as Percent of Total,
by Color, by Region, 1960

Region	White	Negro
United States	69.5	73.2
Northeast	79.1	95.7
North Central	66.8	95.7
South	58.6	58.4
West	77.6	92.6

Source: *U.S. Census of Population*, PC
(1) 1D, 1960, *U.S. Summary*, tables 155 and 233;
PC (2) 1C, *Nonwhite Population by Race*, table 1.

Percent of Negro Families with Female
Head, by Region and Area, 1960

Region	Urban	Rural Nonfarm	Rural Farm
United States	23.1	19.5	11.1
Northeast	24.2	14.1	4.3
North Central	20.8	14.7	8.4
South	24.2	20.0	11.2
West	20.7	9.4	5.5

Source: *U.S. Census of Population, 1960, Nonwhite
Population by Race*, PC (2) 1C, table 9, pp. 9–10.

civilization seem to baffle any attempt to discover order and direction in their mode of life.

In many cases, of course, the dissolution of the simple family organization has begun before the family reaches the northern city. But, if these families have managed to preserve their integrity until they reach the northern city, poverty, ignorance, and color force them to seek homes in deteriorated slum areas from which practically all institutional life has disappeared. Hence at the same time that these simple rural families are losing their internal cohesion, they are being freed from the controlling force of public opinion and communal institutions. Family desertion among Negroes in cities appears, then, to be one of the inevitable consequences of the impact of urban life on the simple family organization and folk culture which the Negro has evolved in the rural South. The distribution of desertions in relation to the general economic and cultural organization of Negro communities that have grown up in our American cities shows in a striking manner the influence of selective factors in the process of adjustment to the urban environment.

Frazier concluded his classic study, *The Negro Family,* with the prophecy that the "travail of civilization is not yet ended."

First, it appears that the family which evolved within the isolated world of the Negro folk will become increasingly disorganized. Modern means of communication will break down the isolation of the world of the black folk, and, as long as the bankrupt system of southern agriculture exists, Negro families will continue to seek a living in the towns and cities of the country. They will crowd the slum areas of southern cities or make their way to northern cities where their family life will become disrupted and their poverty will force them to depend upon charity.

In every index of family pathology — divorce, separation, and desertion, female family head, children in broken homes, and illegitimacy — the contrast between the urban and rural environment for Negro families is unmistakable.

Harlem, into which Negroes began to move early in this century, is the center and symbol of the urban life of the Negro American. Conditions in Harlem are not worse, they are probably better than in most Negro ghettos. The social disorganization of central Harlem, comprising ten health areas, was thoroughly documented by the HARYOU report, save for the illegitimacy rates. These have now been made available to the Labor Department by the New York City Department of Health. There could hardly be a more dramatic demonstration of the crumbling — the breaking — of the family structure on the urban frontier.

Estimated Illegitimacy Ratios Per
1,000 Livebirths for Nonwhites in
Central Harlem, by Health
Area, 1963

Health area [1]	Nonwhite
Total	434.1
No. 8	367.6
No. 10	488.9
No. 12	410.1
No. 13	422.5
No. 15	455.1
No. 16	449.4
No. 19	465.2
No. 24	424.8
No. 85.10	412.3
No. 85.20	430.8

[1] Statistics are reported by geographical areas designated "Health Areas."
Source: Department of Health, New York City.

Unemployment and Poverty

The impact of unemployment on the Negro family, and particularly on the Negro male, is the least understood of all the developments that have contributed to the present crisis. There is little analysis because there has been almost no inquiry. Unemployment, for whites and nonwhites alike, has on the whole been treated as an economic phenomenon, with almost no attention paid for at least a quarter-century to social and personal consequences.

In 1940, Edward Wight Bakke described the effects of unemployment on family structure in terms of six stages of adjustment. Although the families studied were white, the pattern would clearly seem to be a general one, and apply to Negro families as well.

The first two stages end with the exhaustion of credit and the entry of the wife into the labor force. The father is no longer the provider and the elder children become resentful.

The third stage is the critical one of commencing a new day-to-day existence. At this point two women are in charge:

Consider the fact that relief investigators or case workers are normally women and deal with the housewife. Already suffering a loss in prestige and authority in the family because of his failure to be the chief bread winner, the male head of the family feels deeply this obvious transfer of planning for the family's well-being to two women, one of them an outsider. His role is reduced to that of errand boy to and from the relief office.

If the family makes it through this stage Bakke finds that it is likely to survive, and the rest of the process is one of adjustment. *The critical element of adjustment was not welfare payments, but work.*

Having observed our families under conditions of unemployment with no public help, or with that help coming from direct [sic] and from work relief, we are convinced that after the exhaustion of self-produced resources, work relief is the only type of assistance which can restore the strained bonds of family relationship in a way which promises the continued functioning of that family in meeting the responsibilities imposed upon it by our culture.

Work is precisely the one thing the Negro family head in such circumstances has not received over the past generation.

The fundamental, overwhelming fact is that *Negro unemployment,* with the exception of a few years during World War II and the Korean War, *has continued at disaster levels for 35 years.*

Once again, this is particularly the case in the northern urban areas to which the Negro population has been moving.

The 1930 Census (taken in the spring, before the depression was in full swing) showed Negro unemployment at 6.1 percent, as against 6.6 percent for whites. But taking out the South reversed the relationship: white 7.4 percent, nonwhite 11.5 percent.

By 1940, the 2 to 1 white-Negro unemployment relationship that persists to this day had clearly emerged. Taking out the South again, whites were 14.8 percent, nonwhites 29.7 percent.

Since 1929, the Negro worker has been tremendously affected by the movements of the business cycle and of employment. He has been hit worse by declines than whites, and proportionately helped more by recoveries.

From 1951 to 1963, the level of Negro male unemployment was on a long-run rising trend, while at the same time following the short-run ups and downs of the business cycle. During the same period, the number of broken families in the Negro world was also on a long-run rise, with intermediate ups and downs.

Divorce is expensive: those without money resort to separation or desertion. While divorce is not a desirable goal for a society, it recognizes the importance of marriage and family, and for children some family continuity and support is more likely when the institution of the family has been so recognized.

The conclusion from these and similar data is difficult to avoid: During times when jobs were reasonably plentiful (although at no time during this period, save perhaps the first 2 years, did the unemployment rate for Negro males drop to anything like a reasonable level) the Negro family became stronger and more stable. As jobs became more and more difficult to find, the stability of the family became more and more difficult to maintain.

This relation is clearly seen in terms of the illegitimacy rates of census tracts in the District of Columbia compared with male unemployment rates in the same neighborhoods.

In 1963, a prosperous year, 29.2 percent of all Negro men in the labor force were unemployed at some time during the year. Almost half of these men were out of work 15 weeks or more.

The impact of poverty on Negro family structure is no less obvious, although again it may not be widely acknowledged. There would seem to be an American tradition, agrarian in its origins but reinforced by attitudes of urban immigrant groups, to the effect that family morality and stability decline as income and social position rise. Over the years this may have provided some consolation to the poor, but there is little evidence that it is true. On the contrary, higher family incomes are unmistakably associated with greater family stability — which comes first may be a matter for conjecture, but the conjunction of the two characteristics is unmistakable.

The Negro family is no exception. In the District of Columbia, for example, census tracts with median incomes over $8,000 had an illegitimacy rate one-third that of tracts in the category under $4,000.

The Wage System

The American wage system is conspicuous in the degree to which it provides high income for individuals, but is rarely adjusted to insure that family as well as individual needs are met. Almost without exception, the social welfare and social insurance systems of other industrial democracies provide for some adjustment or supplement of a worker's income to provide for the extra expenses of those with families. American arrangements do not, save for income tax deductions.

The Federal minimum wage of $1.25 per hour provides a basic income for an individual, but an income well below the poverty line for a couple, much less a family with children.

The 1965 Economic Report of the President revised the data on the number of persons living in poverty in the United States to take account of the varying needs of families of different sizes, rather than using a flat cutoff at the $3,000 income level. The resulting revision illustrates the significance of family size. Using these criteria, the number of poor families is smaller, but the number of large families who are poor increases, and the number of children in poverty rises by more than one-third — from 11 million to 15 million. This means that one-fourth of the Nation's children live in families that are poor.

Ratio of Nonwhite to White Family Median Income, United States and Regions, 1960–1963

Region	1960	1961	1962	1963
United States	55	53	53	53
Northeast	68	67	66	65
North Central	74	72	68	73
South	43	43	47	45
West	81	87	73	76

Source: U.S. Department of Commerce. Bureau of the Census, Current Population Reports, Series P-60, *Income of families and persons in the United States,* No. 37 (1960), No. 39 (1961), No. 41 (1962), No. 43 (1963). Data by region, table 11 in P-60, No. 41, for 1962, table 13 in P-60, No. 43, for 1963 and, for 1960 and 1961, unpublished tabulations from the Current Population Survey.

A third of these children belong to families in which the father was not only present, but was employed the year round. In overall terms, median family income is lower for large families than for small families. Families of six or more children have median incomes 24 percent below families with three. (It may be added that 47 percent of young men who fail the Selective Service education test come from families of six or more.)

During the 1950–60 decade of heavy Negro migration to the cities of the North and West, the ratio of nonwhite to white family income in cities increased from 57 to 63 percent. Corresponding declines in the ratio in the rural nonfarm and farm areas kept the national ratio virtually unchanged. But between 1960 and 1963, median nonwhite family income slipped from 55 percent to 53 percent of white income. The drop occurred in three regions, with only the South, where a larger proportion of Negro families have more than one earner, showing a slight improvement.

Because in general terms Negro families have the largest number of children and the lowest incomes, many Negro fathers literally cannot support their families. Because the father is either not present, is unemployed, or makes such a low wage, the Negro woman goes to work. Fifty-six percent of Negro women, age 25 to 64, are in the work force, against 42 percent of white women. This dependence on the mother's income undermines the position of the father and deprives the children of the kind of attention, particularly in school matters, which is now a standard feature of middle-class upbringing.

The Dimensions Grow

The dimensions of the problems of Negro Americans are compounded by the present extraordinary growth in Negro population. At the founding of the nation, and into the first decade of the 19th century, 1 American in 5 was a Negro. The proportion declined steadily until it was only 1 in 10 by 1920, where it held until the 1950's, when it began to rise. Since 1950, the Negro population has grown at a rate of 2.4 percent per year compared with 1.7 percent for the total population. If this rate continues, in seven years 1 American in 8 will be nonwhite.

These changes are the result of a declining Negro death rate, now approaching that of the nation generally, and a fertility rate that grew steadily during the postwar period. By 1959, the ratio of white to nonwhite fertility rates reached 1:1.42. Both the white and nonwhite fertility rates have declined since 1959, but the differential has not narrowed.

Family size increased among nonwhite families between 1950 and 1960 — as much for those without fathers as for those with fathers. Average family size changed little among white families, with a slight increase in the size of husband-wife families balanced by a decline in the size of families without fathers.

Negro women not only have more children, but have them earlier. Thus

Average Number of Family Members by Type of
Family and Color, Conterminous United States,
1960 and 1950

Type of family	1950		1960	
	White	Non-white	White	Non-white
All families	3.54	4.07	3.58	4.30
Husband-wife	3.61	4.16	3.66	4.41
Other male head	3.05	3.63	2.82	3.56
Female head	3.06	3.82	2.93	4.04

Source: *U.S. Census of Population, 1960, U.S. Summary
(Detailed Characteristics)*, table 187, p. 469.

in 1960, there were 1,247 children ever born per thousand ever-married nonwhite women 15 to 19 years of age, as against only 725 among white women, a ratio of 1.7:1. The Negro fertility rate over-all is now 1.4 times the white, but what might be called the generation rate is 1.7 times the white.

Population and Labor Force Projections, by Color

	Percent increase	
	Actual 1954–64	Projected * 1964–70
Civilian population age 14 and over		
White	15.6	9.7
Nonwhite	23.9	19.9
Civilian labor force		
White	14.6	10.8
Nonwhite	19.3	20.0

* Population and labor force projections by color were made by the Bureau of Labor Statistics. They have not been revised since the total population and labor force were re-estimated, but are considered accurate measures of the relative magnitudes of increase.
Source: Bureau of Labor Statistics.

This population growth must inevitably lead to an unconcealable crisis in Negro unemployment. The most conspicuous failure of the American social system in the past 10 years has been its inadequacy in providing jobs for Negro youth. Thus, in January 1965 the unemployment rate for Negro teenagers stood at 29 percent. This problem will now become steadily more serious.

Family income in 1959	Number of Children per Nonwhite Mother Age 35–39, 1960
Under $2,000	5.3
$2,000 to $3,999	4.3
$4,000 to $4,999	4.0
$5,000 to $5,999	3.8
$6,000 to $6,999	3.5
$7,000 to $9,999	3.2
$10,000 to $14,999	2.9
$15,000 and over	2.9

Source: 1960 Census, *Women by Number of Children Ever Born*, PC (2) 3A, table 38, p. 188.

During the rest of the 1960's the nonwhite civilian population 14 years of age and over will increase by 20 percent — more than double the white rate. The nonwhite labor force will correspondingly increase 20 percent in the next 6 years, double the rate of increase in the nonwhite labor force of the past decade.

As with the population as a whole, there is much evidence that children are being born most rapidly in those Negro families with the least financial resources. This is an ancient pattern, but because the needs of children are greater today it is very possible that the education and opportunity gap between the offspring of these families and those of stable middle-class unions is not closing, but is growing wider.

A cycle is at work; too many children too early make it most difficult for the parents to finish school. (In February, 1963, 38 percent of the white girls who dropped out of school did so because of marriage or pregnancy, as against 49 percent of nonwhite girls.) An Urban League study in New York reported that 44 percent of girl dropouts left school because of pregnancy.

Low education levels in turn produce low income levels, which deprive children of many opportunities, and so the cycle repeats itself.

The Tangle of Pathology

That the Negro American has survived at all is extraordinary — a lesser people might simply have died out, as indeed others have. That the Negro community has not only survived, but in this political generation has entered national affairs as a moderate, humane, and constructive national force is the highest testament to the healing powers of the democratic ideal and the creative vitality of the Negro people.

But it may not be supposed that the Negro American community has not paid a fearful price for the incredible mistreatment to which it has been subjected over the past three centuries.

In essence, the Negro community has been forced into a matriarchal structure which, because it is so out of line with the rest of the American society, seriously retards the progress of the group as a whole, and imposes a crushing burden on the Negro male and, in consequence, on a great many Negro women as well.

There is, presumably, no special reason why a society in which males are dominant in family relationships is to be preferred to a matriarchal arrangement. However, it is clearly a disadvantage for a minority group to be operating on one principle, while the great majority of the population, and the one with the most advantages to begin with, is operating on another. This is the present situation of the Negro. Ours is a society which presumes male leadership in private and public affairs. The arrangements of society facilitate such leadership and reward it. A subculture, such as that of the Negro American, in which this is not the pattern, is placed at a distinct disadvantage.

Here an earlier word of caution should be repeated. There is much evidence that a considerable number of Negro families have managed to break out of the tangle of pathology and to establish themselves as stable, effective units, living according to patterns of American society in general. E. Franklin Frazier has suggested that the middle-class Negro American family is, if anything, more patriarchal and protective of its children than the general run of such families. Given equal opportunities, the children of these families will perform as well or better than their white peers. They need no help from anyone, and ask none.

While this phenomenon is not easily measured, one index is that middle-class Negroes have even fewer children than middle-class whites, indicating a desire to conserve the advances they have made and to insure that their children do as well or better. Negro women who marry early to uneducated laborers have more children than white women in the same situation; Negro women who marry at the common age for the middle class to educated men doing technical or professional work have only four-fifths as many children as their white counterparts.

It might be estimated that as much as half of the Negro community falls into the middle class. However, the remaining half is in desperate and deteriorating circumstances. Moreover, because of housing segregation it is immensely difficult for the stable half to escape from the cultural influences of the unstable one. The children of middle-class Negroes often as not must grow up in or next to the slums, an experience almost unknown to white middle-class children. They are therefore constantly exposed to the pathology of the disturbed group and constantly in danger of being drawn into it. It is for this reason that the propositions put forth in this study may be thought of as having a more or less general application.

Children Born per Woman Age 35 to 44: Wives of Uneducated Laborers who Married Young, Compared with Wives of Educated Professional Workers who Married After Age 21, White and Nonwhite, 1960 [1]

	Children per Woman	
	White	Nonwhite
Wives married at age 14 to 21 to husbands who are laborers and did not go to high school	3.8	4.7
Wives married at age 22 or over to husbands who are professional or technical workers and have completed 1 year or more of college	2.4	1.9

[1] Wives married only once, with husbands present.
Source: 1960 Census, *Women by Number of Children Ever Born*, PC (2) 3A, tables 39 and 40, pp. 199–238.

In a word, most Negro youth are in *danger* of being caught up in the tangle of pathology that affects their world, and probably a majority are so entrapped. Many of those who escape do so for one generation only: as things now are, their children may have to run the gauntlet all over again. That is not the least vicious aspect of the world that white America has made for the Negro.

Obviously, not every instance of social pathology afflicting the Negro community can be traced to the weakness of family structure. If, for example, organized crime in the Negro community were not largely controlled by whites, there would be more capital accumulation among Negroes, and therefore probably more Negro business enterprises. If it were not for the hostility and fear many whites exhibit towards Negroes, they in turn would be less afflicted by hostility and fear and so on. There is no one Negro community. There is no one Negro problem. There is no one solution. Nonetheless, at the center of the tangle of pathology is the weakness of the family structure. Once or twice removed, it will be found to be the principal source of most of the aberrant, inadequate, or antisocial behavior that did not establish, but now serves to perpetuate, the cycle of poverty and deprivation.

It was by destroying the Negro family under slavery that white America broke the will of the Negro people. Although that will has reasserted itself in our time, it is a resurgence doomed to frustration unless the viability of the Negro family is restored.

Matriarchy

A fundamental fact of Negro American family life is the often reversed roles of husband and wife.

Robert O. Blood, Jr., and Donald M. Wolfe, in a study of Detroit families, note that "Negro husbands have unusually low power," and while this is characteristic of all low-income families, the pattern pervades the Negro social structure: "the cumulative result of discrimination in jobs . . . , the segregated housing, and the poor schooling of Negro men." In 44 percent of the Negro families studied, the wife was dominant, as against 20 percent of white wives. "Whereas the majority of white familes are equalitarian, the largest percentage of Negro families are dominated by the wife."

The matriarchal pattern of so many Negro families reinforces itself over the generations. This process begins with education. Although the gap appears to be closing at the moment, for a long while, Negro females were better educated than Negro males, and this remains true today for the Negro population as a whole.

The difference in educational attainment between nonwhite men and women in the labor force is even greater; men lag 1.1 years behind women.

The disparity in educational attainment of male and female youth age 16 to 21 who were out of school in February 1963 is striking. Among the nonwhite males, 66.3 percent were not high school graduates, compared with 55.0 percent of the females. A similar difference existed at the college level, with 4.5 percent of the males having completed 1 to 3 years of college compared with 7.3 percent of the females.

The poorer performance of the male in school exists from the very beginning, and the magnitude of the difference was documented by the 1960 Census in statistics on the number of children who have fallen one or more grades below the typical grade for children of the same age. The boys have more frequently fallen behind

Educational Attainment of the Civilian
Noninstitutional Population 18 Years of
Age and Over, March 1964

Color and Sex	Median School Years Completed
White	
Male	12.1
Female	12.1
Nonwhite	
Male	9.2
Female	10.0

Source: Bureau of Labor Statistics, unpublished data.

at every age level. (White boys also lag behind white girls, but at a differential of 1 to 6 percentage points.)

In 1960, 39 percent of all white persons 25 years of age and over who had completed 4 or more years of college were women. Fifty-three percent of the nonwhites who had attained this level were women.

However, the gap is closing. By October 1963, there were slightly more Negro men in college than women. Among whites there were almost twice as many men as women enrolled.

Percent of Nonwhite Youth Enrolled in School
Who are 1 or More Grades Below Mode for
Age, by Sex, 1960

Age	Male	Female
7 to 9 years old	7.8	5.8
10 to 13 years old	25.0	17.1
14 and 15 years old	35.5	24.8
16 and 17 years old	39.4	27.2
18 and 19 years old	57.3	46.0

Source: 1960 Census, *School Enrollment*, PC (2) 5A, table 3, p. 24.

There is much evidence that Negro females are better students than their male counterparts.

Daniel Thompson of Dillard University, in a private communication on January 9, 1965, writes:

As low as is the aspirational level among lower-class Negro girls, it is considerably higher than among the boys. For example, I have examined the honor roles in Negro high schools for about 10 years. As a rule, from 75 to 90 percent of all Negro honor students are girls.

Fall Enrollment of Civilian Noninstitutional Population in College,
by Color and Sex, October 1963 (in thousands)

Color and Sex	Population, age 14–34, Oct. 1, 1963	enrolled Number	Percent of youth, age 14–34
Nonwhite			
Male	2,884	149	5.2
Female	3,372	137	4.1
White			
Male	21,700	2,599	12.0
Female	20,613	1,451	7.0

Source: U.S. Bureau of the Census, *Current Population Reports*, Series
P-20, No. 129, July 24, 1964, tables 1, 5.

Dr. Thompson reports that 70 percent of all applications for the National Achievement Scholarship Program financed by the Ford Foundation for outstanding Negro high school graduates are girls, despite special efforts by high school principals to submit the names of boys.

The finalists for this new program for outstanding Negro students were recently announced. Based on an inspection of the names, only about 43 percent of all the 639 finalists were male. (However, in the regular National Merit Scholarship program, males received 67 percent of the 1964 scholarship awards.)

Inevitably, these disparities have carried over to the area of employment and income.

In 1 out of 4 Negro families where the husband is present, is an earner, and someone else in the family works, the husband is not the principal earner. The comparable figure for whites is 18 percent.

More important, it is clear that Negro females have established a strong position for themselves in white collar and professional employment, precisely the areas of the economy which are growing most rapidly, and to which the highest prestige is accorded.

The President's Committee on Equal Employment Opportunity, making a preliminary report on employment in 1964 of over 16,000 companies with nearly 5 million employees, revealed this pattern with dramatic emphasis. In this work force, Negro males outnumber Negro females by a ratio of 4 to 1. Yet Negro males represent only 1.2 percent of all males in white collar occupations, while Negro females represent 3.1 percent of the total female white collar work force. Negro males represent 1.1 percent of all male professionals, whereas Negro females represent roughly 6 percent of all female professionals. Again, in technician occupations, Negro males represent 2.1 percent of all male technicians while Negro females represent roughly 10 percent of all female technicians. It would appear therefore that there are proportionately 4 times as many Negro females in significant white collar jobs than Negro males.

Although it is evident that office and clerical jobs account for approximately 50 percent of all Negro female white collar workers, it is significant that 6 out of every 100 Negro females are in professional jobs. This is substantially similar to the rate of all females in such jobs. Approximately 7 out of every 100 Negro females are in technician jobs. This exceeds the proportion of all females in technician jobs — approximately 5 out of every 100.

Negro females in skilled jobs are almost the same as that of all females in such jobs. Nine out of every 100 Negro males are in skilled occupations while 21 out of 100 of all males are in such jobs.

This pattern is to be seen in the Federal government, where special efforts have been made recently to insure equal employment opportunity for Negroes. These efforts have been notably successful in Departments such as Labor, where some 19 percent of employees are now Negro. (A not disproportionate percentage, given the composition of the work force in the areas where the main Department offices are located.) However, it may well be that these efforts have redounded mostly to the benefit of Negro women, and may even have accentuated the comparative disadvantage of Negro men. Seventy percent of the Negro employees of the Department of Labor are women, as contrasted with only 42 percent of the white employees.

Among nonprofessional Labor Department employees — where the most employment opportunities exist for all groups — Negro women outnumber Negro men 4 to 1, and average almost one grade higher in classification.

The testimony to the effects of these patterns in Negro family structure is widespread, and hardly to be doubted.

Whitney Young: Historically, in the matriarchal Negro society, mothers made sure that if one of their children had a chance for higher education the daughter was the one to pursue it.

The effect on family functioning and role performance of this historical experience [economic deprivation] is what you might predict. Both as a husband and as a father the Negro male is made to feel inadequate, not because he is unlovable or unaffectionate, lacks intelligence or even a gray flannel suit. But in a society that measures a man by the size of his pay check, he doesn't stand very tall in a comparison with his white counterpart. To this situation he may react with withdrawal, bitterness toward society, aggression both within the family and racial group, self-hatred, or crime. Or he may escape through a number of avenues that help him to lose himself in fantasy or to compensate for his low status through a variety of exploits.

Thomas Pettigrew: The Negro wife in this situation can easily become disgusted with her financially dependent husband, and her rejection of him further alienates the male from family life. Embittered by their experiences with men, many Negro mothers often act to perpetuate the mother-centered pattern by taking a greater interest in their daughters than in their sons.

Deton Brooks: In a matriarchal structure, the women are transmitting the culture.

Dorothy Height: If the Negro woman has a major underlying concern, it is the status of the Negro man and his position in the community and his need for feeling himself an important person, free and able to make his contribution in the whole society in order that he may strengthen his home.

Duncan M. MacIntyre: The Negro illegitimacy rate always has been high—about eight times the white rate in 1940 and somewhat higher today even though the white illegitimacy rate also is climbing. The Negro statistics are symptomatic of some old socioeconomic problems, not the least of which are underemployment among Negro men and compensating higher labor force propensity among Negro women. Both operate to enlarge the mother's role, undercutting the status of the male and making many Negro families essentially matriarchal. The Negro man's uncertain employment prospects, matriarchy, and the high cost of divorces combine to encourage desertion (the poor man's divorce), increases the number of couples not married, and thereby also increases the Negro illegitimacy rate. In the meantime, higher Negro birth rates are increasing the nonwhite population, while migration into cities like Detroit, New York, Philadelphia, and Washington, D.C., is making the public assistance rolls in such cities heavily, even predominantly, Negro.

Robin M. Williams, Jr., in a study of Elmira, New York: Only 57 percent of Negro adults reported themselves as married—spouse present, as compared with 78 percent of native white American gentiles, 91 percent of Italian-American, and 96 percent of Jewish informants. Of the 93 unmarried Negro youths interviewed, 22 percent did not have their mother living in the home with them, and 42 percent reported that their father was not living in their home. One-third of the youths did not know their father's present occupation, and two-thirds of a sample of 150 Negro adults did not know what the occupation of their father's father had been. Forty percent of the youths said that they had brothers and sisters living in other communities; another 40 percent reported relatives living in their home who were not parents, siblings, or grandparent.

The Failure of Youth

Williams' account of Negro youth growing up with little knowledge of their fathers' occupations, still less of family occupational traditions, is in sharp contrast to the experience of the white child. The white family, despite many variants, remains a powerful agency not only for transmitting property from one generation to the next, but also for transmitting no less valuable contracts with the world of education and work. In an earlier age, the Carpenters, Wainwrights, Weavers, Mercers, Farmers, Smiths acquired their names as well as their trades from their fathers and grandfathers. Children today still learn the patterns of work from their fathers even though they may no longer go into the same jobs.

White children without fathers at least perceive all about them the pattern of men working.

Negro children without fathers flounder — and fail.

Not always, to be sure. The Negro community produces its share, very possibly more than its share, of young people who have the something extra that carries them over the worst obstacles. But such persons are always a minority. The common run of young people in a group facing serious obstacles to success do not succeed.

A prime index of the disadvantage of Negro youth in the United States is their consistently poor performance on the mental tests that are a standard means of measuring ability and performance in the present generation.

There is absolutely no question of any genetic differential: Intelligence potential is distributed among Negro infants in the same proportion and pattern as among Icelanders or Chinese or any other group. American society, however, impairs the Negro potential. The statement of the HARYOU report that "there is no basic disagreement over the fact that central Harlem students are performing poorly in school" may be taken as true of Negro slum children throughout the United States.

Eighth grade children in central Harlem have a median IQ of 87.7, which means that perhaps a third of the children are scoring at levels perilously near to those of retardation. IQ *declines* in the first decade of life, rising only slightly thereafter.

The effect of broken families on the performance of Negro youth has not been extensively measured, but studies that have been made show an unmistakable influence.

Martin Deutsch and Bert Brown, investigating intelligence test differences between Negro and white 1st and 5th graders of different social classes, found that there is a direct relationship between social class and IQ. As the one rises so does the other: but more for whites than Negroes. This is surely a result of housing segregation, referred to earlier, which makes it difficult for middle-class Negro families to escape the slums.

The authors explain that "it is much more difficult for the Negro to attain identical middle- or upper-middle-class status with whites, and the social class gradations are less marked for Negroes because Negro life in a caste society is considerably more homogeneous than is life for the majority group."

Therefore, the authors look for background variables other than social class which might explain the difference: "One of the most striking differences between the Negro and white groups is the consistently higher frequency of broken homes and resulting family disorganization in the Negro group."

Further, they found that children from homes where fathers are present have significantly higher scores than children in homes without fathers.

The influence of the father's presence was then tested *within* the social classes and school grades for Negroes alone. They found that "a consistent trend within

Percentage of Time Father Absent from the Home

	Lowest social class level	Middle social class level	Highest social class level
White	15.4	10.3	0.0
Negro	43.9	27.9	13.7

(Adapted from authors' table)

Mean Intelligence Scores

	Mean Intelligence Scores
Father present	97.83
Father absent	90.79

Mean Intelligence Scores of Negro Children by School, Grade, Social Class, and by Presence of Father

Social Class and School Grade	Father present	Father absent
Lowest social class level:		
Grade 1	95.2	87.8
Grade 5	92.7	85.7
Middle social class level:		
Grade 1	98.7	92.8
Grade 5	92.9	92.0

(Adapted from authors' table)

both grades at the lower SES [social class] level appears, and in no case is there a reversal of this trend: for males, females, and the combined group, the IQ's of children with fathers in the home are always higher than those who have no father in the home."

Percent of Nonwhite Males Enrolled in School, by Age and Presence of Parents, 1960

Age	Both parents present	One parent present	Neither parent present
5 years	41.7	44.2	34.3
6 years	79.3	78.7	73.8
7 to 9 years	96.1	95.3	93.9
10 to 13 years	96.2	95.5	93.0
14 and 15 years	91.8	89.9	85.0
16 and 17 years	78.0	72.7	63.2
18 and 19 years	46.5	40.0	32.3

Source: 1960 Census, School Enrollment, PC (2) 5A, table 3, p. 24.

The authors say that broken homes "may also account for some of the differences between Negro and white intelligence scores."

The scores of fifth graders with fathers absent were lower than the scores of first graders with fathers absent, and while the authors point out that it is cross sectional data and does not reveal the duration of the fathers' absence, "What we might be tapping is the cumulative effect of fatherless years."

This difference in ability to perform has its counterpart in statistics on actual school performance. Nonwhite boys from families with both parents present are more likely to be going to school than boys with only one parent present, and enrollment rates are even lower when neither parent is present.

When the boys from broken homes are in school, they do not do as well as the boys from whole families. Grade retardation is higher when only one parent is present, and highest when neither parent is present.

The loneliness of the Negro youth in making fundamental decisions about education is shown in a 1959 study of Negro and white dropouts in Connecticut high schools.

Only 29 percent of the Negro male dropouts discussed their decision to drop out of school with their fathers, compared with 65 percent of the white males (38 percent of the Negro males were from broken homes). In fact, 26 percent of the Negro males did not discuss this major decision in their lives with anyone at all, compared with only 8 percent of white males.

A study of Negro apprenticeship by the New York State Commission Against Discrimination in 1960 concluded:

Negro youth are seldom exposed to influences which can lead to apprenticeship. Negroes are not apt to have relatives, friends, or neighbors in skilled occupations. Nor are they likely to be in secondary schools where they receive encouragement and direction from alternate role models. Within the minority community, skilled Negro 'models' after whom the Negro youth might pattern himself are rare, while substitute sources which could provide the direction, encouragement, resources, and information needed to achieve skilled craft standing are nonexistent.

Percent of Nonwhite Males Enrolled in School Who Are 1 or More Grades Below Mode for Age, by Age Group and Presence of Parents, 1960

Age group	Both parents present	One parent present	Neither parent present
7–9 years	7.5	7.7	9.6
10–13 years	23.8	25.8	30.6
14–15 years	34.0	36.3	40.9
16–17 years	37.6	40.9	44.1
18–19 years	60.6	65.9	46.1

Source: 1960 Census, *School Enrollment*, PC (2) 5A, table 3, p. 24.

Delinquency and Crime

The combined impact of poverty, failure, and isolation among Negro youth has had the predictable outcome in a disastrous delinquency and crime rate.

In a typical pattern of discrimination, Negro children in all public and private orphanages are a smaller proportion of all children than their proportion of the population although their needs are clearly greater.

On the other hand Negroes represent a third of all youth in training shcools for juvenile delinquents.

Children in Homes for Dependent and Neglected Children, 1960

	Number	Percent
White	64,807	88.4
Negro	6,140	8.4
Other races	2,359	3.2
All races	73,306	100.0

Source: 1960 Census, *Inmates of Institutions,* PC (2) 3A, table 31, p. 44.

It is probable that at present, a majority of the crimes against the person, such as rape, murder, and aggravated assault, are committed by Negroes. There is, of course, no absolute evidence; inference can only be made from arrest and prison population statistics. The data that follow unquestionably are biased against Negroes, who are arraigned much more casually than are whites, but it may be doubted that the bias is great enough to affect the general proportions.

	Number of Arrests in 1963	
	White	Negro
Offenses charged, total	31,988	38,549
Murder and nonnegligent manslaughter	2,288	2,948
Forcible rape	4,402	3,935
Aggravated assault	25,298	31,666

Source: *Crime in the United States* (Federal Bureau of Investigation, 1963), table 25, p. 111.

Again on the urban frontier the ratio is worse: 3 out of every 5 arrests for these crimes were of Negroes.

In Chicago in 1963, three-quarters of the persons arrested for such crimes were Negro; in Detroit, the same proportions held.

In 1960, 37 percent of all persons in Federal and State prisons were Negro. In that year, 56 percent of the homicide and 57 percent of the assault offenders committed to State institutions were Negro.

	Number of city arrests in 1963 [1]	
	White	Negro
Offenses charged, total	24,805	35,520
Murder and nonnegligent manslaughter	1,662	2,593
Forcible rape	3,199	3,570
Aggravated assault	19,944	29,357

[1] In 2,892 cities with population over 2,500.
Source: *Crime in the United States* (Federal Bureau of Investigation, 1963), table 31, p. 117.

The overwhelming number of offenses committed by Negroes are directed toward other Negroes: the cost of crime to the Negro community is a combination of that to the criminal and to the victim.

Some of the research on the effects of broken homes on delinquent behavior recently surveyed by Thomas F. Pettigrew in *A Profile of the Negro American* is summarized below, along with several other studies of the question.

Mary Diggs found that three-fourths — twice the expected ratio — of Philadelphia's Negro delinquents who came before the law during 1948 did not live with both their natural parents.

In predicting juvenile crime, Eleanor and Sheldon Glueck also found that a higher proportion of delinquent than nondelinquent boys came from broken homes. They identified five critical factors in the home environment that made a difference in whether boys would become delinquents: discipline of boy by father, supervision of boy by mother, affection of father for boy, affection of mother for boy, and cohesiveness of family.

In 1952, when the New York City Youth Board set out to test the validity of these five factors as predictors of delinquency, a problem quickly emerged. The Glueck sample consisted of white boys of mainly Irish, Italian, Lithuanian, and English descent. However, the Youth Board group was 44 percent Negro and 14 percent Puerto Rican, and the frequency of broken homes within these groups was out of proportion to the total number of delinquents in the population.

In the majority of these cases, the father was usually never in the home at all, absent for the major proportion of the boy's life, or was present only on occasion.

(The final prediction table was reduced to three factors: supervision of boy by mother, discipline of boy by mother, and family cohesiveness within what family, in fact, existed, but was, nonetheless, 85 percent accurate in predicting delinquents and 96 percent accurate in predicting nondelinquents.)

Researchers who have focussed upon the "good" boys in high-delinquency neighborhoods noted that they typically come from exceptionally stable, intact families.

Recent psychological research demonstrates the personality effects of being reared in a disorganized home without a father. One study showed that children from fatherless homes seek immediate gratification of their desires far more than children with fathers present. Others revealed that children who hunger for immediate gratification are more prone to delinquency, along with other less social behavior. Two psychologists, Pettigrew says, maintain that inability to delay gratification is a critical factor in immature, criminal, and neurotic behavior.

Finally, Pettigrew discussed the evidence that a stable home is a crucial factor in counteracting the effects of racism upon Negro personality.

A warm, supportive home can effectively compensate for many of the restrictions the Negro child faces outside of the ghetto; consequently, the type of home life a Negro enjoys as a child may be far more crucial for governing the influence of segregation upon his personality than the form the segregation takes — legal or informal, Southern or Northern.

A Yale University study of youth in the lowest socioeconomic class in New Haven in 1950 whose behavior was followed through their 18th year revealed that among the delinquents in the group, 38 percent came from broken homes, compared with 24 percent of nondelinquents.

The President's Task Force on Manpower Conservation in 1963 found that of young men rejected for the draft for failure to pass the mental tests, 42 percent of those with a court record came from broken homes, compared with 30 percent of those without a court record. Half of all the nonwhite rejectees in the study with a court record came from broken homes.

Juvenile Delinquents—Philadelphia by Presence of Parents, 1949–54

	White			Negro		
	All Court cases	First Offenders	Recidivists	All Court cases	First Offenders	Recidivists
Number of cases	20,691	13,220	4,612	22,695	11,442	6,641
Number not living with both parents	7,422	4,125	2,047	13,980	6,586	4,298
Percent not living with both parents	35.9	31.2	44.4	61.6	57.6	64.7

Source: Adapted from table 1, p. 255, "Family Status and the Delinquent Child," Thomas P. Monahan, *Social Forces*, March 1957.

An examination of the family background of 44,448 delinquency cases in Philadelphia between 1949 and 1954 documents the frequency of broken homes among delinquents. Sixty-two percent of the Negro delinquents and 36 percent of white delinquents were not living with both parents. In 1950, 33 percent of nonwhite children and 7 percent of white children in Philadelphia were living in homes without both parents. Repeaters were even more likely to be from broken homes than first offenders.

The Armed Forces

The ultimate mark of inadequate preparation for life is the failure rate on the Armed Forces mental test. The Armed Forces Qualification Test is not quite a mental test, nor yet an education test. It is a test of ability to perform at an acceptable level of competence. It roughly measures ability that ought to be found in an average 7th or 8th grade student. A grown young man who cannot pass this test is in trouble. Fifty-six percent of Negroes fail it. This is a rate almost four times that of the whites.

The Army, Navy, Air Force, and Marines conduct by far the largest and most important education and training activities of the Federal Government, as well as provide the largest single source of employment in the nation.

Military service is disruptive in some respects. For those comparatively few who are killed or wounded in combat, or otherwise, the personal sacrifice is inestimable. But on balance service in the Armed Forces over the past quarter-century has worked greatly to the advantage of those involved. The training and experience of military duty itself is unique; the advantages that have generally followed in the form of the G.I. Bill, mortgage guarantees, Federal life insurance, Civil Service preference, veterans hospitals, and veterans pensions are singular, to say the least.

Although service in the Armed Forces is at least nominally a duty of all male citizens coming of age, it is clear that the present system does not enable Negroes to serve in anything like their proportionate numbers. This is not a question of discrimination. Induction into the Armed Forces is based on a variety of objective tests and standards, but these tests nonetheless have the effect of keeping the number of Negroes disproportionately small.

In 1963 the United States Commission on Civil Rights reported that "A decade ago, Negroes constituted 8 percent of the Armed Forces. Today . . . they continue to constitute 8 percent of the Armed Forces."

In 1964 Negroes constituted 11.8 percent of the population, but probably remain at 8 percent of the Armed Forces.

The significance of Negro under-representation in the Armed Forces is greater than might at first be supposed. If Negroes were represented in the same proportions in the military as they are in the population, they would number 300,000 plus. This would be over 100,000 more than at present (using 1964 strength figures). If the more than 100,000 unemployed Negro men were to have gone into the military the Negro male unemployment rate would have been 7.0 percent in 1964 instead of 9.1 percent.

In 1963 the Civil Rights Commission commented on the occupational aspect of military service for Negroes. "Negro enlisted men enjoy relatively better opportunities in the Armed Forces than in the civilian economy in every clerical, technical, and skilled field for which the data permit comparison."

Enlisted Men:	Percent Negro
Army	12.2
Navy	5.2
Air Force	9.1
Marine Corps	7.6

Officers:	
Army	3.2
Navy	.2
Air Force	1.2
Marine Corps	.2

There is, however, an even more important issue involved in military service for Negroes. Service in the United States Armed Forces is the *only* experience open to the Negro American in which he is truly treated as an equal: not as a Negro equal to a white, but as one man equal to any other man in a world where the category "Negro" and "white" do not exist. If this is a statement of the ideal rather than reality, it is an ideal that is close to realization. In food, dress, housing, pay, work — the Negro in the Armed Forces *is* equal and is treated that way.

There is another special quality about military service for Negro men: it is an utterly masculine world. Given the strains of the disorganized and matrifocal family life in which so many Negro youth come of age, the Armed Forces are a dramatic and desperately needed change: a world away from women, a world run by strong men of unquestioned authority, where discipline, if harsh, is nonetheless orderly and predictable, and where rewards, if limited, are granted on the basis of performance.

The theme of a current Army recruiting message states it as clearly as can be: "In the U.S. Army you get to know what it means to feel like a man."

At the recent Civil Rights Commission hearings in Mississippi a witness testified that his Army service was in fact "the only time I ever felt like a man."

Yet a majority of Negro youth (and probably three-quarters of Mississippi Negroes) fail the Selective Service education test and are rejected. Negro participation in the Armed Forces would be less than it is, were it not for a proportionally larger share of voluntary enlistments and reenlistments. (Thus 16.3 percent of Army sergeants are Negro.)

Alienation

The term alienation may by now have been used in too many ways to retain a clear meaning, but it will serve to sum up the equally numerous ways in which large numbers of Negro youth appear to be withdrawing from American society.

One startling way in which this occurs is that the men are just not there when the Census enumerator comes around.

According to Bureau of Census population estimates for 1963, there are only

87 nonwhite males for every 100 females in the 30-to-34-year age group. The ratio does not exceed 90 to 100 throughout the 25-to-44-year age bracket. In the urban Northeast, there are only 76 males per 100 females 20-to-24 years of age, and males as a percent of females are below 90 percent throughout all ages after 14.

There are not really fewer men than women in the 20-to-40 age bracket. What obviously is involved is an error in counting: the surveyors simply do not find the Negro man. Donald J. Bogue and his associates, who have studied the Federal count of the Negro man, place the error as high as 19.8 percent at age 28; a typical error of around 15 percent is estimated from age 19 through 43. Preliminary research in the Bureau of the Census on the 1960 enumeration has resulted in similar conclusions, although not necessarily the same estimates of the extent of the error. The Negro male *can* be found at age 17 and 18. On the basis of birth records and mortality records, the conclusion must be that he is there at age 19 as well.

Ratio of Males per 100 Females in the
Population, by Color, July 1, 1963

Age	Males per 100 Females	
	White	Nonwhite
Under 5	104.4	100.4
5–9 years	103.9	100.0
10–14 years	104.0	100.0
15–19 years	103.2	99.5
20–24 years	101.2	95.1
25–29 years	100.1	89.1
30–34 years	99.2	86.6
35–39 years	97.5	86.8
40–44 years	96.2	89.9
45–49 years	96.5	90.6

Source: *Current Population Reports*, Series P-25, No. 276, table 1 (Total Population Including Armed Forces Abroad).

When the enumerators do find him, his answers to the standard questions asked in the monthly unemployment survey often result in counting him as "not in the labor force." In other words, Negro male unemployment may in truth be somewhat greater than reported.

The labor force participation rates of nonwhite men have been falling since the beginning of the century and for the past decade have been lower than the rates for white men. In 1964, the participation rates were 78.0 percent for white men and 75.8 percent for nonwhite men. Almost one percentage point of this difference was due to a higher proportion of nonwhite men unable to work because of long-term physical or mental illness; it seems reasonable to assume that the rest of the difference is due to discouragement about finding a job.

If nonwhite male labor force participation rates were as high as the white rates, there would have been 140,000 more nonwhite males in the labor force in 1964.

If we further assume that the 140,000 would have been unemployed, the unemployment rate for nonwhite men would have been 11.5 percent instead of the recorded rate of 9 percent, and the ratio between the nonwhite rate and the white rate would have jumped from 2:1 to 2.4:1.

Understated or not, the official unemployment rates for Negroes are almost unbelievable.

The unemployment statistics for Negro teenagers — 29 percent in January 1965 — reflect lack of training and opportunity in the greatest measure, but it may not be doubted that they also reflect a certain failure of nerve.

"Are you looking for a job?" Secretary of Labor Wirtz asked a young man on a Harlem street corner. "Why?" was the reply.

Richard A. Cloward and Robert Ontell have commented on this withdrawal in a discussion of the Mobilization for Youth project on the Lower East Side of New York.

What contemporary slum and minority youth probably lack that similar children in earlier periods possessed is not motivation but some minimal sense of competence.

We are plagued, in work with these youth, by what appears to be a low tolerance for frustration. They are not able to absorb setbacks. Minor irritants and rebuffs are magnified out of all proportion to reality. Perhaps they react as they do because they are not equal to the world that confronts them, and they know it. And it is the knowing that is devastating. Had the occupational structure remained intact, or had the education provided to them kept pace with occupational changes, the situation would be a different one. But it is not, and that is what we and they have to contend with.

Narcotic addiction is a characteristic form of withdrawal. In 1963, Negroes made up 54 percent of the addict population of the United States. Although the Federal Bureau of Narcotics reports a decline in the Negro proportion of new addicts, HARYOU reports the addiction rate in central Harlem rose from 22.1 per 10,000 in 1955 to 40.4 in 1961.

There is a larger fact about the alienation of Negro youth than the tangle of pathology described by these statistics. It is a fact particularly difficult to grasp by white persons who have in recent years shown increasing awareness of Negro problems.

The present generation of Negro youth growing up in the urban ghettos has probably less personal contact with the white world than any generation in the history of the Negro American.

Until World War II it could be said that in general the Negro and white worlds lived, if not together, at least side by side. Certainly they did, and do, in the South.

Since World War II, however, the two worlds have drawn physically apart. The symbol of this development was the construction in the 1940's and 1950's of the vast white, middle- and lower-middle-class suburbs around all of the Nation's cities. Increasingly the inner cities have been left to Negroes — who now share almost no community life with whites.

In turn, because of this new housing pattern — most of which has been financially assisted by the Federal government — it is probable that the American school system has become *more,* rather than less, segregated in the past two decades.

School integration has not occurred in the South, where a decade after *Brown v. Board of Education* only 1 Negro in 9 is attending school with white children.

And in the North, despite strenuous official efforts, neighborhoods and therefore schools are becoming more and more of one class and one color.

In New York City, in the school year 1957–58 there were 64 schools that were 90 percent or more Negro or Puerto Rican. Six years later there were 134 such schools.

Along with the diminution of white middle-class contacts for a large percentage of Negroes, observers report that the Negro churches have all but lost contact with men in the Northern cities as well. This may be a normal condition of urban life, but it is probably a changed condition for the Negro American and cannot be a socially desirable development.

The only religious movement that appears to have enlisted a considerable number of lower class Negro males in Northern cities of late is that of the Black Muslims; a movement based on total rejection of white society, even though it emulates white mores.

In a word: the tangle of pathology is tightening.

The Case For National Action

The object of this study has been to define a problem, rather than propose solutions to it. We have kept within these confines for three reasons.

First, there are many persons, within and without the Government, who do not feel the problem exists, at least in any serious degree. These persons feel that, with the legal obstacles to assimilation out of the way, matters will take care of themselves in the normal course of events. This is a fundamental issue, and requires a decision within the Government.

Second, it is our view that the problem is so inter-related, one thing with another, that any list of program proposals would necessarily be incomplete, and would distract attention from the main point of inter-relatedness. We have shown a clear relation between male employment, for example, and the number of welfare dependent children. Employment in turn reflects educational achievement, which depends in large part on family stability, which reflects employment. Where we should break into this cycle, and how, are the most difficult domestic questions facing the United States. We must first reach agreement on what the problem is, then we will know what questions must be answered.

Third, it is necessary to acknowledge the view, held by a number of responsible persons, that this problem may in fact be out of control. This is a view with which we emphatically and totally disagree, but the view must be acknowledged. The persistent rise in Negro educational achievement is probably the main trend that belies this thesis. On the other hand our study has produced some clear indications that the situation may indeed have begun to feed on itself. It may be noted, for example, that for most of the post-war period male Negro unemployment and the number of new AFDC cases rose and fell together as if connected by a chain from 1948 to 1962. The correlation between the two series of data was an astonishing .91. (This would mean that 83 percent of the rise and fall in AFDC cases can be statistically ascribed to the rise and fall in the unemployment rate.) In 1960, how-ever, for the first time, unemployment declined, but the number of new AFDC cases rose. In 1963 this happened a second time. In 1964 a third. The possible implications of these and other data are serious enough that they, too, should be understood before program proposals are made.

However, the argument of this paper does lead to one central conclusion: Whatever the specific elements of a national effort designed to resolve this problem, those elements must be coordinated in terms of one general strategy.

What then is that problem? We feel the answer is clear enough. Three centuries of injustice have brought about deep-seated structural distortions in the life of the Negro American. At this point, the present tangle of pathology is capable of per-petuating itself without assistance from the white world. The cycle can be broken only if these distortions are set right.

In a word, a national effort towards the problems of Negro Americans must be directed towards the question of family structure. The object should be to strengthen the Negro family so as to enable it to raise and support its members as do other families. After that, how this group of Americans chooses to run its affairs, take advantage of its opportunities, or fail to do so, is none of the nation's business.

The fundamental importance and urgency of restoring the Negro American family structure has been evident for some time. E. Franklin Frazier put it most succinctly in 1950:

As the result of family disorganization a large proportion of Negro children and youth have not undergone the socialization which only the family can provide. The disorganized families have failed to provide for their emotional needs and have not provided the discipline and habits which are necessary for personality development. Because the disorganized family has failed in its function as a socializing agency, it has handicapped the children in their relations to the institutions in the commu-nity. Moreover, family disorganization has been partially responsible for a large amount of juvenile delinquency and adult crime among Negroes. Since the wide-spread family disorganization among Negroes has resulted from the failure of the father to play the role in family life required by American society, the mitigation of this problem must await those changes in the Negro and American society which will enable the Negro father to play the role required of him.

Nothing was done in response to Frazier's argument. Matters were left to take care of themselves, and as matters will, grew worse not better. The problem is now more serious, the obstacles greater. There is, however, a profound change for the better in one respect. The President has committed the nation to an all-out effort to eliminate poverty wherever it exists, among whites or Negroes, and a militant, organized, and responsible Negro movement exists to join in that effort. Such a national effort could be stated thus:

The policy of the United States is to bring the Negro American to full and equal sharing in the responsibilities and rewards of citizenship. To this end, the programs of the Federal government bearing on this objective shall be designed to have the effect, directly or indirectly, of enhancing the stability and resources of the Negro American family.

The Family: Resources for Change

Hylan Lewis
Elizabeth Herzog

This planning session has a concern for the influences on contemporary family life, especially family life among Negroes. It is assumed that the aims of the working session are to propose policies and programs for the immediate future as well as long-term directions and programs. The agenda paper refers to some of the issues and some of the facts having to do with

1. The effects of low income on family life
2. Family composition among Negroes — its characteristics, factors influencing it, and its consequences
3. Plans and programs aimed at strengthening family life, especially among the low-income population.

Among the issues: the nature and extent of family disorganization among Negroes, the reasons given for it, the outlook for it, and of course what to do about it.

The measures of family disorganization most frequently used are the incidence of families headed by females, illegitimacy, and the attributes and behavior of the disadvantaged male. The nature of the prognosis and programs proposed are heavily conditioned by whether the indications of "family breakdown" are seen primarily as a heritage of slavery or as responses to current conditions.

Among the facts:

Over-all, two-thirds of Negro families include two parents. The increase in the proportion of female-headed households has been less than five percentage points in 15 years, with no rise in the last five years. The evidence is that Negro-white differences in family structure diminish when controlled for income and that differences by income are more striking than differences by color; that factors attributable

Hylan G. Lewis, Elizabeth Herzog, et al., *Agenda Paper No. V: The Family: Resources for Change — Planning Session for the White House Conference. "To Fulfill These Rights,"* November 16–18, 1965. The authors wish to acknowledge the invaluable assistance of Bonita Valien, Alvin Schorr, Marian Chase, and Jack Lefcowitz.

to the effects of inequities in housing, employment, health, and education account for a large amount of the difference between the figures for Negroes and whites.

The family and family behavior among Negroes show great range and variability; especially overlooked and underrated is the diversity among low-income Negro families. When these are overlooked for any reason, there is danger that the depreciated, and probably more dramatic and threatening, characteristics of a small segment of the population may be imputed to an entire population.

Family and personal strengths, resiliencies and demonstrated capacities for change found at all levels are a prime resource to be taken into account in planning programs aimed at strengthening family life among Negroes.

Questions

1. What are the goals for *all* families?
   Are there special goals for different categories of families? — e.g., Negro families? Negro low-income families? Negro families in urban ghettos? urban problem families? rural problem families?
2. What is the most important single thing that needs to be done now to improve the quality of family life generally? For low-income families?
3. What should be the general objective with regard to low-income Negro families:
   (a) to propose a model to which all families should conform?
   (b) to offer the kinds of economic and social supports that seem best suited to allow families to work out their own forms and functions?
4. Among the Federal Government's efforts to strengthen the family, which programs seem to be moving effectively in needed directions? — i.e., programs such as the following:
   Aid to Families of Dependent Children
   public housing, and other Federal aid to housing
   day care
   vocational training and rehabilitation
   employment counseling and services
   training and use of non-professional aids
   family counseling and education
   medical and survivors' insurance
   foster family and group family care
   social and protective services for children
   federal aids to education

The Family: Resources for Change

. . . the family is rooted in human nature — in human nature conceived not as a bundle of instincts but as a product of social life; . . . the family may take protean forms as it survives or is reborn in times of cataclysmic social change; and . . . we can predict with some assurance the persistence of the family but not the specific forms which it may take in the future.[1]

The viability of families, especially low-income families, is critically relevant to our national design and commitment "to fulfill these rights." The purpose of this agenda paper is to serve the working group's examination of stresses and potentials for contemporary families. The discussion is cued to "outside" as well as "inside," and to contemporary as well as historical, factors affecting the course and quality of family life, particularly among low-income Negroes. The aim is to focus attention on the policy and program implications of current family facts and issues. The agenda paper has been prepared with these goals of the planning session in mind: (1) the proposal of directions and long-term programs that seem most promising for eliminating or reducing the factors that make for family stress and instability, and for maximizing the realization of family potentials; (2) the proposal of some specific programs, services or activities to be accomplished within a stated time.

It is through the family that the individual enters into the privileges and liabilities bestowed upon him as a citizen. And it is through the family that the effects of his citizen status first impinge on his inner circle and his inner self. The family acts, not merely as conduit, but rather as agent, reagent and catalyst. It defines the child's world for him; and it, initially, defines him to himself.

The functions of the family are discussed chiefly in terms of what it does for children, and the emphasis is accurate. Yet the viability of the family depends on the satisfactions and supports it offers to adults, since it is they who determine whether a family unit survives or dissolves. Moreover, what the family can offer to its children depends on the psychological, social, physical and economic status of the adults who preside over it.

It is often claimed that the United States is a child-centered country and, like most claims, this one is occasionally challenged. If we were child-centered, ask the challengers, would we be spending on education only a fraction of what we spend for defense? Would our most family-labeled program, Aid to Families of Dependent Children, have focused for so many years on the sex morality and employability of the mother, with so little official regard for the care of children while the mother works?

Contemporary Family Forms

A major issue in any discussion of the Negro family is the higher proportion of female-headed households among Negroes compared with whites.[2] The genesis of such families is, by some, attributed to slavery. Others reject or place little emphasis on slavery as an explanation, as compared with current conditions. For example, it has been suggested that

. . . not enough is known about . . . present family forms and functions and about the behavior patterns which are distinctly urban products with a dynamic and history of their own. The forms, as in the case of the family headed by the female, may be the same but the context in which they fit and function has probably changed in important details.[3]

In one sense, the disagreement about the influence of the slavery heritage on current family forms and practices appears largely academic. We are dealing with the problems and potentials of today, as they are manifested today. Although historical influences may affect kind and degree of potential for growth, it is not necessary to agree on underlying causes in order to perceive present problems and build upon present potentials.

In another sense, the controversy is not academic, for it colors opinions about the nature and extent of differences and similarities between Negro and white families at very low income levels. Those who emphasize the historical influence point to differences; those who emphasize post-slavery influences point to similarities between the two.

The habit of analyzing data by color rather than by income level has tended to support the slavery-specific hypothesis. Since a much larger proportion of Negroes than of whites are on the lowest income levels, what look like statistically significant differences between Negroes and whites may actually be differences between socio-economic levels. [See Figures 1a and 1b] But if the figures are presented only in one way, the other possibility is obscured. Studies of prenatal care, for example, indicate that in effect one is comparing the prosperous with the poor in all three of the following comparisons: white mothers with nonwhite mothers; married mothers with unmarried mothers; all mothers who do with all mothers who do not obtain prenatal care.[4]

The Lefcowitz paper compares a variety of qualities for Negroes and whites who are poor and for Negroes and whites who are not poor.[5] In effect, Negro and white comparisons are made after a rough standardization for income. These data suggest that

1. When controlled for income, Negro-white differences in family structure diminish. Differences by income are more striking than differences by color.
2. When Negro and white children with similar incomes are compared, differences between them in educational achievement diminish and the differences by class appear more striking than the differences by color.
3. There is far more difference in employment status by income than by color.
4. The relative position of men with respect to women, economically and educationally, is the same for whites as for nonwhites.

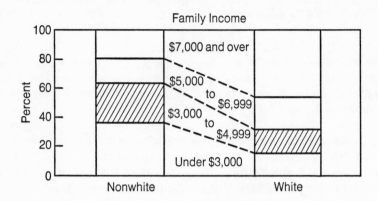

Figure 1a: Two out of five nonwhite families had incomes below $3,000 in 1964. (*Source*: U.S. Bureau of the Census.)

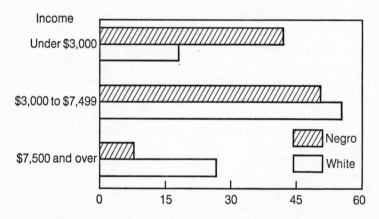

Figure 1b: About half of the Negro and white urban families (after taxes, 1960–1961; includes single consumers) had incomes of $3,000–$7,500. But most of the remaining Negroes had lower incomes whereas most of the remaining whites had higher incomes. (*Source*: U.S. Department of Labor, Bureau of Labor Statistics.)

In short, some differences diminish and others disappear. On the other hand, even within income classes, some striking differences remain, differences that may be attributed to two qualities. First, a time-consuming, sophisticated analysis may be required to discern what quality that overlaps with ethnic status is operating. For example, the number of children born per 1,000 mothers is greater for Negroes than for whites. However, the migration pattern of Negroes is different from whites and rural background, like income level, appears to be a powerful factor affecting fertility. If one could standardize white-Negro fertility figures for rural background and for income, would a difference continue to appear?

A second quality that creates difference between Negroes and whites is, obviously, the impact of discriminatory treatment. If the rate of home ownership is higher for whites than for Negroes, even within income classes, can there be any doubt that discrimination by real estate and financing firms is responsible? As another example, the mortality rate of young Negro men exceeds that of white men.[6] Obviously, this increases the incidence of Negro broken families.

We may come to three general conclusions:

1. Plainly, and overlooking the fact that most Negroes are poor, there are more female-headed families among Negroes than among whites.
2. Poverty accounts for a large measure of this difference. If the qualities of poverty were removed from statistical comparisons, figures for Negroes would move much closer to those for whites.
3. Locatable factors emerging in general from discrimination — health, housing, employment, and so forth — account for a large measure of the difference between figures for Negroes and for whites.

Opinions differ about the rate of increase in the proportion of female-headed families.[7] Some, citing the increase in the proportion of nonwhite families headed by women, from 1949 (18.8%) to 1962 (23.2%), see a headlong deterioration, a rapid "crumbling" of the low-income Negro family. Others point out that the rise from 1949 to 1964 was 4.4 percentage points in all (that is, less than one-third of one percentage point a year); that it was gradual from 1949 (18.8%) to 1959 (23.6%) and that from 1959 to 1964 it has remained relatively stable. They conclude that there exists a plateau, or perhaps a gradual but not acute increase in the over-all proportion of broken homes among low-income Negroes.

Those who hold the rapid-deterioration view urge strong action to halt an accelerating breakdown. Those who hold the plateau view urge strong action to remedy adverse conditions that have existed far too long. There is consensus between the two schools of thought with regard to the existence of a long-standing disparity between white and nonwhite rates, and the need for strong and prompt intervention. Differences lie: (a) in interpreting the current situation as a crisis vs. a long-term manifestation; (b) in the attitudes of alarm and hostility that may be held with regard to an erupting crisis, as compared with the problem-solving approach that is more likely with regard to a long-continued situation.

The Father — Present and Absent

The two-parent family is modal in the United States, which is to say that it is the norm for American Negroes. [See Figures 2a and 2b.] Over-all, two-thirds of Negro families include two parents. At the upper income levels the proportion rises and at the lower income levels it falls. Nevertheless, it is useful to remember that when we speak of the female-headed household we are talking about a minority, even among the poor. The fact that family composition is especially flexible among the very poor means that, although at any given moment two-thirds of the Negro families in the urban slums include two parents, individual children at various times of their lives may move from two-parent to one-parent homes and vice versa.[8]

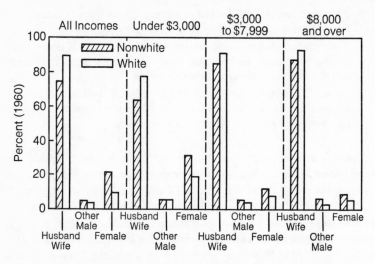

Figure 2a: All families at all income levels. Most families have male heads, but female heads are more prevalent among nonwhites. (*Source*: U.S. Bureau of the Census.)

At the same time, outside the slum areas, family stability is the rule rather than the exception. In focusing on family homes, as Erikson has pointed out, the present father tends to be forgotten. Forgotten also is the fact that we know very little about him. We do not even know whether there is evidence to support an occasionally voiced impression that the stable Negro home is more patriarchal than the stable white home.

The great majority of our children — some 87 per cent — live in a home with two parents. Most of the rest live in a one-parent home, and in most cases that parent is the mother.

Few would deny that a harmonious two-parent home offers the best prospect for a child to reach his full potential. On the other hand, a substantial minority of American children, over six and a half million of them, live in a home headed by a woman. It is reasonable, therefore, to review current assumptions about the one-parent home and what it means for the developmental prospects of the children who grow up in it.

It has been our habit to view any deviation from our modal family pattern as an aberration. A number of research findings have tended to reinforce this habit. The question may be raised, however, whether a form that includes so many children and has produced so many effective and apparently happy adults deserves a less negative status. Perhaps the time has come to recognize the one-parent family as a family form in its own right.

Among reasons urged for reassessment of the one-parent family as a family form in its own right are the following:

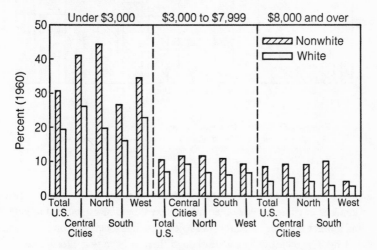

Figure 2b: Families with female heads. The proportion of female family heads falls sharply with rising income. It is most prevalent among the poorest families in large cities and in the North. (*Source*: U.S. Bureau of the Census.)

1. The one-parent family is with us and shows no sign of becoming less frequent. [See Figure 3.]
2. There is reason to believe that children in such families are adversely affected by the negative assumptions which cluster around it.
3. Through time and space the family has absorbed a vast array of different forms and still has continued to function as the family.
4. The modal American family may not be as functionally two-parent or as "patriarchal" as is sometimes assumed.
5. Analysis of research findings concerning the one-parent family fails to support a sweeping indictment of its potential for producing children capable of fruitful and gratifying lives.

1. The first proposition is supported by a vast array of statistics. The march of these figures is reminiscent of figures concerning the working mother. Not many years ago, conferences were discussing whether mothers should or should not be

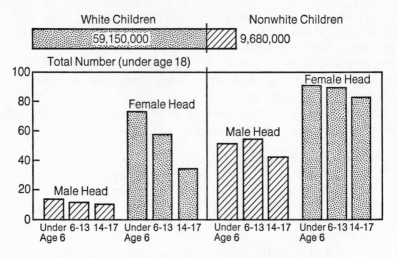

Figure 3: Over 80% of the nonwhite children living in families headed by females and 40–50% of those in families with male heads were poor in 1963. (*Source*: Mollie Orshansky, "Who's Who Among the Poor," *Social Security Bulletin,* July 1965.)

permitted or encouraged to work. At present, the main focus of discussion is, rather, what kinds of daytime care or other supervision should be established to help the working mother fulfill her dual role (a subject which is touched upon at somewhat greater length below). In any case, although there is hope that effective economic and social measures can reduce the frequency of one-parent homes, it seems unlikely that the numbers will be drastically reduced in the very near future.

2. With regard to effects on children of popular assumptions about the one-parent home, the evidence is chiefly presumptive. Specialists in child development provide persuasive discussions and data bearing on the growth of positive and negative identity. There is no lack of evidence that children are alert to the classifications implicit in questions at school about father's occupation, in social differences between mothers who do and do not have a spouse, in the activities of children who do and do not have a father to take them places and do things with them. The fact of a father's presence or absence is ineluctable; the subtle or overt responses to that fact on the part of adults and other children are in themselves responsive to popular assumptions, and are capable of change as those assumptions change.

3. Although relatively few have made an intensive study of family forms through time and space, most students of problems relating to families are aware that, as Witmer and Kotinsky put it:

All the evidence points to the infinite capacity of the family to change — to change its composition, to redefine the way it shares the care of children with other social institutions — and yet to retain its over-all responsibility for them.[9]

4. The extent to which children in two-parent homes are reared at home and taught at school by women, during their formative years, has been the subject of extensive comment. Without assuming that this is to their advantage, some raise questions about the extent to which it reduces the contrast between children in one-parent and in two-parent homes.

5. Correlation between undesired behavior or attributes and the one-parent home has been a repetitive research finding. The broken home has been reported as associated with emotional maladjustment, poor school achievement, juvenile delinquency, and illegitimacy. However, when data are controlled for socio-economic status, such correlations often fade out. The relationship is more often apparent in studies that have not made a point of such control. Its occurrence is too frequent to require documentation here. Its absence under adequate statistical controls is less familiar but is reported in a number of studies.[10]

In this connection it is sometimes pointed out that studies which claim adequate controls also have shown children doing better in warm, stable one-parent homes than in two-parent homes with tension and friction. If such findings are trusted, the implication may be an underlining of the need to offer to one-parent homes the kinds of support that would enhance the mother's ability to be a competent, unharried and undefeated mother.[11]

The proponents of the views summarized above do not by any means advocate the one-parent family as the most desired type. What they do advocate is: (1) recognition of the one-parent family as an existing and fairly common form rather than a sick form or a strange deviation from normality; (2) recognition that a sound one-parent home may be better for a child than a torn and strife-ridden two-parent home; (3) devising of ways to enhance the ability of parents without partners to provide a sound one-parent home.

The choice, unfortunately, is not necessarily between a warm, stable, adequate two-parent home and a one-parent home. No one would hesitate to prefer the former for any American child. To avoid the separation of the parents does not, however, insure for the child a "good" or "adequate" home. Evidence available so far does not justify the assumption that any two-parent home is better for a child than any one-parent home; or that the intactness or broken-ness of the home is, in itself, the variable that determines whether or not a child will reach his full potential. As in so many cases, it is an extremely important variable, the net effect of which depends on a number of other important variables. And as in so many cases, the net effect can be helped or hindered by community attitudes and supports.

The relatively frequent dissolution of marriages among low-income Negro families is generally attributed, by students of the subject, to the disadvantaged economic position of the Negro male and the consequent downgrading of his role and status within the family, his own self-esteem, and his readiness to struggle with continuing and insuperable family responsibilities.[12] A new determination to improve the economic status of Negro men coincides with a widening of information about and access to the means of birth control. Some see in this convergence a likelihood of mutual reinforcement. A man with a stable income is more ready to accept the responsibilities of family head than one whose economic position is precarious. At the same time, the responsibilities of a family head are more manageable if the size of the family can be planned. The most optimistic prognosticators add that marital stability is likely to be enhanced by the convergence of male ego satisfaction, female respect for him as a breadwinner, and ability of each to give and to receive sex satisfactions without fear of undesired pregnancy.

Early indications suggest that in general people will reach out for services when they believe the services will meet a felt need, and specifically that birth control information and assistance can increase the interest in receiving prenatal health care. "Our experience so far in the maternity and infant care programs gives us hopeful indications that the institution of family planning services more than doubles attendance at postpartum clinics and, in some programs at least, seems to have a favorable influence in attracting women to prenatal clinics early as word gets around that the services are available."[13]

The Present Mother

In a fatherless home, the mother carries a multiple burden: as head of family, as breadwinner, as homemaker, as mentor, comforter and caretaker of children. Some psychologists hold that, during the first two years of a child's life, the father's presence is more important for his psychological, physical and economic help to the mother than for his direct effect on the child's well-being. (This assumes, of course, that he does give such support.)

The one-parent mother of very low income is likely to be either a working mother or a relief recipient. In either case she is likely to be more fatigued, less healthy physically and more subject to depression than a prosperous mother. If she is "on relief," she and her family may be living on less than a subsistence budget — although recent modifications in welfare practices and policies may bring about some modification of this situation.

If she is a working mother, the same comparisons would hold, plus the problem of arranging supervision for the children while she is out of the home. Mothers without husbands are far more likely to work than other mothers with children under eighteen; and nonwhite mothers are more likely to work than white mothers. They are also likely to receive lower pay.

The effects on children of having their mothers work outside the home are hotly debated. Research findings show strong convergence on three conclusions: (1) that almost no generalization holds true for all working mothers or all their children;

(2) that many popular assumptions about working mothers and their children do not stand up under challenge; (3) that the mother's working, in itself, is only one among many factors impinging on children, and may well be a secondary factor.

Primary factors appear to condition its impact on children and family life in three chief ways:

1. The type of arrangements made for the child's care and supervision during the mother's absence. These are partly the result of attitudes, assumption and behavior, which affect the child whether the mother works or not. But to a large extent they are the result of resources available to her.
2. The way the child perceives and reacts to the mother's absence. This is also a result of basic factors — including his own special needs — which again affect the child in any case.
3. Parental attitudes and behavior, including specific reactions to the mother's outside work. These, once more, are largely the product of basic factors which would affect the child in any case, although in special instances the working mother situation may have a secondary influence on their impact and interaction.[14]

The conclusions listed above have been reported by a number of independent investigators. They leave unanswered a good many questions that cannot be discussed here. They also drive home a realization that the very mothers most likely to have no option about working outside the home are the ones least able to arrange for adequate supervision of children while the mother is out of the home.

Some of their problems were highlighted by studies conducted in the late fifties and mid-sixties. The Children's Bureau and the Women's Bureau contracted with the Bureau of Census in February 1965 for a new survey to obtain information on the child-care arrangements of one specific group of working mothers: those women who worked 27 weeks or more in 1964, either full- or part-time, and who had at least one child under 14 years of age living at home. There were 6.1 million mothers in this group. These mothers had a total of 12.3 million children under 14, one-fifth of all U.S. children in this age group. The number of mothers in the labor force with children under six numbered 3.6 million.

A number of different child-care arrangements were reported:

Almost one-half of the children (46 per cent) were cared for in their own homes, usually by a father (15 per cent) or by another relative (21 per cent) and less frequently by a nonrelative (10 per cent). For 5 per cent the relative caring for the children at home was a child under 16 years of age.
Care in someone else's home (15 per cent) was reported much less frequently than care in own home and was equally divided between care by a relative and by a nonrelative.
Group care (in day centers, after school centers, etc.) was reported for 2 per cent

of the children but this type of arrangement also varied by age, being 4 per cent for children under 3, 7 per cent for children 3 to 5, and 1 per cent or less for children 6 years of age or older.

Eight per cent of the children in the survey were expected to care for themselves, an arrangement that varied by age, amounting to 1 per cent for the children under 6, 8 per cent for those 6 to 11, and 20 per cent for children 12 or 13 years of age.[15]

The picture is not reassuring, especially if one considers that the "latchkey" children for whom no arrangements are made are probably over-represented among the lowest-income families, that the proportion of children in group care remains very low, and that some of the arrangements reported are sketchy in the extreme. Studies of children under the AFDC program show a larger proportion of children with no daytime care arrangements. It should be added that some of these studies also have revealed great concern on the part of some mothers about the lack of child supervision, and ingenious arrangements by a few of them to have the children report regularly by telephone.

Children and Daytime Care

In recent years, new and systematic efforts have been made to increase the quantity and quality of day-care facilities for children of working mothers, and new legislation has given impetus to these efforts. Nevertheless, the 1965 figures suggest a large gap to be filled.[16]

Although research results indicate that outside employment of the mother does not, in and of itself, affect children adversely, a good many believe that it is better for children to be in their own homes with their own mothers during the first two years. Even if present measures do not demonstrate adverse effects, they say, we are not able to tell whether the own mother's care would be better for them. This discussion, invoking "the Bowlby thesis" on the one hand, and, on the other, accounts of the many "fulfilled" men and women who were raised by nurses and governesses, will probably not be resolved in the near future.

Meanwhile, new controversies are flaring about the need of preschool children to obtain training for school adjustment and achievement of a kind believed not to be provided in their own homes. Should day care centers offer not only custodial care and opportunities for socialization, but also cognitive enrichment to enhance school readiness? The hotly debated and many-faceted subject of preschool for children of low-income families is equally pertinent to discussions of education and discussions of family life. It includes consideration of what mothers offer to children and what a specific mother offers to a specific child under specific circumstances, as compared with what trained and responsive day-care attendants or nursery school teachers can offer. It includes questions about whether cognitive enrichment is being sought at the expense of social and emotional development; of whether nursery school cooperativeness is cultivated at the expense of independence and coping abilities; of whether the intellectual gains reported after preschool training are stable, or fade away under the impact of unfortunate school experiences in over-crowded classes, with split shifts, and teachers often hampered by inadequate teaching or by their own unconsciously acquired habits.[17]

Closely linked to problems of preschool and later education is the role of the parent in his child's schooling. There is ample evidence that low-income Negro parents have high educational aspirations for their children; and that they (like the rest of the American public) see education as the magic key to wealth and happiness. It is equally clear, however, that they tend to view themselves as having no role in the child's education, aside from housing and feeding him while he goes to school. The school is seen as a foreign and fearsome place, where a parent goes chiefly when summoned because his child has failed in his work or gotten into trouble.

There is a widely accepted dictum that small children cannot be helped toward school readiness and social competence if their parents are not involved. Many programs are based on this principle, some very ingenious and apparently effective. Nevertheless, on-the-spot visits often reveal that glowingly described programs in fact are able to "reach" very few parents, at great cost and investment of staff. The great breakthrough in parent and family life education has yet to be made, at least for the low income groups. Pending it, the question remains whether one must assume that any child whose parent is unable or unwilling to be "reached" is himself beyond the reach of programs designed to open up for him the way to the kind of life that most people in this country consider a good life.

The use of nonprofessional aides in nursery schools and daycare centers is urged as one means of combatting both the problem of parental involvement and the problem of insufficient adequate male models. Some centers for daytime care of children from low-income families encourage the mothers to serve as aides, thus increasing their involvement, giving them practice in enhancing intellectual stimulation and interpersonal response, establishing them as active collaborators in the school program, and — in some instances — augmenting their income a little. Some of these centers strive to promote active school-home partnership by arranging for parents to visit the schools their children will later attend and to become acquainted with the teachers in whose classes the children will be.

Some success has been reported in the use of teen-age boys as nursery school aides, including "delinquents" and "near-delinquents." The children respond with eager warmth to these "big men" in their lives. The youthful "big men," in turn, appear to derive great pleasure and profit from the response of the children, who treat them as responsible adults and thus evoke warmth, responsibility and enhanced self-respect.

Recently some parents whose children are in a preschool enrichment program met with the teachers to express their concern about the lax discipline in the school. Children were not smacked when they failed to obey adults, and were not scolded if they were "ugly" to each other. The teachers explained that they were trying to instill inner controls that would continue to operate when the children were too old to spank, and when so many low-income parents feel their children have moved beyond parental control. After considerable discussion, both parents and teachers expressed satisfaction.

The observers, however, were left with a number of questions that echoed concerns expressed by others: Are the children being "socialized" in a way that will be a disadvantage to them in their own neighborhoods?

Are the school and home environments incompatible in a way that will be detrimental to the children and to family cohesion?

Will the encouragement of spontaneity and autonomy in the nursery school equip them badly for the atmosphere of the usual public schoolroom?

Is the cognitive being stressed at the expense of other elements?

Births Out of Wedlock

A number of statements frequently made about births out of wedlock are supported by evidence which — even allowing for vagaries of national reporting that includes over-reporting and under-reporting, as well as lack of reporting from some 15 states — still affords solid support for these particular generalizations.

It is solidly established, for example, that numbers of births out of wedlock have increased strikingly in the past twenty years and that rates have tripled since 1933. Rates are far higher among Negroes than among whites. In fact, the majority of children born out of wedlock are nonwhite, although only 12 per cent of the population are nonwhite.

There is also ample and unchallenged evidence that illegitimacy rates are much higher among the poor than among the prosperous. If further evidence were needed on a virtually unchallenged generalization, figures on rates in high and low income tracts should be sufficient. Pakter and associates, for example, found that the proportion of births out-of-wedlock in relation to total nonwhite births varied from a high of 37.5 per cent in the Central Harlem district to a comparative low of 8.9 per cent in the Pelham Bay district.[18] It is difficult to say to what extent differences should be ascribed to greater use of contraception and abortion by the nonpoor, to more frequent marriage because of pregnancy among the nonpoor, to higher fertility rates among the poor and among nonwhites, and to differential reporting.

A few points, also based on available figures, are less recognized and publicized. Some of these relate to the increase in rates of illegitimacy, by which is meant the number of births out of wedlock per 1,000 unmarried women of child-bearing age. The rise in *rates* (as differentiated from *numbers*) has been relatively steady over several decades, and has paralleled to a considerable degree changes in birth rates generally. This rise represents a long-term trend and not a sudden upsurge. Moreover, in the last six years reported (1957–1963) the rates have oscillated at about the same level, rising or falling one or two points or less, but in effect representing a six-year plateau. Thus, the current picture is a rise in numbers and a leveling off in rates of nonwedlock births.[19]

The rates for teen-agers have increased *less* than the rates for other age groups over the past twenty years, and in the last eight years reported their rates have remained relatively constant. The rates for those fourteen and under have not increased since 1947. The population explosion has multiplied *numbers* in that age group, but rates have remained constant. True, the figures derive from estimates, but this is true of all figures on unmarried mothers and there is as much reason to trust one part of them as to trust another part. Thus any recent increase in the magnitude of problems relating to births out of wedlock is attributable to increase in population rather than to changes in the way people are behaving.

The figures just cited refer to all births out of wedlock, since rates for white and nonwhite are not available separately. Until recently, rates were undoubtedly increasing faster among nonwhites than among whites. Recently, however, nonwedlock births have increased faster among whites than among nonwhites.[20] This minor shift in relative rate of increase does not, of course, alter the large and long-standing difference between white and nonwhite illegitimacy rates nor answer the question noted above, concerning it.

Although rates of illegitimacy have not increased during the past six years, numbers have multiplied, reaching 259,000 in 1963. Unfortunately, social and medical service have not kept pace. It has been estimated roughly that probably less than one-third of our unmarried mothers receive social services near the time of the child's birth. Presumably still fewer receive them at other times.

No careful observer asserts that the insufficient services we do have are distributed evenly or efficiently. With regard to social services, it has been estimated that in 1961 about one unmarried mother in six received services from a public or voluntary child welfare agency.[21] Three-fourths of the mothers served by such agencies in 1961 were white, although the majority of the children born out of wedlock in that year were nonwhite. From this we can estimate that nearly one-third of the white unmarried mothers and less than one-tenth of the nonwhite were served by public or private child welfare agencies.

On the whole, the unmarried mothers served by voluntary child welfare agencies, maternity homes and family service agencies tend to be of higher socio-economic status (including somewhat higher education) than the average for all unmarried mothers in the United States. They also tend, as do those served by public agencies, to be younger and more likely to place their children in adoption. About 70 per cent of the white babies born out of wedlock and less than 10 per cent of the nonwhite are legally adopted.

Failure to receive services does not necessarily mean that service has been sought and refused. On the contrary, a major deterrent to receiving social services is that the unmarried mother-to-be sees no need of them. It should be added that her definition of her needs and her conception of the kind of help social agencies give seldom coincide with agency definition. Moreover, if all unmarried mothers did seek agency help, the agencies would be unable to cope with the demand.

In the case of medical services, problems of eligibility and of arranging for care bulk far larger than with social services, and many women — married or unmarried — wait until they are in labor in order to obtain emergency service because they are not eligible to receive prenatal care. Far too few mothers, married or unmarried, receive adequate prenatal care and many receive none at all. However, still fewer unmarried than married mothers-to-be receive such care.[22]

Those who have studied the problems of low-income Negro unmarried mothers on the whole subscribe to the belief that the most effective way to decrease nonwedlock births in this group would be to improve the economic situation of the low-income Negro male. Census tract data and special studies show that as income increases rates of nonwedlock birth, like the frequency of female-headed homes, decrease.[23]

How illegitimacy rates will respond to dissemination of birth control information and devices remains to be seen. Some predict that, after moderate delay, there will be a radical decrease in the number of births out of wedlock. Those who question the prediction hold that among low-income Negroes a positive value attaches to having a child, both as an affirmation of masculinity or femininity and because children are prized in themselves. This view, in turn, is countered by reminders of nonwedlock children left in hospitals by mothers who do not want to keep them. It seems reasonable to assume that given the information and materials they need, at least some unmarried women will take steps to avoid pregnancy. It is possible also that the possibility of family planning would encourage men to enter and maintain the continuing obligations of marriage — the more so if, at the same time, their own economic stability is improved.

Recent changes in policies with regard to AFDC are also cited as a possible influence in decreasing illegitimacy rates. Among other features, these changes modify the "man in the house" rule, which is said to discourage marriage, on the one hand, and, on the other, to encourage over-reporting of illegitimacy through fear of losing the relief check if it is known that there is a stable relation with a man.

The often-heard statement that no stigma attaches to illegitimacy among low-income Negroes usually carries the implication that no stigma means no penalty, and that this means it doesn't matter whether one is born in or out of wedlock. This implication runs contrary to abundant evidence. To be born in wedlock and to have your children born in wedlock is a decided social plus, and a gratification.

The plus value of regular marriage is stronger than the minus value of no marriage. The lack of marriage is by no means a matter of indifference. Some low-income mothers pray for boys in order to avoid "trouble" for their daughters, and when trouble comes there is grief and anger, even though you stick to your own, take care of your own, and never turn them away. There is also a revulsion against forcing a marriage between a girl pregnant out of wedlock and the putative father, unless they really love each other. The question is — is an unhappy marriage more desirable than an out-of-wedlock birth? A girl may wait until she is "sure she loves him" — even though the assurance comes after the baby is born.

Both national statistics and special studies make it clear that women move in and out of married and unmarried motherhood, so that many families include both legitimate and illegitimate children. The pattern is familiar also among middle- and high-income whites, although with them it is more usual to have one illegitimate child (which may or may not be placed in adoption) and then marry and have children only in wedlock.

Attitudes toward illegitimacy and toward marriage are clearly linked with the economic position of the Negro male. A male head of house who is not a bread-winner and provider is a hazard to the happiness of the marriage, and his loss of economic status is so great a hazard to his intra-family status that he may decamp, either to protect his own ego or to make his family eligible for support from AFDC. Recent changes in the AFDC program are aimed against the second reason for family desertion.

One reason why it is difficult for middle-class observers to fathom attitudes toward sex and marriage among the poor is failure to recognize that values may be honored by people who do not adhere to them in daily life. This discrepancy between what one believes and what one does may arise from conflict between different sets of values observed by the same individual, and different hierarchies of values held by different nations, socio-economic classes, or individuals. Food and shelter for self or family may rank higher than scrupulous honesty; avoidance of an unhappy marriage may rank higher than legitimate birth status, and the value hierarchy may be constant in an individual's life or may change according to the situation.

Rodman posits the "value stretch," which he describes as broader among the poor than among the prosperous. The very poor, he says, "share the general values of the society with members of other classes, but in addition they have stretched these values or developed alternative values, which help them to adjust to their deprived circumstances."[24] Thus, the "lower-class value stretch" refers to "the wider range of values, and the lower degree of commitment to these values, to be found within the lower class." Some commentators raise a question whether the "stretch" is wider among the low-income groups than among those with middle or high incomes, or merely more perceptible to middle-class observers. The behavior of the prosperous with regard to taxes is mentioned in this connection, as are sharp business practices, sexual infidelity, and the frequent placing of career advancement before the needs of family or country. No one has devised an accurate measure of stretch-difference. It seems clear, however, that on all socio-economic levels people can consciously believe in certain values, even while they continue to act as if those values did not exist.[25]

Child-Rearing Practices

A number of differences between the poor and the prosperous with regard to child-rearing practices have been described, and attempts have been made to relate some of them directly to school achievement, social satisfactions and later vocational adequacy. Among the differences frequently cited: The poor are less likely to encourage a child's interest in exploration, discovery, inquiry; they are more likely to reward inactivity and passivity as attributes of a "good child"; they are less likely to enhance and reward development of verbal skills through precept and approval; they are more likely to display repressive and punitive attitudes toward sex, sex questioning and experimentation, and a view of the sex relationship as basically exploitative; they are more likely to rely on authoritarian methods of child rearing; they are more likely to discipline by corporal punishment, harshly and inconsistently applied.

Little challenge is raised against these generalizations, although many are quick to point out that some of them are almost inevitable in crowded dwellings where adults are harried, depressed and fatigued.

Some other generalizations about child-rearing practices, as about attributes of the poor generally, arouse more objections. Some of the objections relate to the investigators' use of "culture-bound instruments"; some to the claim that the traits involved are direct products of the "reality world" in which both parents and children dwell. These kinds of challenges have been raised against statements that children are reared to low esteem of selves and parents, present time-orientation, impulse gratification, fatalism, emphasis on "keeping out of trouble" rather than positive achievement, lack of goal commitment.

Objections are raised also to implications that some of the attitudes and psychological sets listed in the preceding paragraph are basic traits rather than responses to immediate environment; and that they apply globally to an income category or neighborhood. For example, a study of child-rearing practices among low-income families in Washington, D.C., reports that the amount of diversity among low-income families is overlooked and underrated in popular and scientific thinking.[26] In addition, the study supports the following propositions:

1. The life chances and the actual behavior of low-income families are not to be confused with the cultural values and the preferences of families so classified.
2. A great deal of behavior among low-income urban families reflects a straddling of behavior and of goals associated with deprivation and poverty on the one hand, and of behavior and of goals associated with higher socioeconomic status and affluence on the other hand.
3. Among a considerable proportion of low-income urban families observed,

failures to conform in overt behavior to the so-called middle-class values are due less to any lack of recognition of, and affirmation of, middle-class values than they are due to such factors as (a) lack of money to support these values, (b) a process of diminution in the will to do so, and (c) a lessened confidence in their own, and especially their children's, life chances in the present and future.

4. Most parents in low-income families tend to show greater conformity to and convergence with the ascribed standards of parents of middle and upper income in what they indicate they want than in their actual behavior.

5. The range and the specifics of the child-rearing concerns of low-income parents approximate closely the range and the specifics of child-rearing concerns ascribed to upper- and middle-income families. The specifics of child-rearing concerns and the priorities attached to particular concerns vary from family to family.

6. The amount of family income and the evenness of its flow makes a significant difference in child-rearing priorities acted upon by parents.

7. Major priority among families with low income tends to be given to meeting basic physical needs — food, clothing, and shelter.

8. The need to invest a significant proportion of energies into meeting basic physical needs on inadequate income can result in a kind of compartmentalization of child-rearing concerns.

9. With few exceptions, low-income parents do not approve of the circumstances in which they now live or in which their children are being brought up.

10. A major aspiration of low-income parents for their children is to see their children do better in life — especially in jobs, education, and family behavior — than they have been able to do themselves.

11. Many low-income parents assess their own child-rearing performances in terms of whether they have made advances over the child-rearing circumstances and performances of their own parents.

12. The economic and social roles wished of, and expected of, the low-income male as husband and father by wives, mothers, and children are not different from those of the middle and upper classes, but his abilities — and the family and community consequences of his inabilities — to fulfill these roles are different.

Some Familiar Generalizations

A great many generalizations are made about the poor, often without differentiating among various categories of people and life styles found on the lower income levels. [See Figures 4 and 5.] In general, the ill-defined group referred to as "the poor" does not include the stable, respectable working class. Nevertheless, certain

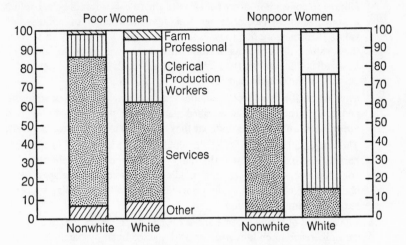

Figure 4: Among white as well as nonwhite poor women, most were in service occupations; among the nonpoor the majority of the non-white were still in services, but the majority of the white were crafts-men, clerical or production workers. *Poor* here derives from Social Security Administration criteria, based on a 1963 income of $1,580 a year for a nonfarm single person under 65 ($1,470 aged 65 and over), to $5,090 for a nonfarm family of 7 or more persons. The poverty line for single persons and families living on a farm was put at 60 percent of the above. (*Source*: Office of Economic Opportunity.)

characteristics are reported in inverse relation to income from top to bottom (e.g., education, physical and mental health, regular employment, adequate housing, privacy, membership in organizations).[27] Some of the attributions come from studies based on inadequate breakdowns, so that in our studies as in our life, class distinctions become blurred.

The term "culture of poverty" is used by Oscar Lewis in a dynamic sense to express the interplay of circumstance and attitude. There is no special issue when the term is used in this way. Issues arise when the term is used to mean a world outlook or style of life that has become a thing in itself. At this edge of the term, there is an implication that the source of such a world outlook lies in other people — parents, peers — who hold the same attitudes, and that the attitudes persist, whatever their relation to reality.

Many of the attitudes and much of the behavior of persons enmeshed in "the culture of poverty" are a response to facts of life. One author writes about the effects of prolonged malnutrition:

. . . various functional changes occur. These functional changes are manifested clinically by symptoms usually placed in the neurasthenic syndrome. They include such common complaints as excessive fatigability, disturbances in sleep, inability

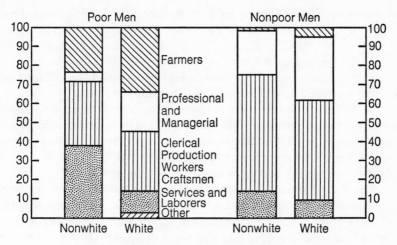

Figure 5: Among poor men, the largest proportion of nonwhite were in farm, service and laborer occupations; the largest proportion of white were in crafts, production or clerical work. Among the nonpoor, there are few in farming and the bulk of both nonwhite and white workers are in crafts, clerical or production work. *Poor* here derives from Social Security Administration criteria, based on a 1963 income of $1,580 a year for a nonfarm single person under 65 ($1,470 aged 65 and over) to $5,090 for a nonfarm family of 7 or more persons. The poverty line for single persons and families living on a farm was put at 60 per cent of the above. (*Source*: Office of Economic Opportunity.)

to concentrate, "gas," heart consciousness, and various queer bodily sensations . . . Occurrences [of these symptoms] as a manifestation of tissue depletion of certain nutrients is undoubted.

As for drive and ambition, a study describes "depression, apathy, and lethargy" as consequences of malnutrition. The tendency to blame others rather than one's self has also been attributed to inadequate nutrition.[28]

The following effects have been attributed to poor housing:

. . . a perception of one's self that leads to pessimism and passivity, stress to which the individual cannot adapt, poor health, and a state of dissatisfaction; pleased in company but not in solitude, cynicism about people and organizations, a high degree of sexual stimulation without legitimate outlet, and difficulty in household management and child rearing; . . . relationships that tend to spread out in the neighborhood rather than deeply into the family.[29]

The ways in which some of these effects are produced are almost self-evident. Poor health is a consequence of the effects of poor housing in contributing to accidents, to respiratory and skin diseases, and so forth. Poor health has its attitudinal and behavioral consequences, of course. The effects of crowding are possibly less apparent but are felt through their effects on privacy, on time and opportunity for communication, and on the tendency to live out-of-doors. Living in congested neighborhoods, where tenants are transient and physical hazards are real, produces in many a constant sense of loneliness, helplessness and anxiety.

With regard to the higher level of aggression attributed to the poor, one report comments that, in encouraging their children to fight back, slum dwellers show a realistic perception of the social problems in their neighborhoods. This view receives support from a low-income father who said of his son: "I . . . knock the hell out of him, 'cause he can't be no sissy and grow up in this here jungle."

One frequent generalization made about the poor is that they have less belief in their control over their own destinies than the prosperous — less sense of autonomy. And to this, another commentator responds — why wouldn't they?

Perhaps the most frequent generalization of all is that the poor have a shorter time perspective than the prosperous, that they are present-oriented rather than future-oriented. A number of challenges to this one have been heard lately, especially with regard to the Negro poor. Those who question the blanket accuracy of the present time-orientation generalization, add that in many instances future time-orientation just doesn't make sense for many of the poor. Nevertheless, they claim, when it does make sense to people of any income level, they plan for the future.

Many of the middle class have been recruited from the poor, many of the poor have middle-class tastes and preferences. Time orientation may not be a culture trait or a unitary trait. It may be rather a multiple and realistic response to the multiple aspects of life as it presents itself, with future-oriented planning and performance where that makes sense, and present-oriented response where the future is unpromising and unpredictable.

It has been argued from cases and from large-scale but partial experiences (e.g., moving poor people into public housing, which rapidly turn into slums) that the attitudes and behavior — however they began — persist well beyond the need for them. Virtually all evidence lies in a contrary direction, that upward mobility is accompanied by change in values. The difference between the impression and the evidence may depend on whether a shorter or longer time span is considered or whether one element of reality (housing) or several (schools, nutrition, job opportunity) are changed.

There is abundant evidence of resources for change among Negro families, particularly among children. Dr. Robert Coles writes:

. . . I was constantly surprised at the endurance shown by children we would all call poor or, in the current fashion, "culturally disadvantaged."

What enabled such children from such families to survive, emotionally and educationally, ordeals I feel sure many white middle-class boys and girls would find impossible? What has been the source of the strength shown by the sit-in students, many of whom do not come from comfortable homes but, quite the contrary, from rural cabins or slum tenements? Why do some Negro children — like the ones I have studied — behave so idealistically and bravely, while others go on to lives of uselessness and apathy, lives filled with hate, violence and crime?[30]

Notes

[1] Ernest W. Burgess, Preface to E. Franklin Frazier, *The Negro Family in the United States* (New York, 1957).

[2] Office of Policy Planning and Research, U.S. Department of Labor, *The Negro Family: The Case for National Action* (March 1965), pp. 9 ff.

[3] Hylan Lewis, "The Changing Negro Family" in *The Nation's Children*, Vol. 1 (New York, 1960), p. 126.

[4] Elizabeth Herzog and Rose Bernstein, *Health Services for Unmarried Mothers*, Children's Bureau Publication No. 425, Welfare Administration, U.S. Department of Health, Education, and Welfare (Washington, D.C., 1964), p. 32.

[5] Jack Lefcowitz, "Poverty and Negro-White Family Structure," unpublished paper, Research and Planning Division, Office of Economic Opportunity (1965).

[6] At ages 25–30, 7 per 1,000 white males and 16 per 1,000 Negro males are likely to die. These figures are not adjusted for income. White young women can marry-up into a comparatively large pool of non-poor white young men. The relative opportunity for Negro young women has been much smaller.

[7] Office of Policy Planning and Research, U.S. Department of Labor, *The Negro Family: The Case for National Action* (March 1965), pp. 9 ff.

[8] The section entitled "The Father — Present and Absent" is part of an unpublished manuscript by Elizabeth Herzog, Children's Bureau, Welfare Administration, U.S. Department of Health, Education, and Welfare.

[9] Helen Leland Witmer and Ruth Kotinsky, *Personality in the Making* (New York, 1962), p. 209.

[10] Ivan F. Nye, *Family Relationships and Delinquent Behavior* (New York, 1958). Clark Vincent, *Unmarried Mothers* (New York, 1961).

[11] Ivan F. Nye, "Child Adjustment in Broken and in Unhappy Unbroken Homes," *Marriage and Family Living*, Vol. 19 (1957); and Virginia Wimperis, *The Unmarried Mother and Her Child* (London, 1960).

[12] E. Franklin Frazier, *The Negro Family in the United States* (New York, 1957). St. Clair Drake and Horace R. Cayton, *Black Metropolis* (New York, 1954). Thomas F. Pettigrew, *A Profile of the Negro American* (Princeton, 1964). Hylan Lewis, "The Changing Negro Family," in *The Nation's Children* (New York, 1960). Office of Policy Planning and Research, U.S. Department of Labor, *The Negro Family: The Case for National Action* (March 1965).

[13] Katherine B. Oettinger, "This Most Profound Challenge," U.S. Department of Health, Education, and Welfare, Welfare Administration, Children's Bureau (1965). Address before the Fall Conference on Public Family Planning Clinics, Hotel Roosevelt, New York, New York, September 9, 1965.

[14] Elizabeth Herzog, *Children of Working Mothers*, U.S. Department of Health, Education, and Welfare, Welfare Administration, Children's Bureau Publication No. 382 (1960); reprinted 1964. See also Alberta Engvall Siegel, Lois Meek Stolz, Ethel Alice Hitchcock, and Jean Adamson: "Dependence and Independence in the Children of Working Mothers," *Child Development* (1959) Vol. 30, pp. 533–546.

[15] U.S. Department of Health, Education, and Welfare, Welfare Administration, Chil-

dren's Bureau, and U.S. Department of Labor, Women's Bureau, *Child Care Arrangements of the Nation's Working Mothers — a preliminary report* (Washington, D.C., 1965), (Processed) pp. 1–4.

[16] Kathryn Close, "Day Care as a Service for All Who Need It," *Children* (July–August 1965), pp. 157–160.

[17] Kenneth B. Clark, *Dark Ghetto* (New York, 1965). S. M. Miller and Ira E. Harrison, "Types of Dropouts: 'The Unemployables,' " presented at the Annual Meeting of the American Orthopsychiatric Association, Washington, D.C., March 1963 (Syracuse University Youth Development Center, Syracuse, New York).

[18] Jean Pakter, el al., "Out-of-Wedlock Births in New York City: I — Sociological Aspects," *American Journal of Public Health,* LI (1961).

[19] The section entitled "Births Out of Wedlock" is based on the following papers: Elizabeth Herzog, "The Chronic Revolution," *Journal of Clinical Pediatrics,* December 1965 or January 1966; "Unmarried Mothers: Some Questions to be Answered and Some Answers to be Questioned," *Child Welfare* (October 1962); Hylan Lewis and Elizabeth Herzog, "Priorities in Research on Unmarried Mothers," in *Research Perspectives on the Unmarried Mother,* Child Welfare League of America, Inc. (New York, 1961).

[20] National Center for Health Statistics, Public Health Service, U.S. Department of Health, Education and Welfare: *Vital Statistics of the United States, 1963:* Vol. 1, *Natality.*

[21] Hannah M. Adams, *Social Services for Unmarried Mothers and Their Children Provided through Public and Voluntary Child Welfare Agencies.* Child Welfare Report No. 12. Children's Bureau, Social Security Administration, U.S. Department of Health, Education, and Welfare (Washington, D.C., 1962).

[22] Elizabeth Herzog and Rose Bernstein, *Health Services for Unmarried Mothers,* Children's Bureau Publication 425, Welfare Administration, U.S. Department of Health, Education, and Welfare (1964).

[23] Paul H. Gebhard, et al., *Pregnancy, Birth and Abortion* (New York, 1958).

[24] Hyman Rodman, "The Lower-Class Value Stretch," *Social Forces,* Vol. 42, No. 2 (December 1963), pp. 205–215. See also Hylan Lewis, "Culture, Class and the Behavior of Low Income Families," prepared for Conference on Lower Class Culture, Barbizon Plaza Hotel, New York City, June 27–29, 1963.

[25] William J. Goode, "Illegitimacy in the Caribbean Social Structure," *American Sociological Review,* Vol. 25 (1960). Elizabeth Herzog, "Some Assumptions About the Poor," *Social Services Review* (1962). Oscar Lewis, *Children of Sanchez* (New York, 1961). Hortense Powdermaker, *After Freedom: A Cultural Study in the Deep South* (New York, 1939).

[26] From Hylan Lewis, "Culture, Class and Child Rearing among Low Income Urban Negroes," prepared for inclusion as a chapter in a forthcoming volume, Arthur Ross (ed.), *Jobs and Color,* to be published by Harcourt, Brace, and World. The paper is based on materials from a 5-year project, "Child Rearing Practices Among Low Income Families in the District of Columbia," sponsored by the Health and Welfare Council of the National Capital Area, and supported by NIMH Grants, MH 278–5.

[27] Seymour Martin Lipset, "Democracy and Working-Class Authoritarianism," *American Sociological Review,* Vol. 24:4, pp. 482–501 (August 1959). Elizabeth Herzog, "Some Assumptions About the Poor," *Social Service Review,* Vol. 37, 4 (December 1963).

[28] J. Jolliffe, "The Pathogenesis of Deficiency Disease." A. Keys, "Caloric Deficiency and Starvation," and F. F. Tisdall, "The Relation of Nutrition to Health," in J. Jolliffe, F. F. Tisdall, and P. R. Cannon, *Clinical Nutrition* (1950).

[29] Alvin L. Schorr, *Slums and Social Insecurity,* Division of Research and Statistics, Social Security Administration, U.S. Department of Health, Education, and Welfare, 1963.

[30] Robert Coles, "There's Sinew in Negro Family," *The Washington Post* (October 10, 1965).

New Approaches

5

"Black Matriarchy" Reconsidered: Evidence from Secondary Analysis of Sample Surveys

Herbert H. Hyman
John Shelton Reed

The American Negro family has been characterized as a *matriarchy* so often that the assertion is widely accepted as a truth rather than a proposition still in need of empirical evidence and critical analysis. Moynihan was only a recent, albeit prominent, example of the many scholars, both Negro and white, who have continued to the growth of such belief.[1] Is it not significant that most critics of his report attacked what they took to be its policy implications or implicit moral judgments, rather than its factual content?[2]

If the conception of a matriarchy referred solely to the physical datum, father's absence from the family, adequate evidence could be extracted from the Census, although its proper interpretation is not so simple. The fact is indisputable that father-absent families are relatively more frequent among Negroes. But how common does the situation have to be, and how *much more* frequent among Negroes than whites, perhaps of equivalent status, for the characterization to be valid and peculiarly applicable to the Negro family?[3]

The conception, however, usually implies that even when a father is present, the mother is the dominant member of the intact Negro family. Evidence adequate to support this more subtle aspect of the concept is much harder to find.[4] To be sure, many Negroes believe this to be true of the Negro family. In 1966 Louis Harris asked a national sample of Negroes: "In most Negro families do you think the mother or the father is usually the one who teaches the children to behave right?" Fifty-one per cent replied that the mother is; only 6 per cent said the father. But

Herbert H. Hyman and John Shelton Reed, " 'Black Matriarchy' Reconsidered: Evidence from Secondary Analysis of Sample Surveys," *Public Opinion Quarterly,* Vol. 33 (Fall 1969), 346–354. Reprinted by permission of the publisher and authors. The research was supported by a grant from the National Science Foundation for a program of studies in secondary analysis. That support is gratefully acknowledged.

this may be unfounded belief — perhaps even a *stereotype* — rather than a knowledgeable report, let alone proof. Among the small sample of "Negro community leaders" whom Harris also questioned, 60 per cent mentioned the mother, but this group may not be fully knowledgeable about the situation that prevails in the general population, although it may be highly informed by the literature on the subject.[5]

On this aspect of the problem more searching inquiry of a social psychological nature is needed which adequately samples the general population. In the absence of such a specially designed study, we present a secondary analysis of three existing surveys which fortunately contained relevant data. The major limitation of these surveys is that the samples, although national in scope, include only small numbers of Negro respondents. But for reasons which will become dramatically clear, the large numbers of white respondents are a most valuable resource. Apart from the efficiency and economy of secondary analysis, we also benefit from the replication of our findings over three independent studies, from the fact that several aspects of the broad domain within which maternal dominance might operate are covered by the various questions, and from the fact that the observations are not drawn from one narrow point in time.[6] Some brief description of the three studies from which we have drawn our data is essential background.

For the larger cross-national inquiry on *The Civic Culture* by Almond and Verba, the National Opinion Research Center interviewed in 1960 a probability sample of Americans over the age of eighteen. The sample of approximately 1,000 individuals included about 100 Negro respondents. All were asked in the course of the inquiry who had made each of a number of decisions in their families of origin, and, if married, whether they or their spouses made each of the decisions. In the South, interviewers and respondents were explicitly matched racially; elsewhere, interviewer assignment patterns made such matching quite likely, although not certain. The total sample agrees very closely with census estimates on population in metropolitan areas, population with little schooling, and is slightly overweighted on low-income families, the very stratum in which matriarchy is supposed to be most prevalent.[7]

The second survey was a Gallup Poll conducted in 1951 in which a national sample of about 1,400 adults (21 and older) was interviewed and asked one general question on which parent had been most influential during their childhood. The sample was drawn by quota control methods, and included about eighty Negro respondents, of whom an undeterminable number were interviewed by Negro interviewers.[8]

In 1965 the Survey Research Center conducted a series of studies directed by Kent Jennings of political socialization among national samples of high school seniors. Our data are drawn from a self-administered questionnaire taken by almost 20,000 students. To test one aspect of the theory of matriarchy we have limited ourselves to the smaller group of about 2,500 students, including some 150 Negro youth, who live in intact families where the father and mother have definite and different political party loyalties, as perceived and reported by the student. Since the youth also reported on their own political preferences, the relative influence of the two parents on this dimension of political socialization can be determined and regarded as one test of a theory of matriarchy.[9]

All three surveys were selected for secondary analysis without any prior knowledge of the relevant results, thus providing a fair test.

Given the ages spanned by the samples, the timing of the inquiries, and the retrospective nature of the questioning, the Gallup Poll reconstructs the family patterns that prevailed in a much earlier era and one battery in the Almond and Verba survey re-creates the patterns of a somewhat more recent, but still distant, past. Their other battery of questions and the Jennings inquiry explore the contemporary situation. The data are summarized in Table 1, and the limitations specific to each inquiry will be treated below.

We urge the reader to imagine the primary survey he might well have undertaken to explore the problem of matriarchy in which he invested all of his resources in the study of a large, and exclusively Negro, sample. He might have then generated only the column of figures for Negro respondents presented in Table 1. Note that an examination limited to those data might have given considerable support to the theory. Women's influence exceeds that of men in a number of instances. Even in the area of politics, where male dominance has long been assumed, Negro children are more likely to side with the mother when the parents disagree on party choice. But the phenomenon of a "Black Matriarchy" revealed in the several areas is seen to be an illusion when viewed in the perspective of the second column of findings on white respondents. It appeared as a product of what Hyman has called elsewhere the "pseudo-comparative design" or "fictitious comparison," in which the comparative data, in this case for whites, are imputed on the basis of the analyst's beliefs rather than by measurement.[10]

The actual white pattern, contrary to expectation, is almost identical to that for Negro families. The plausible notion that the father dominates the transmission of party preference has been cast into serious doubt by a number of studies, and is demonstrated in the Jennings inquiry not to apply to the aggregate sample.[11]

Over the three studies and all the aspects examined, the differences between white and Negro respondents are small and inconsistent. When the Almond and Verba data are arranged in terms of their temporal reference to past or present, there is some suggestion that matriarchal power has grown in the recent era, but if true, this applies to both Negro and white families. There seems to be little evidence for any social-psychological pattern of matriarchy peculiarly characteristic of the Negro family, on the basis of which social theorizing or social policy could be formulated.

This evidence goes so contrary to the literature that one must examine it most critically. Certainly, one must be tentative in light of the small number of Negro respondents in each of the samples — no smaller individually, however, than the statistical base of the Detroit study of the problem cited earlier, and considerably larger when pooled. The small numbers prevent an examination of the pattern

Table 1: Patterns of Male and Female Influence in Negro and White Families

Surveys and Questions		Negro	White
Gallup — 1951 [a]			
Per cent reporting that most important influence on them when growing up was:			
Father		27%	31%
Mother		73	69
	N =	(68)	(1,367)
NORC *(Almond and Verba) — 1960* [b]			
Per cent reporting that the important family decisions were made by:			
Father		28	23
Mother		14	13
	N =	(93)	(858)
Per cent reporting that decisions about child discipline were made by:			
Father		16	19
Mother		28	25
	N =	(97)	(855)
Per cent of married respondents reporting that important family decisions are made by:			
Husband		9	6
Wife		10	7
	N =	(67)	(628)
Per cent of married respondents with children reporting that decisions about child discipline are made by:			
Husband		4	7
Wife		37	28
	N =	(56)	(474)
Per cent reporting that decision as to how husband and wife vote are made by:			
Husband		11	7
Wife		2	—
	N =	(66)	(627)
JENNINGS — 1965 [c]			
Per cent of youth from politically divided homes who agree with:			
Father		32	34
Mother		40	40
	N =	(151)	(2,384)

[a] Negro respondents were considerably less likely to *volunteer* "both parents equally." Those who gave this response have been excluded from this table.
[b] Other possible responses were "Both . . . *together*" and "Each . . . *individually.*"
[c] A "politically divided home" is one in which the child reported one parent Democrat and the other Republican or one "Independent" and the other partisan.

separately for such subgroups as the urban lower classes, where matriarchy is supposed to be most prevalent. But, as was noted earlier, such subgroups are strongly represented in the Negro sample, whereas the white respondents tend to be drawn from higher strata. Thus the gross comparisons in Table 1 probably overstate the differences that would be found if whites and Negroes were equated in class position.

One must also entertain the possibility of response error. In the instance of the Gallup and the Almond and Verba surveys, the respondent is cast in the role of an *informant* about the family. The hypothesis immediately suggested is that the *sex* of the respondent making that report is relevant. Women might be inclined to inflate their own power when reporting on the battle of the sexes. And the lady survey analyst might add: men would be inclined to an equivalent self-aggrandizement.[12] But as will be recalled, the sex distribution in the Almond and Verba study is almost 50-50 in both the Negro and the white samples. Any bias of report would presumably be balanced out and would not obscure the racial comparison.

In the Gallup survey, the situation is not so fortunate. Women constitute a considerably higher proportion of the Negro sample than men, whereas there is parity in the white sample. An ideal test of bias would be to obtain independent reports from a sample of husbands and wives from the same family units, or from male and female offspring of the same families. An approximate test was made by comparing the answers of men and women in the Gallup survey. The numbers are very small and too few to equate the informants in social characteristics to insure that they are describing the patterns in families from the same stratum. Among the white respondents, the sex of the informant clearly made no difference. Among Negro respondents, differences by sex could easily be due to sampling variation.

The findings must also be interpreted in relation to one other feature of the surveys. Families where there was prolonged father-absence cannot be eliminated from the Gallup data, nor from the Almond and Verba data pertaining to patterns in the families of origin. Thus any evidence of matriarchy in these data reflects two phenomena: objective absence of father plus his low power, when present. Since father-absence is more frequent among Negroes, it seems a reasonable inference that the racial comparison presented overstates the Negro-white difference in maternal power in intact families.

The Jennings data (and the Almond and Verba data on the contemporary situation) describe the balance of power in intact families. However, the sample of high school seniors obviously excludes academic dropouts, who are known to come disproportionately from poorer households. The findings must be qualified in the light of this restriction on the universe.[13]

Our evidence is tentative, but it certainly casts the issue into doubt. If the concept of a culturally linked Negro-white difference in family organization has been weighty enough to generate debate about social policy and action, it deserves the conclusive evidence that primary research could provide.[14] We hope our secondary analysis will give guidance in the design of such research and impetus for it to be undertaken. Although the economy of secondary analysis will have to be forsaken, there is a halfway strategy to be recommended. Since race and family composition are routine face-sheet items in surveys, a few indicators of the balance of power can be "piggy-backed" or "hitchhiked" onto surveys of the general population. Provided some basic cautions are observed, the pool of data will soon grow large enough to permit substantial and sound analysis at modest cost.

Notes

¹ For example, Hortense Powdermaker concluded from her field work in rural Mississippi in the 1930's that "among the middle- and lower-class Negroes . . . , the woman is usually the head of the house in importance and authority." (*After Freedom: A Cultural Study in the Deep South,* New York, Atheneum Reprint NL3, 1968, p. 145.) E. Franklin Frazier also dealt with this theme, drawing on his field work in Chicago and on documentary and census sources. (See his chapter "The Matriarchate" in *The Negro Family in the United States,* Chicago, University of Chicago Press, 1939, pp. 125–145. See also pp. 108–124, 325–357.) In the same period, Charles Johnson, in *The Shadow of the Plantation,* Chicago, University of Chicago Press, 1966, pp. 35–39, reached similar conclusions. (See also his *Growing Up in the Black Belt,* New York, Schocken Books, 1967.)

More recently, matriarchal organization of the Negro family has been discussed by, among others, Abram Kardiner and Lionel Ovesey, in *The Mark of Oppression: Explorations in the Personality of the American Negro,* Cleveland, Meridian Books, 1962, pp. 60 ff.; Kenneth Clark, in *Dark Ghetto: Dilemmas of Social Power,* New York, Harper and Row, 1965, pp. 70–74; and Whitney M. Young, Jr., *To Be Equal,* New York, McGraw-Hill, 1964, pp. 174–175. Billingsley's recent essay reviews critically these and other scholarly works on the Negro family. (Andrew Billingsley, *Black Families in White America,* Englewood Cliffs, Prentice-Hall, 1968, pp. 197–215.)

Data on father-absence can be found in Lee Rainwater, "Crucible of Identity: The Negro Lower Class Family," *Daedalus,* Vol. 95, No. 1, 1966, p. 181, and in Martin Deutsch and Bert Brown, "Social Influences in Negro-White Intelligence Differences," *Journal of Social Issues,* Vol. 20, No. 2, 1964, p. 28. Leonard Broom and Norval Glenn also note the high frequency of father-absent Negro families, but their treatment is highly qualified and their observation that "the stereotype is grossly inaccurate when generally applied, since Negro families are now as varied as white families" is worth repeating (*The Transformation of the Negro American,* New York, Harper Colophon CN117, 1967, p. 15). For a thoughtful critique of the concept and fruitful analysis of the data, see also Jessie Bernard, *Marriage and Family among Negroes,* Englewood Cliffs, Prentice-Hall, 1966, especially pp. 21–23, 83–84. Another researcher who questions the accuracy of the matriarchal image, on the basis of intensive study of ten families, is David A. Schulz, in "Variations in the Father Role in Complete Families of the Negro Lower Class," *Social Science Quarterly,* Vol. 49, 1968, pp. 651–659.

The celebrated "Moynihan Report" (Daniel Patrick Moynihan, *The Negro Family: The Case for National Action,* Washington, U.S. Department of Labor, Office of Policy Planning and Research, 1965) is reprinted in full, with its original pagination, in Lee Rainwater and William L. Yancey, *The Moynihan Report and the Politics of Controversy,* Cambridge, M.I.T. Press, 1967.

² See Rainwater and Yancey, *op. cit.,* pp. 185–186, 195–200, 215–219, 235–236, *et passim.*

³ A paper by Lee Rainwater illustrates the complexity of interpretation. Data from the Census of 1960 are presented showing that among urban Negroes (non-whites) with incomes under $3,000, 47 per cent of the families with children have female heads. Rainwater stresses the consequences of such a "matriarchal" situation, but makes no reference in his text to the finding he presents in the same table that in the equivalent white stratum, 38 per cent of the families have female heads, a difference of 9 percentage points. In the other strata tabled, the differences between Negroes and whites are less than 5 per cent and the matriarchal pattern is exceedingly rare (*loc. cit.*). Moynihan charts trends in this datum from census sources (*op. cit.,* p. 11). For data on the situation as recently as 1966, see *Report of the National Advisory Commission on Civil Disorders,* Washington, U.S. Government Printing Office, 1967, pp. 129, 337–338. The Commission is careful to emphasize that most Negro families are headed by men.

⁴ On this score, it should be stressed that although the Moynihan report provides most elaborate statistical evidence on the physical datum, father-absence, the only *empirical* evidence presented on the psychological datum, husband's subordination to the wife, is one study

conducted in Detroit in 1955. The *wives* in a sample of 103 Negro families and 554 white families answered a series of questions on who made the decisions in each of 8 spheres. A scale score of 10 indicates that power lies completely in the hands of the husband, and a score of 4 indicates that husband and wife share equally in power. While the distribution can be examined in various ways, and cut at different points to define particular types of family structure, it should be noted that the mean score for whites was 5.2 and for Negroes 4.4. A not unreasonable interpretation of these findings is that the average white family studied was slightly patriarchal, and the Negro family equalitarian, rather than matriarchal, in pattern. For the data and the authors' somewhat different appraisal, see Robert O. Blood, Jr., and Donald M. Wolfe, *Husbands and Wives,* New York, Free Press, 1960, pp. 22–36. The other evidence Moynihan summarized on this aspect is in the nature simply of learned opinions or generalizations (*op. cit.,* pp. 30, 34). That "harder" evidence is very rare cannot be doubted. And the kind of evidence required for a test of theories of matriarchy that would convince all advocates would be even more difficult to collect, given the elusive nature of the argument. Highly aggressive behavior within the family is sometimes regarded as a defense or reaction on the part of the Negro male to his inferior status. If both submission *and* ascendance can be regarded as indicators of the feeling of subordination, it is hard to see how the theory could ever be refuted. On such psychodynamic consequences of inferior status, see Whitney Young, *op. cit.,* pp. 174–175, or Kenneth Clark, *op. cit.,* p. 70.

⁵ William Brink and Louis Harris, *Black and White,* New York, Simon and Schuster, 1967, pp. 268–269. The authors apparently share this belief, referring in the text to "the matriarchal character of Negro society today . . ." (p. 150). That the leaders were not reflecting their higher socioeconomic status and the corresponding circles in which they move is suggested by the fact that higher income respondents in the general sample were less likely to credit the mothers with dominance.

⁶ That social change might operate in this sphere is likely as one realizes that rising economic position and educational level might affect the dominance of one or another parent and the prevalence of matriarchy in the particular population.

⁷ G. Almond and S. Verba, *The Civic Culture,* Princeton, Princeton University Press, 1963, pp. 519–522. From a secondary analysis of the Negro sample reported by Marvick, we may add that 57 per cent of the Negro respondents reported family incomes less than $5,000 a year; 37 per cent were unskilled workers and 39 per cent operatives and service workers; 89 per cent were born in the South; 37 per cent reported only some grammar school, and another 19 per cent had completed only grammar school; 53 per cent lived in big cities. The white respondents, as Marvick reports, were considerably less likely to be big city dwellers, poor, in low occupations, or poorly educated. Relevant to our later discussion is the fact that 49 per cent of the Negro sample and 47 per cent of the white sample was male. See D. Marvick, "The Political Socialization of the American Negro," *Annals,* Vol. 361, 1965, p. 116. The data were made available to us through the courtesy of the Inter-University Consortium for Political Research, Ann Arbor.

⁸ Of the Negro respondents, 19 per cent were unskilled or domestic workers, 49 per cent semi-skilled or service workers, and 4 per cent skilled workers; 30 per cent resided in the South; 53 per cent reported education of eight grades or less; 53 per cent lived in cities of over 100,000 population. The white respondents were considerably less likely to be southern, poorly educated, big city residents, and in low-status occupations. The data for these analyses were provided by the Roper Center for Public Opinion Research, whose cooperation is gratefully acknowledged. They are from the American Institute of Public Opinion (Gallup) Poll 478K.

⁹ These unpublished data were kindly made available to us by M. Kent Jennings and are gratefully acknowledged. For some of his basic findings on political socialization see, for example, M. Kent Jennings and R. G. Niemi, "Patterns of Political Learning," *Harvard Educational Review,* Vol. 38, 1968, pp. 443–467.

¹⁰ Herbert H. Hyman, "Research Design," ch. 8 of Robert E. Ward, ed., *Studying Politics Abroad: Field Research in the Developing Areas,* Boston, Little, Brown, 1964, p. 162. Cross-national data from the Almond and Verba study also show that American white and Negro families are more like each other in respect to family decision-making than either is like the

more patriarchal German family, but even in the German family, maternal dominance is evident in some areas of family life. (We shall not present these data, but they were made available to us by the Inter-University Consortium for Political Research.)

[11] Herbert H. Hyman, *Political Socialization: A Study in the Psychology of Political Behavior,* New York, Free Press, 1959, pp. 82–84; John Shelton Reed, "The Transmission of Party Preference by Identification," paper read at the conference of the American Association for Public Opinion Research, Santa Barbara, California, May 11, 1968; M. Kent Jennings and Kenneth P. Langton, "Mothers versus Fathers: The Formation of Political Orientations among Pre-Adults," mimeographed, University of Michigan, March 1968. In an inquiry into political socialization among college students in Puerto Rico, drawn mainly from the urban middle classes, it was found that 40 per cent of the sample deviated from the party preferences of their fathers. This finding was most unexpected, not only because of the usual theory, but because the culture is presumed to produce a strong propensity to defer to authority generally, and to paternal authority in particular. See P. Bachrach, "Attitude toward Authority and Party Preference in Puerto Rico," *Public Opinion Quarterly,* Vol. 22, 1958, pp. 68–73.

[12] The analyst of a psychoanalytical persuasion might prefer an Oedipal model of such response error, suggesting that the daughter would inflate the power of the father, and the son the mother. In any case, the sex of the informant would be at issue. [Findings from a study of 179 couples, in which the husbands and wives were questioned separately, were reported in the Summer issue of the *Quarterly,* after the present article was received. Each partner tended to attribute more importance to his or her own role in disciplining their child than was attributed to it by the spouse. See John A. Ballweg, "Husband-Wife Response Similarities on Evaluative and Non-Evaluative Survey Questions," *Public Opinion Quarterly,* Vol. 33, 1969, pp. 249–254. *Editor's Note.*]

[13] The analysis was also restricted to those students who were able to report a political position for *both* parents. Since it was not possible unambiguously to separate "Don't know" responses due to parent absence from those attributable to other causes, all cases where such a response was given for either parent were excluded. It is possible that differential awareness of parental political positions could be an indicator of a subtle aspect of relative parental influence which has eluded us.

[14] Several surveys conducted by the National Opinion Research Center in 1966 for the U.S. Civil Rights Commission, but not as yet published, may provide additional data on the phenomenon.

Family and Childhood in a Southern Negro Community[1]

Virginia Heyer Young

Current interpretations of American Negro personality formation have been hampered by lack of field data and by faulty conceptualization. Personality formation has been studied through interviews with children and adolescents, through interviews with adults concerning childrearing practices, and through psychoanalytic interpolation from persons in therapy (Davis and Dollard 1940; Davis and Havighurst 1946; Kardiner and Ovesey 1951). Field observations of childhood, however, have never been undertaken, and there has never been a check on what mothers say they did and what is recalled from childhood. Furthermore, the applicability of psychoanalytic interpretations to American Negro life has been assumed with a minimum of knowledge about prevailing styles of interpersonal behavior and the way these might modify the psychoanalytic scheme of cause and effect. An additional interpretative problem arises from the fact that the Negro family has been widely analyzed with a strong bias toward White American family values, its functionality being judged by the degree to which it exemplifies White forms. American Negro life styles generally have been seen as impoverished versions of White American culture, impoverished by dependency and dehumanization under slavery and impoverished by lack of access to many of the rewards of American culture. Herskovits' (1941) demonstration of the retention of African forms especially in the areas of interpersonal behavior and deep levels of communication was ignored to a surprising degree by anthropologists and sociologists who have interpreted American Negro life. Many intellectual currents and habits have contributed to this bias, not the least of which is the common emphasis on institutions at the expense of interpersonal behavior. In this case we are witnessing a people wrongly pigeonholed who are protesting and declaring they have a culture of their own. That there are distinctive American Negro cultural styles of interpersonal behavior was one conclusion of a field study of Negro childhood conducted in a Georgia town during the summers of 1961, 1962, and 1966. Negro family organization also was

Virginia Heyer Young, "Family and Childhood in a Southern Negro Community," *American Anthropologist,* Vol. 72 (April, 1970), 269–288. Reprinted by permission of the American Anthropological Association and the author.

found to be so different from the current stereotypes about it that the literature on the subject was reviewed to seek a resolution of the apparent contradiction. These two subjects are the substance of this paper.

Georgiatown is a county seat of under ten thousand population, approximately twenty percent to twenty-five percent Negro.[2] Milling of cotton products and light manufacturing provide most of the jobs in the town, and farming has dwindled to minor importance in the county (U.S. Department of Labor 1965). The 1960 Census shows forty percent of the Negro men in the county labor force employed as nonfarm laborers, twenty-six percent as operatives and twelve percent as service workers. Among Negro women in the labor force sixty-six percent are employed as private household workers and sixteen percent as other service workers. There is little Negro-owned business and no Negro upper class. One Negro doctor and the teachers of the centralized Negro elementary school and high school are the only professional persons. In settlement pattern and social habits Georgiatown Negroes resemble the people of Kent described by Hylan Lewis (1955).

The method of this study was to observe and record in detail the behavior of parents and children in their own houses and yards. Conversations were used to establish rapport and to obtain information, but the primary aim was always to avoid disrupting the natural social situation as much as possible. Visits lasted as long as they could be comfortably prolonged, sometimes only thirty minutes, usually an hour and a half, often three hours. Almost all families were visited at least twice, and most were observed four or more times. The subjects of closest study were the members of thirty-four households. Twelve additional households were known less well but well enough to yield information on some subjects. Forty-two children under the age of three and sixteen children between the ages of three and six were observed. Older brothers and sisters between six and fourteen numbered twenty-eight. Four of the closely studied households and one of the less closely studied were middle class, the heads of four out of these five being schoolteachers. The other forty-one households were lower class, the heads of family being employed at unskilled or semi-skilled jobs or unemployed. Class designation is on the basis of prestige of occupation, a small difference in standard of living, and observed deference-superiority behavior. The main bias in the sample is toward families with young children since this was the family composition sought.

These subjects lived in the three Negro sections of town and in one rural hamlet adjoining the town. Housing ranged from brick two-story row houses with five rooms in a public housing project to the more usual two- or three-room frame house with porch that is typical of this section of the country. As in the town of Kent, all rooms but the kitchen usually serve as bedrooms. Television sets are common but few comforts or decorations enhance these houses. A county clinic in Georgiatown is used widely for children's medical care, and all births of the children in this study had taken place in the county hospital, also located in town.

Family Organization

Central to all interpretations of Negro personality has been the contention that the Negro man plays a relatively insignificant role in family life in the lower class. It was therefore surprising to find the large majority of Georgiatown Negro families in this study had husbands present and supporting them. Among forty-one lower-class families, men are the main providers or coequal providers with their wives in thirty-eight of the households, as Table 1 shows. The basis for selection of families to be studied, the presence of young children, would tend to give an under-representation of complete families in this community because marriages of older couples are the most stable.

Table 1: Sources of Household Support

Household Support Type	Lower class	Middle class
Husband's employment sole support	20	1
Husband's pension sole support	3	0
Husband main support, wife contributes much less	2	0
Husband and wife contribute about equal amounts	13	4
Husband present, wife contributes more than husband	0	0
Female-headed household, no male provider	3	0
Total	41	5

Not only do Georgiatown Negro men support their families, but their earning ability far exceeds women's as is demonstrated by U.S. Census figures for 1950 and 1960 (Table 2). Women earn approximately forty percent of what men earn in Georgia cities and towns despite a slight tendency between 1949 and 1959 for Negro women's incomes to increase in relation to Negro men's incomes. Georgiatown County in 1959 conforms to the 1949 income ratios for cities and towns, perhaps reflecting conservatism in wage scales or the fact that the county was a depressed area at the time (being so classified by the U.S. Department of Labor). That Georgia Negroes are in this respect typical of Negroes in the nation is also seen in Table 2. Wages in industry, which employs many more men than women, far exceeded wages for domestic work, the main occupation for women. While industrial wages are not matched in other forms of male employment, they have had the effect of raising men's wages in general. Yard work, for instance, offers a higher wage for men than domestic work does for women. There have been periods when jobs for men have been scarcer than domestic work for women and some male employment is seasonal and subject to lay-offs, but in general men are at present, and have been in the recent past, able to provide for their families better than their wives and have the prestige that goes with better-paying jobs. Since Georgiatown County was in economic depression during this study, the favorable income of Negro men compared to Negro women cannot be laid to prosperity, a relationship some observers have conjectured. One cornerstone of the prevailing interpretation of the lower-class Negro family as female-headed is a supposed advantage of Negro women over Negro men in wage earning (Davie 1949:207; Powdermaker 1939:145; Kardiner and Ovesey 1951:54), but such an advantage has never been found to be substantiated by factual data. Lewis (1955:121) estimates Kent Negro women's annual incomes to be about half of Negro men's incomes. Table 2 shows the fallacy of assuming women's superior earning power in the recent period.

Table 2: Median Income of Nonwhite Persons with Income *

	1949			1959		
	Male Median Income	Female Median Income	Fe Med Inc as % of M Med Inc	Male Median Income	Female Median Income	Fe Med Inc as % of M Med Inc
U.S.A.†	$1571	$672	42.8	$2254	$905	40.1
Georgia	919	389	42.3	1489	660	44.3
G'tn County	‡	‡	‡	1780	647	36.3
Ga. Urban	1259	477	37.9	1947	785	40.3
Ga. Rural NF§	855	322	37.8	1153	478	41.5
Ga. Rural F	459	288	62.7	770	368	47.4

* Source: U.S. Census of Population, 1950, Vol. II, Pt. 11, table 88, p. 343; Vol. II, Pt. 1, table 139, p. 302; U.S. Census of Population, 1960, Vol. I, Pt. 12, table 67, p. 209, and table 88, p. 351; Vol. I, Pt. 1, table 218, p. 578.
† 1949 U.S.A. figures are for all non-White; 1959 U.S.A. figures are for Negroes.
‡ Not available for 1949.
§ Georgiatown is classified as a Rural Non-Farm place in both Censuses.

Other evidence for an important male role in Georgiatown families is abundant. Rural family traditions are still close to the people of the town since many are of the first generation to have left the countryside. In informants' reminiscenses of rural life there is frequently a strict authoritarian father who supervised the whole family in their farm chores, punished the children, read aloud from the Bible daily, and said he could spell better than the schoolteacher. Some men in the community today are spoken of in a similar vein, as hardworking and authoritarian. In family behavior, men are usually accorded or assume authority in the house. Women act as though their husbands had authority, and children are respectful of them. Women observed in casual behavior with their husbands and with male visitors are deferent. Especially indicative of the important familial role of men in Georgiatown is the fact that the grandmothers who supervise large households of children, grandchildren, and great-grandchildren all have husbands supporting them.

Since men head a large proportion of households it is not surprising that illegitimate and orphaned children are often cared for in the households of male kinsmen — the paternal grandfather, a paternal uncle, a maternal uncle, and a maternal great-uncle in cases known. Responsibility for a son's illegitimate children as well as a daughter's may be assumed by older stable couples. In one case an illegitimate child's mother regularly visited the child where he lived in his father's parents' household with the father absent. Care of children while their mothers work is extended by older women and men to a son's children as well as daughter's children. Thus family ties through men and emotional attachments of men to their kinsmen are socially important in this town, as well as mother-daughter ties.

At the same time there are many illegitimate births, multiple sequential marriages, and frequent dissolution of marriage; practices the prevailing literature on the American Negro associates with family breakdown and the female-headed family.

These apparent incongruities point up the confused state of analysis of American Negro culture and especially of the lower-class family. The widespread construct that interprets the lower-class Negro family as disorganized and dysfunctional, represented in the work of E. Franklin Frazier and Daniel P. Moynihan and dominating the social work and sociological perspectives in this field, has been called into question by several writers (Lewis 1960; Bernard 1966; Valentine 1968). Valentine has demonstrated many of the sources of misconception and bias in their analyses and has pointed out that statistical data showing high frequencies of female-headed families fail to show the whole pattern of the Negro family for the very reason that it does not take into consideration the external stimulation for male absence provided by the welfare system. As Valentine points out, the female-headed family is viewed as a broken family, as a product of failure to achieve a norm. The norm is explicitly assumed to be the nuclear family of a generalized American culture: "On the institutional side, the family structure of the lower-class Negro is the same as the White. However, in the actual process of living, the vicissitudes of the lower-class family are greater and its stability much less" (Kardiner and Ovesey 1951:307). The validity of a generalized American White family pattern is itself open to question, but what concerns us here is the assumption that there is no distinctive American Negro family system. That assumption rests on the explicit rejection of Herskovits' thesis of the retention of African cultural elements by New World Negroes and the denial that there could be significant independent social and cultural development of Negroes in this country.

New constructs and new data are needed. M. G. Smith's analysis of family organization in five Negro communities in the West Indies (1962) establishes a model for the family system of the New World Negro culture area, showing basic patterning and variant forms and placing the female-headed family in perspective in the systematic whole. The functionality of Negro family types in the United States, including those headed by women, has been advocated before but this point has been forgotten in the popular despair over the Negro's lack of a middle-class style family. Johnson (1934a, 1934b) and Powdermaker (1939) point out that Negro families, whether headed by males or females, provide secure groups for child raising and that marriage patterns accommodate the accepted styles of interpersonal behavior between men and women. Johnson's analysis of egalitarian values and behavior patterns of men and women in mating customs is especially relevant to the attempt in this paper to define the distinctive aspects of the Negro family (Johnson 1934a:29 ff). Johnson's sample of 612 households in rural Alabama contained two-thirds complete nuclear families, yet high rates of illegitimacy and marital break-up. The pattern is similar to Georgiatown's and suggests that the variable of male or female head of the house does not necessarily alter the occurrence of illegitimacy and the customs of marriage. Even Frazier (1939) must be credited with describing functional systems in the matriarchal family and in the male-headed tenant farm family, all useful data in spite of the shortcomings of his general analysis.

In Georgiatown, the Negro family is functional and systematic. The potential for social dysfunction in the high illegitimacy rate and frequent marital dissolutions is compensated for by other parts of the system, so that as a whole the patterns of family organization are functional. Indeed, illegitimacy and separation are necessary concomitants of the emotional underpinning of the system. Illegitimate births are especially common before the first marriage. Of forty-four women who gave life histories, at least twenty-one had one or more children before marriage. The unwed mother almost never forms a separate household, but remains with her own childhood family, sometimes working and relying on her family for help in child care. Having children out of wedlock is not approved, even though it is so common. The father is almost always known, but opinion is likely to weigh less heavily against the boy than against the girl, and the girl is almost always said to be the instigator of the union. She is criticized within her family and by others for a time, but she bears the shame rather lightly, showing typical independence of public opinion. Her mother may demonstrate scorn for her or may accept the embarrassment lightly.

The child probably does not suffer from its illegitimacy. Its mother shows the immense pride in her baby that is typical of all births in this community. The baby has the mother's surname and her household dotes over it. One proud authoritarian man took his daughter's new-born illegitimate son to show the mother of the baby's father, who was himself working in the North, and said, "I have a real pretty baby here and I'm going to name him after your boy so he'll grow up to be as smart as your boy." The grandmother, who related the story, was embarrassed, as she was expected to be, but the grandfather was doing more than embarrassing her: he was showing his own intention to care for the child. By the time this story was told the boy had become the paternal grandmother's indulged favorite and a frequent visitor to the maternal grandfather. Sometimes the father of the illegitimate baby helps support it and, as it grows, sends for it to visit him. The child usually has two or even three households where he has a berth — the paternal and maternal relatives who helped to raise him and his own mother's house after she marries. The first two are most likely to be secure homes. In his own mother's home the potentiality of a hostile relationship with the stepfather seemed little developed, and the useful role that oldest children play in households provides them with a means of creating a secure position for themselves.

The first child is the most fondled and most stimulated and often becomes the most self-confident and capable of all the children in a family, whether or not he is illegitimate as many first children are. Because illegitimacy is common and because there is little derogation of the child born out of wedlock, these children themselves seem relatively undisturbed by their status. The children know their real father's name and where he lives. Overt signs of anxiety about being deserted by their father were occasionally seen, but there is also a casual acceptance of the multiplicity of fathers that characterizes most families. Children explain about themselves, "We're halves," meaning half-siblings. They can be heard comparing their relatives and are quick to deny a half-sibling's claim to a cousin who is really only theirs. Although many Georgiatown children do not have their own father's care, they usually have the example of a male provider in the home and a man filling an authoritative role in the home. The grandfather often fills the affectional role that the father deserts.

In Georgiatown illegitimacy does not endanger the child, nor does it force the mother into a disadvantageous social position or reduce her prospects for forming a stable marriage. The inconsequentialness of illegitimacy to both mother and child was observed by Johnson (1934b:214–215) in rural Alabama in the 1920's and by Powdermaker (1939:204–206) in Mississippi, and the pattern in this manufacturing town in the 1960's is essentially the same.

Georgiatown Negro family life is relatively secure despite the instability of some of its phases. Although many families achieve stability well after childrearing is underway, the grandparental families usually serve as secure social units for children until their mothers make a stable marriage. Childbearing usually begins in the middle or late teens, and most women have achieved a relatively stable marriage by their midtwenties. The sequence is essentially the same as Smith (1962) found in the two more stable family systems in his sample, from extra-residential mating to consensual union to marriage, with the exception that consensual union is not acknowledged openly, and in Georgiatown it would be more accurate to speak of a sequence of extraresidential mating, unstable marriage, and stable marriage. In many families the mother is thus the permanent figure. Her children may have a series of fathers as she first has children out of wedlock and then may have one or more marriages. The family is centered on her in this sense, but not in the sense that she provides the main support for the family or is a stronger authority than the man who supports her and her children.

Marriage and family in Negro society differ culturally and structurally from their counterparts in other American groups. Marriage is thought of as a relationship concerning only the couple and neither the community nor individual families attempt to regulate marriage beyond a qualified adherence to an ethic of obligations between mating couples. Adolescents are free to engage in sexual behavior, but marriage as an acceptance of enduring obligations and as an economic arrangement comes about with more maturity and primarily as a matter of choice and with a minimum of social pressure. In the family, husband and wife both contribute economically, both have authority, both can take the initiative to bring about separation, and both may find separation advantageous. Although many marriages dissolve, remarriage is usual, and middle-aged persons not living in a married state are uncommon. In contrast to the two-generation White nuclear family, the Negro family maintains strong ties over three or four generations. It is not organized as a multigenerational household, but the grandparental tie on either side is easily and often invoked in a variety of arrangements. These multigenerational ties lend stability to the system by protecting unmarried mothers and children born outside of marriage.

Children usually remain with their mother while she may have a series of unions; this makes the ties between mother and child strong and culturally significant. The Negro man, however, has a role in the system. His absence from the household of his own children and his periodic moves to different households, at least while he is young, is not a measure of psychic inadequacy. It is his role in a functional system, the values of which, judging from Liebow's and C. S. Johnson's material, are free response to emotions and true and continuing compatibility between man and woman.

Negro marriage and family practices provide social and psychological security for childbearing and child training; they embody cultural values and serve human needs. As such they deserve to be recognized as functionally integral parts of an American Negro culture. To interpret these practices as deteriorated forms of a general American culture introduces an ethnocentric bias and obscures some of the values and inner workings of Negro society.

Childhood

Within the Negro family, this loose yet structured group, this group geared to emotional compatibility of egalitarian spouses, what are interpersonal relations like? Little research on American Negro interpersonal relations has been done. Davis and Dollard (1940), Davis and Havighurst (1946), Kardiner and Ovesey (1951), Rohrer and Edmonson (1960), and Liebow (1967) almost alone among social scientists have explored the question. Liebow's participant observation is unique, and the results invaluable. Rohrer and Edmonson's work presents welcome new typologies but lacks the perspective of observational study and child-training data. The two earlier studies use stereotyped sociological frameworks and depend on clinical interviews to reconstruct life experiences, and from this method they draw a picture of distressed human relations. "The mother is ill tempered, imposes severe and rigid disciplines, demands immediate obedience, and offers only sporadic affection. . . . Mothers in this group [Negro lower class] are often loveless tyrants. Coldness, scoldings, and frequent beatings are the rule" (Kardiner and Ovesey 1951:65). "Fathers are either seclusive, taciturn, violent, punitive, and without interest in the children or they are submissive to the mother" (Kardiner and Ovesey 1951:66). "Sibling attitudes in the lower class show that animosity and hatred are the rule, with complete severance of relations" (Kardiner and Ovesey 1951:67). "Lower-class Negro children grow up to be fighters, cutters, and shooters and they are reinforced in this behavior by their parents" (Davis and Dollard 1940:270). "Early controls upon the child's use of his erogenous zones are equally effective in all classes [White and Negro] and . . . the rigors of this training give rise to the same kind of personality strain [in all classes]" (Davis and Dollard 1940:270).

Interpersonal relations within the Negro family were considered the product of psychological maladjustment resulting from White society's definition of the Negro as a lesser human being and its systematic deprivation of his wants. Racial discrimination was thought to determine fundamentally the character of relationships between Negro parents and children and husbands and wives. The Negro was assumed to have no life style of his own and to make no adjustments to society except the destructive ones based on his sharing of Whites' judgments of him. Certainly self-hatred and inward-directed aggression have played their part in the personalities of American Negroes, and there is much psychological evidence and many considered statements to support this point. The perspective which is lacking, however, is that institutional patterns and modes of interpersonal behavior in Negro culture have a genuine character and inner consistency of their own deriving from the historical separateness of the group and that this culture deeply affects psychic processes. The clinical studies have failed to establish an accurate cultural base. In the present field study many of the generalizations about Negro parent-child relationships which derive from clinical studies were not found evident, and other types of experience were found to be significant, experiences which generally do not come to attention in clinical interviews.

In their relations with their young children the Negroes of Georgiatown find perhaps the greatest pleasures of their lives. Everyone with the slightest claim to do so holds and plays with the baby. The unmarried mother of fifteen displays her baby as proudly as does the veteran child-bearer sitting on her porch and giving orders to her flock of offspring. The baby finds that its environment is almost wholly human. Cribs, baby carriages, and highchairs are almost never seen. The baby is held and carried most of the time, and when it is laid down it is seldom without company.[3]

Being held is an active relationship between holder and baby, a highly personal experience. Most mothers hold babies with relaxed posture, usually cradling the baby on one arm or in the lap. As she cradles him the mother's free hand wipes, pets, pokes, investigates, and her eyes explore the baby's face and body. Newborn and very young babies are often laid in the groove between the legs as the mother sits, with the baby's feet toward the mother. In either position mother and baby look into each other's faces and the mother's hands caress the baby. She talks to it, expressing in her manner pride and amusement and enjoyment in it. When not being held young babies are laid on a bed, usually lying on their backs, and children and adults lean over the young baby and talk to it. Babies old enough to turn over and pull themselves along are laid on a folded blanket on the floor, where the little children are likely to join them, leaning over or on top of them and testing the baby's responses. Seldom is a baby seen held against the shoulder and looking behind the mother, and seldom does the mother hold it while doing chores. These more impersonal ways of holding a baby, where the mother's main attention is directed at something other than the baby, are not characteristic. In the mother's care there is typically a high degree of personal involvement.

This highly personal, highly active relationship between mother and baby takes place in a crowded household. Household composition varies widely, but one aspect of the human environment is almost certain, a full and crowded house. The baby experiences many different types of people of all ages, all of whom hold the baby and play with it. The father and male relatives play with it as readily as the women and children, and although they are not home much of the time, they enjoy babies and are competent in handling them.

Patterns of sleep are distinctive. The interest in playing with babies not uncommonly interferes with the infant's own inclination to sleep. Naps are characteristically short and irregular, since they are taken in the midst of the many disturbances of normal household activities, and usually are ended by the household commotion or by a person seeking the napper to play with. Long periods of sleep at night are usually established very early. The infant sleeps next to the mother in the mother's and father's bed, or sometimes with either parent alone. The mother may have both the infant and the knee-baby sleeping in her bed with her, but if there are older children the knee-baby is more likely to join them in their bed. The environment does not respond to the baby's own periodicity of rest and activity, tending to prevent establishment of natural rhythms in this area. Sleep does, however, reinforce the usual state of physical closeness.

Infant feeding habits vary widely, but certain attitudes about eating and about the giving and receiving of food run through the variations in behavior. Some mothers breastfeed a few weeks or months and then wean to a bottle. Most use a bottle entirely, while some use the breast and bottle concurrently, depending on convenience and privacy. Whether the baby is fed by breast or bottle the periods of eating are typically brief and the milk is offered frequently. When the baby shows discomfort the mother almost invariably offers the bottle. She typically says: "I know you not hungry. You hungry? You just ate a while ago." But she offers the bottle. The feeding is casually interrupted at any sign of decreased demand from the baby and as casually begun again at any interval. The rhythm of eating is like the rhythm of napping, short periods of each activity and frequent repetition. The environment is ever ready to interrupt and ever ready to offer gratification. This rhythm is very different from the disciplined long spans of attention cultivated in middle-class childrearing and expected in schools.

Mothers speak as though weaning occurred abruptly, but toddlers keep their bottles until three in the face of strong parental resistance and teasing. The mother may stop the bottle and the father accede to the baby's demand to have it, and the mother casually accepts the situation. One sees a mother repeatedly refuse the bottle to a demanding knee-baby, even while going to the kitchen to prepare it. It is not fixed habits of eating and feeding with which one is impressed, but rather that mothers and children act on whim and willfully in these matters. The wide variation in practice and in feelings about different practices gives much leeway for idiosyncratic behavior, in fact requires it. The behavioral constant is will on both the mother's and child's part. Neighbors' practices and neighbors' opinions are not thought to have any bearing on what any individual mother does. She sees herself as acting on sudden personal decisions. Being decisive and abrupt is admired and is one aspect of these people's strong sense of individualism.

Related also to decisiveness is the emphasis on giving and demanding food. The mother does not speak of infant feeding and weaning in terms of the infant's needs but of her own giving of food. She deemphasizes two objective aspects of eating, nourishment and routineness, and emphasizes two other aspects of eating, the giving and the receiving. The mother gives the satisfaction of eating and the child demands and receives it. It is the giving and the receiving, the demanding and the choosing to satisfy the demand — that is, the interpersonal exchange aspects of eating — that seem most important. Need, nourishment, succoring, routine — all possible aspects of eating and emphasized in White culture — are not usual concepts.

Family food habits also represent food as a voluntary gift from the parents. The hour of eating is not routinized within families, nor are there habitual meal times within the community. Meals are geared to the hours of work of the father and mother, which are irregular and varied since men work different shifts and domestic work keeps women away at conventional meal times. It is typical for a family to have two cooked meals a day, one in the morning or midday and the other at evening. The mother cooks at her convenience, not at a routine time, neither routinely for her family nor in coordination with the community. Between these times pick-up meals are gotten by each child for himself and eaten while walking around. During the day the mother may bring out sweet snacks or send children to a nearby store with money to buy a soft drink or popsicle. Mothers enjoy these treats and give them with largess. Occasionally the family will have to wait for its first meal of the day until the father wakes up after bringing his pay home the night before from a late shift job. When he wakes he walks to town to buy food, then all wait while the mother cooks it. In this situation the parents' roles as providers are abundantly clear. Eating is less a matter of routine than of individualistic voluntary giving and receiving.

Babies who are held so much of the time urinate and have their bowel movements while being held, and these actions are responded to immediately and directly. The action and response may be clearly associated in the baby's mind from a very early age. The diaper is usually changed quickly and quietly as soon as it is soiled or wet. If the mother's clothes get wet she usually shows her annoyance with a jerk and a long, penetrating scolding look into the baby's eyes. A five-month-old baby was told reproachfully: "You should have gotten down to pee-pee." The quick wiping away of the urine and feces is a forerunner of bladder and bowel training usually begun and quickly accomplished between nine and fifteen months. Some mothers wait until twenty or twenty-two months to begin it, showing the idiosyncratic tendency seen in the widely varied feeding habits. The highly personal conditions for care of these functions in early infancy may make the mother's expectations for control later an easier transition than for infants whose functions have occurred typically alone. The mother's intrusion in the functioning of bladder and bowel has been established from birth. In contrast, among middle-class white Americans the mother begins to interfere with the infant's bladder and bowel release only after many months of paying no attention to these functions. The greater continuity in the Negro mother's behavior undoubtedly eases the effects of early and stringent toilet training, which is commonly reported for American Negroes (Davis and Dollard 1940; Davis and Havighurst 1946) and which is the practice of many but not all mothers in this group.

Cleanliness, as distinguished from control of sphincters, is emphasized not only in the immediate wiping away of urine and feces, but also in the wiping of the mouth. The young baby's regurgitated milk is quickly wiped away and clothing soiled in this way is changed. A teething baby's mouth is wiped whenever drooling is noticed. Wiping is both a measure of cleanliness and also a tactile experience similar to the caressing with fingers that is so commonly done while holding the baby. The tactile experiences of the bath are similar. The baby is laid on the mother's lap and wiped with a cloth that is wetted and lathered in a small basin of water; it is then wiped again with the cloth rinsed clean of soap. The baby is never stood or seated in the basin. Young babies are sponged in this manner twice a day and this form of bath is usual throughout early childhood. The rubbing with a damp cloth is analogous to the caressing hand. The communication of a sense of care and attention through the skin is maximized while there is no opportunity for water play and the exploration of its properties.

The most usual kind of play with babies revolves around pretending the baby is aggressive. The young baby's reflexive extensions of its arms and legs are called hitting and kicking and its explorations with its lips are called biting. It is a great joke and everyone enjoys it. The mother will duck the flying two-month-old fist and say: "She sure is mad at me." Two babies will be propped beside each other and their wavering lunges and grasps and leaning on one another are laughingly called fighting.

The playful accusations of biting are the most usual form of the game. The mother brings the baby to her face and caresses its face lightly with her lips or forehead, and when the baby tries to suck or feel with its mouth the mother jerks it away in mock anger saying, "Don't you bite me." She brings the baby to her face again and repeats the thrust and accusation. She laughs admiringly while accusing it over and over. This episode is played with boy and girl babies, fathers play it with babies, and older nurse-girls play it with their charges, although not with as much pleasure as the adults. It is one of the most specifically stylized and most often observed forms of behavior with babies. In contrast to this game, babies' attempts to suck on the mother's fingers or other exposed areas of skin bring reactions of strong disgust. She jerks her hand away and reprimands with a harsh tone and angry look. This type of spontaneous oral incorporative behavior brings an angry reaction, whereas teasing the baby to the point of, but not the fulfillment of, similar mouth activity is a pleasurable game. There is only sporadic interference with young babies sucking and chewing their own fingers.

As babies gain control of the extensor muscles, the playful accusations of kicking and hitting are no longer made, but the interpretation of lip explorations as biting begins before babies have teeth and reaches a peak at about eight to ten months. By fifteen months, or by the time the baby walks well, the face-to-face play is no longer seen, but the child of that age is regularly told not to bite the new baby or the borrowed baby who is held up for it to kiss. By this time lip explorations seem to have ceased, and when urged to kiss a young baby a child in his second year is very cautious, hardly touching its lips to the baby and keeping its arms stiffly at its sides. The linkage of kissing and biting, of love and aggression, is understood by the fifteen-month-old baby but not mastered as a form of play. It is mastered by six, the earliest age at which children play the game almost like adults. Infantile oral pleasures are frustrated and replaced by structured parental demonstrativeness.

Frustrations for infants in this culture arise from less vital experiences than the satisfaction of hunger and the provision of attentive care. Frustration is undoubtedly experienced from interference with oral pleasures, from disruption of the natural rhythms of sleep, and from the frequently stringent restrictions on bowel and bladder movements. Rich compensation is offered for these frustrations, all of it interpersonal. The mother frustrates the lip explorations and at the same time rewards them with playfulness and admiration. The mother who toilet-trains early requires difficult control and yet her frequent physical contact and accustomed attentiveness, which enable her to get compliance, are themselves satisfactions. The aggression that is generated is admired and tolerated to a great extent, and yet the mother even as she is encouraging and admiring aggressiveness indicates that she is regulating its expression. There is a complex interplay of permissiveness and regulation, of indulgence and frustration, and all are carried out with a deep level of interpersonal involvement.

When the infant is accused of biting, the young children who surround it learn that the baby is an individual capable of bold initiative. The baby is attributed these characteristics in many other ways also. There is much talk about babies' meanness. Mothers and nurse-children will sigh about how mean a baby was who would not nap, while they are greatly enjoying holding and displaying the mean baby. A four-month-old baby who held tight to a glass of water after drinking was told, "Uh-uh, stop trying to fight. You's a mean little old girl." The mother was admiring the baby's assertiveness and attesting to the highly developed character assumed in babies.

The individuality of the baby is stressed through questioning the baby about its wants, especially its hunger, and though interpreting its random or directed movements as expressions of wants: he wants to get somewhere; he wants a certain person. As Old American Whites might say "Hello" over and over again, a frequent remark to a baby is: "What you want? What you want?" The focusing on wants is an important expression of these people's life experience. An infant's wants are well satisfied, whereas later life is full of unsatisfied wants. The new baby is usually the best-dressed member of the family. Little girls and adolescent girls long for pretty clothes but go without. Small items such as baby brushes, plastic bags for carrying bottles and plastic baby toys are sometimes seen and are conspicuous because of the general lack of paraphernalia and gadgets in this culture. Older children fondle the baby's booties admiringly or defiantly use the baby's hair brush, or plead to play with the baby bag. Having these things enhances the baby's high status.

Babies are taught to be responsive orally. The baby held up before the mother's or father's face is teased about biting for a while, and then is likely to be urged to imitate the parent's sounds. One hears five-month-old babies spontaneously imitating single sounds of their parents, and often babies show precociousness that tends to be lost in later childhood when the stimulus falls off. Babies will be distracted by calling their attention to a person, seldom an object: "Look yonder, who's coming?" "What you want? Jean? You want Jean to come?" Before they can talk babies are said to know the name of a favorite visitor. Parents will say the name of the favorite over and over to bring a smile to the baby's face.

In contrast to this great stimulation of the baby's responsiveness to people, its explorations of the inanimate environment are limited. Few objects are given to babies or allowed them when they do get hold of them. Plastic toys are almost the only objects ever seen in the hands of a prewalker, and their use seems to result from shopping in the supermarkets. Babies' reachings to feel objects or surfaces are often redirected to feeling the holder's face, or the game of rubbing faces is begun as a substitute. Sometimes the reaching is turned into a teasing game in which the baby is said to want to bite what it reaches for, and is teasingly brought up to and away from it. Such a degree of inhibition of exploration is possible only because there are always eyes on the baby and idle hands to take away the forbidden objects and then distract the frustrated baby. The personal is thus often substituted for the impersonal.

Babies are kept from crawling on the floor by holding them and passing them along from one holder to another. Walkers are the one piece of baby gadgetry that is rather commonly seen. The baby who is not safe on a bed and not adequately restricted on a pallet is likely to be put in a walker. He gets little chance to explore since he is usually chaperoned by older children who push him in the walker. It serves more as a restrictive seat than a device for learning to walk. Babies learn to stand on people's laps. They are jumped generously when they want to flex and stiffen their leg muscles. They are stood momentarily on the floor between the mother's or father's legs and jumped. But they are seldom allowed to stand alone, sink down on the floor or pull themselves up. All their standing is done on a lap. Babies are observed to walk at ten months, and claims were recorded of walking at nine months, while those learning to walk after twelve months seem relatively few. The baby who is ready to walk is stood on the floor; in the midst of great excitement it lunges and steps to waiting arms and is stood up when it falls either to try again or to be put in the lap.

The baby on the verge of the great change that walking and toilet training bring, the one-year-old, has been held almost all the waking hours of his first year, has been fed often and allowed to refuse food whenever inclined, has slept close to his parents and has been treated as a willful assertive individual. His natural rhythms of sleep and perhaps also hunger have not been perceived and have been interrupted, probably a very common enculturation experience. His desire to explore his nonhuman environment has been frustrated and human contact substituted. His own tactile expressions both oral and manual have been severely restricted, yet he has been constantly handled. He is taught to be passive in tactile experiences. He is urged to precocious speech development and walking, becomes accustomed to a high level of stimulation and is encouraged to avow an aggressiveness beyond what is probably natural in his situation. He should be a secure baby with confident expectations of gratification, self-assertive, and accustomed to close and continuous human contacts. The restrictions placed on him in tactile exploration and the systematic removal of objects from his range have certainly made him much more a stranger to his material environment than to his human one.

Walking brings an enormous change in the scope of experience of any baby, and especially the baby who has not had much chance to crawl. For people in this community the accomplishments of walking and toilet training, which come at about the same time, signify the transition to different expectations of the baby. His mother now requires him to use a pot or the outdoors for his excretion. Beyond this requirement he has free rein in his behavior, but he is expected to cause his mother no trouble. She punishes him by switching, starting with a light switch but using it frequently and with seriousness, although often with playfulness. The new behavioral expectations bring about a change in attitude toward the one-year-old child. One can speak of the one-year-old as the knee-baby, as the Georgiatown people do, the ambulatory child who leaves the mother and returns to her, who stands at her knee whether there is a new baby in her lap or not.

When there is a new baby, jealousy is usual, sometimes accompanied by psychosomatic symptoms, but it is usually short-lived. The knee-baby's aggressive feelings toward the lap-baby are acknowledged and aggressive expressions toward it tolerated to some extent. The knee-baby can hit or pinch the unwanted infant in his mother's lap and run off with little scolding or punishment. After a month or two the knee-baby's anxiety over the younger child becomes more concerned with the continuance of the mother's attention than with jealousy of the infant. He shares the lap with the newborn, or has it to himself while the newborn sleeps, but he is not treated as an infant in the lap. It is made clear to him what his role is. He is urged to mother the baby as everyone else in the household does. The infant is held out to him and he is asked, "You want the baby?" He looks hostile or puzzled. He is urged to kiss the baby and, if he does so, does it stiffly and frowning. The infant is held up to the knee-baby to dance with him, and joggled in time to music as though held in the knee-baby's arms. I have seen this with knee-babies as young as fifteen months. The eighteen-month-old acts the same when urged to take or kiss the infant. But by twenty to twenty-four months both girls and boys enjoy this game with a baby. The child who is said not to like his sibling is nevertheless offered the baby to kiss and hold. For the child who has no younger sibling, neighbors or relatives or nurse-girls offer their babies. Learning to mother the baby is an important lesson in this culture.

Children in their second year, the knee-babies, seem typically secure. Their close relationship with their mothers continues, but their world expands to include the children's gang, a group of children primarily from the family, sometimes from the neighborhood, ranging in age from the fifteen-month-olds through a nurse-girl or boy of at least six. Usually children up to ten or twelve are included. The youngest child is the toy of all children who are six or older and who can claim the right to carry it. It is the center of attention of the gang, the favorite, never the interferer, for the gang has little to do but look after the young ones. Some children in their second year who have a baby sibling have transferred their main attachments to a substitute mother, to the father if he is home in the daytime, or to the grandmother if she is present, or even to a child nurse who is sufficiently reliable and devoted.

But the strong sense of security of the child in his second year is observed most interestingly in his relations with his mother. She sits, passively enjoying his assertiveness, playing the fetching games that his new-found independence of walking has led him to, and waging contests over innumerable issues, whether he will kiss or pinch the lap baby, whether he will be allowed to go off with someone, whether he will obey his mother's command or not. Mother and child smile slyly as they challenge each other. If the issue must be settled or if she wants to assert her authority, she does so with threat or use of a switch. She asks the little aggressor to bring her a switch and sits flicking it while he provokes her, to her enjoyment, as long as she wants him to. Children watch their mother's face to see whether they must cringe in fear and obey when she gets the switch or whether they can make a new challenge on top of a switching. The knee-baby is the one most likely to be allowed to make a new challenge. The contests between mother and knee-baby are staged for enjoyment and as demonstrations of the toddler's stalwart individualism. The mother is continuing the encouragement of aggression and the control of its expression as she and the father so regularly did in the baby's first year. An occasional mother is overbearing in this play and her knee-baby is unplayful. These mothers wield their authority more strictly than most and rigidly control their baby's responses to them. The result is usually a sullen child.

The first two or three years of life would seem to lay the groundwork for a healthy and resilient self-image. The two-year-old acts out the aggressiveness and assertiveness that are natural for his age and that were stimulated during his first year. It is an age of great self-confidence, mastery over all persons in the environment, and lavish admiration. Interpersonal activity continues to predominate in contrast to the manipulation of objects and the exploration of the environment, and a strong preference for this range of activity seems to have been established already, since restrictions on explorations are no longer seen. This preference continues all through childhood without further restrictions on use of natural materials. The typical two-year-old, the admired, assertive and playful knee-baby, seems to be doing well in terms of developing his potential and adjusting to his environment. But at the end of the knee-baby stage comes a marked change in experience, an almost complete cessation of the close relationship with the mother and father and a shift in orientation to the children's gang.

A change in the mother-child relationship comes when the knee-baby is pushed out of that lordly position by a growing younger sibling, and is expected to transfer his dependence to the gang of older children in the family and to the oldest child in it who is in charge of the gang. This transition to the gang takes place at about three. If the displaced knee-baby is the oldest in the family he becomes attached to a neighboring family group of older children. Only one child at a time is involved with the parents in the typical knee-baby relationship. The youngest child in a family or a set of children often retains the teasing relationship with its parents typical for the knee-baby, which seems to indicate that the third-position child is not thought to outgrow the relationship, but that a younger child is preferred if available. With this exception parents no longer play with children after the knee-baby position. The stimulation that was so intense ends almost entirely. The separation from the mother at this time seems to be taken well in stride except by those displaced very young and by some who show an unusually strong and exclusive dependence on their mother. The gang's forays away from home and the easy-going authority of the nurse-child seem to be attractions that substitute for the old closeness to the mother. Some children seem to prefer the nurse-child to their mothers even while still babies. These are the children of the overly aggressive mothers who so dominate the contests that the knee-babies become unresponsive and sullen. The very independent and assertive child manages best while the insecure child is truly lost, hanging on to the nurse-child or mother, but no one's favorite. He is no longer the toy of the gang because like the parents the gang prefers the knee-baby to play with. Most children seem to manage well by acquiring solemnity and stolidity and quietly following the gang. Others retain the playful and assertive personalities that are typical of the knee-baby, but aggressiveness seems well controlled at this age.

The three-year-old is sometimes intimidated by the toddler. He is told, "You have hands, don't you?" but he seldom fights back effectively and seldom is reprimanded for aggressiveness. Once the baby's aggressiveness was fully managed by the parent, both encouraged and restricted. The older gang members keep up constant pressure for cooperative behavior, and the young ones show remarkably little aggressiveness.

The most apparent loss at this time due to the abrupt ending of parental stimulation is not seen in the form of anxiety, but in loss of precociousness of speech development. Often speech becomes an indistinct children's patois in contrast to the clear enunciation used by the knee-baby with his parents. Children speak less to adults and get along adequately with "Yes'm" and "No'm." Exploration of the environment seems to have been thoroughly inhibited by this age. Children become subsumed in the small community of the family-based gang.

The core of any gang is the children of one family. Single children or several young children of neighbors may also be regular parts of the gang. Nurse-children who are friends sometimes bring their gangs together but for both nurse-child and younger gang members the family orientation of the gang overrides friendship with age mates. The gang is essentially a child-tending group and the oldest child is fully occupied with the responsibility. There is little other activity to attract the nurse-child away and he or she seems content to manage the gang. Boys from about nine years leave the mixed-sex gang if they themselves are not the nurse-child. They range farther from home than the gangs with young children, playing games of athletic skill and keeping their promises to their mothers or older sisters to be back at a certain hour. The gang with young children sits and gossips, runs, climbs, swings, lines up for inspection, teases. Sitting in a circle of chairs, it passes a joke around the group, each one repeating the punch line in much the same way as a group of women tells a joke. Occasionally an imaginary family game will be seen, but most of the play uses only the real relationships of the children. There are almost no toys, almost no use of natural materials, no "projects" such as the middle-class child, whether in the sandbox or supplied with paper and crayons or dress-ups, is usually involved in. Equipment such as swings and slides are used where available, chairs are lined up for the gossip circle, but simple equipment, such as ropes, poles, sticks, balls, and stones, is almost never seen in use. Junebugs are an exception, the one part of the natural environment that is used, creatures, significantly, not objects. They are tied by one leg to fly from a string and raced on the ground. For the most part children are the playthings and the players. The youngest is the center of attention. He is carried and kissed and shepherded and talked to lovingly, and his words and acts are discussed with great interest. Children sit close to one another, rub bare feet with each other, tease, tell stories and jokes. There are few displays of proficiency of the kind learned at school and little use of school as a play model.

Aggression, punishment, and acceptance of authority in Georgiatown childhood diverge markedly from what has been reported before. Fighting is not encouraged as Davis and Dollard's interviewees said it was (1940:270–271). Possibly this is a case in which interviews bring out bragging, or perhaps, since parents' advice to children over three or four was so infrequent in the course of observations, directives to "Fight it out" in Georgiatown may have been given and missed. In the children's gangs, however, quarrels are infrequent and children seldom resort to blows. Word battles and glaring matches take their place. A child may be threatened with exclusion and make counter claims of his right to play. An older child may hit a younger, who usually sulks without hitting back, but this is unusual. No bullies were seen and no wrestling matches. Play was mild and even-tempered. One blow and the other children would take the victim home.

In visiting for a few hours at a time one seldom sees punishments, although occasionally the resounding cracks of prolonged spanking and the steady crying of a child are heard from a neighboring house and the remark is made, "Hear her beating on that girl!" Sometimes a mother reports somberly that she had to "beat on him" for some misdeed and the child sulks on the edges of the household activity. Adolescent boys and girls are also whipped by their mothers. Punishments, however, do not seem to be extreme or more frequent than in middle-class American society. The mother unquestionably has authority over her children but she also cultivates a degree of defiance in them. Even after the games of defiance in knee-babyhood are over, mothers indicate to their children that they will be allowed to get away with things. In so doing they are actually asserting their ultimate authority, like the mother who likes to see her infant bite and fight and likes to scold him for it, but the children are also being taught playful defiance. Children defy their mothers on many small issues, and they watch her closely to see if they will be allowed to get away with it. The behavior is similar to the mother's games with the knee-baby except that the mother is not playful. She quietly watches or looks impassive to indicate that she is allowing whatever small liberties are being taken. Aggression in childhood situations is not an adequate analogy for aggression in adulthood, and childhood experience as observed in this relatively secure community does not show the origins of the aggressiveness found in much adult Negro behavior. These findings do not alter the common perception that the sheer amount of Negro aggression is more directly related to race relations than to other aspects of their experience. The mother's admiring and encouraging attitude toward limited expressions of aggression and defiance may become a prototype for children's expectations of this kind of attitude from other authorities.

The position of nurse-child is held by the oldest in the family, boy or girl. He or she is responsible for all the other children, tends the food the mother may have left cooking before going to work, or makes the sandwiches, serves lunch to the children, diapers the baby and knee-baby if they are left in his charge, fixes bottles for them, puts them in bed for naps. The nurse-children are bossy but gentle and protective and easygoing. The heightened attention that the nurse-girl or boy, as first baby, got prepares him for his responsible position. Their competence demonstrates that illegitimate birth, the lot of so many first babies, and that of many nurse-children observed, does not hamper development.

A girl retains this responsibility as a teenager and until she leaves the household. Boys at thirteen or fourteen are expected to desert their regular responsibilities and go off with age-mates although at home they display deep attachments for the younger children. None of the younger children, even if only a year younger than the nurse-child, has major responsibilities and they tend not to show the managerial personality of the oldest child. They are given tasks by the mother, however, and take over some of the care of the younger children because it is privileged activity, and all children have been exhorted from the first appearance of their own younger sibling to mother the younger child. The training that the one-year-old gets in kissing and holding the newborn is his training for all of childhood. A young child may be demanding of an older child, yet turns to a younger one and mothers it, gives in to it, and protects it. Gestures of love for young children are commonplaces in this culture, from the fourteen-year-old boy who rides home on his bicycle and buries his face against the stomach of the baby in his cousin's lap, to the twenty-two-month-old boy, hungry and distressed because his mother is leaving, diverted to pleasurably kiss his three-month-old half-sister in his aunt's lap.

Since mothering is proper behavior for boys as well as girls and for fathers as well as mothers, the question is raised of the behavioral differences between the sexes. In knee-babyhood boys are expected to be assertive, playful, and "bad," while girls are expected to be assertive, playful, coy, and cooperative. The slight but significant difference is as great a contrast as is made at any time in childhood between boys' and girls' expected behavior. The very common, admiring adjective "bad" is used only through knee-babyhood. After that boys are neither bragged on as bad nor are they unruly. Little boys in the family gang have the same activities as the girls and no patterned differences of behavior are seen. Differences between the sexes are marked only in specifically sex-related behavior, just as coyness in baby girls and greater assertiveness in boys are the main differences in babyhood. Girls are encouraged to dance. A baby boy may be a partner, but young boys are never asked to show off in this way. A coy little girl of four climbed into a visiting young man's lap and wriggled and flirted. "I can get me a big 'un," he said. Children are not considered asexual. Children are knowledgeable about birth, menstruation, and sex at an early age. There is a sense of strong continuity between childhood and adulthood. This seems to reinforce in children their sexual identity even though that identity has few indicators other than dress in the organization of children's activity before the age of nine or ten when boys may be expected to leave the young children's gang. In adulthood sex roles are also similar in authority at home, in supporting the family, in styles of child care, and in initiative in forming and breaking up a marriage. Contrasting behavior, however, is also characteristic as has been described in the deferent, yielding, and flirtatious behavior of women and the assertive behavior of men.

The adolescent girls remain in charge of the younger children, but they now manage their broods with subdued and resigned manner. This behavior characteristic of girls in their early teens is one of the most striking and consistent patterns.

They stay at home and watch television and read fiction magazines and often show a deep attachment for a baby. If there is no baby or young child in their family they attach themselves to a relative's household to care for the baby. They seem to have only weak ties with girl friends, seem to withdraw solemnly and await the beginning of a love affair that comes to so many in the few years after fourteen. The adolescent girls' feelings of resignation seem to foreshadow the whole course of the adulthood they are about to enter, which will lack material security and material pleasures, lack any attainment of status, but will soon bring their first love affair and the pride and pleasure and heavy responsibility of children. It is as though the irony of their culture is suddenly perceived. The most valued experience in life, parenthood, and perhaps also sex, will foreclose the paths to achievement in American society, education and freedom from emotional entanglement, and with this the loss of opportunity to achieve any more of the televised dream than a Southern town offers Negroes. The Negro boy and girl, with their safe and satisfying childhood devoted to care of young children and spent in warm human contacts, and with the threatening and unrewarding world of unskilled work and poverty in prospect, seek their own emotional fulfillment as they have been taught to do.

One theme that keeps recurring in the behavior observed is best reviewed after many appearances. It is a polarity of individuality and interrelatedness. The baby is treated as though willful and assertive beyond his natural inclination and able beyond his natural abilities. He is highly stimulated and admired for his assertiveness, and his acceptance of authority is expected to be defiant. Individualistic behavior is seen also in neighborhood relations. It is striking how separate each family remains from its neighbors, how uncommon the favors exchanged, how independent each family feels of the opinions of others. All of women's work is done inside the houses or in the private backyards, each woman working alone. Shared gardens or communal work of any kind is not undertaken. Only children gather in groups outdoors, playing with neighbor children but seldom involving their mothers in their play or quarrels. Women go to neighbors' houses on brief errands, but are not likely to spend an idle hour. The occasional caller is received on the front porch or in the livingroom if there is no porch, and the visitors sit and talk awhile and never were seen offered food. Interchange of services or hospitality or dependence on these things is at a minimum. Much of religious behavior also is highly individualistic. In social organization there are no strongly organized groups to overshadow the individualistic style of behavior in the loosely structured small groups. The girl and boy in adolescence are remarkably free of any community restraint on premarital relations even though there is general disapproval and criticism of license. Strong individuality,[4] however, is paired with strong interpersonal connectedness, not absorption in a group or acceptance of group identity as higher than individual identity, but merely relatedness as distinguished from the isolation that characterizes individualism in the Western tradition. Human contacts are the whole substance of life for the infant. He learns early to be disinterested in the natural environment and entirely occupied by his human one. When the knee-baby is abruptly expected to merge into the quiet and cooperative children's gang and get along with little attention from his parents, individualistic stimulation lessens but the succoring, playful human environment continues.

There is a quality of mutuality in family relations, often heard in remarks that pass between mothers and children, "I'm tired," the three-year-old girl complains. "I'm tired too," her mother responds. "I want some ice cream," the eight-year-old says wistfully as the ice cream truck passes. "I want some too," is the mother's way of saying no. This echoing of words and tone of voice is a common speech pattern. One does not see mothers and children clash and contend. The minimal amount of verbal exchange that has been remarked in lower-class families is in this group connected with abundant communication in other forms. These Georgiatown people are often seen to look deeply into each other's eyes, not speaking but seeming to communicate fully. Parents use this means to impress a point on a child. The observation has been made that Negroes avoid meeting the eyes of Whites, and this has been interpreted as a gesture of nonequality. It may also, or instead, be a gesture of uncommunicativeness in view of the extensive communication through looking into the eyes within their own group. The mother's idle caressing of the baby and children sitting in a circle rubbing bare feet are other forms of nonverbal communication. The communication of news in this community is rapid and thorough despite the fact that it is physically scattered and has no central organizations of any kind. A mother's communication of directions in household tasks uses few words, and tasks for which she has to give instructions are broken down into small units with brief directions for each short task following on completion of the previous one.[5] The children seem thoroughly familiar with the directions. They respond immediately even when they seem to be napping when an order comes. The rhythm of children's household chores repeats the periodicity of early eating and napping: immediate response to the request, whether for food, to stop napping and play, or to do a task, and brief intervals of the sought activity. Routinized or planned activity with long-range objectives in either household chores or gang activities is minimal. Personal interaction again emerges as the central element in behavior. The combination of interpersonal responsiveness and strong individuality in all this behavior is suggestive for the present day when the modes of individualistic disciplined achievement have been found of limited adaptability in modern society and where inability to relate genuinely to other persons has been found a common personality malformation.

Negro childhood and family represent a distinctive complex both institutionally and behaviorally. They exhibit organization, values, and behavioral styles that differ from the White cultural tradition. The indulgence of the baby, the constant human environment, linking of aggression and love, the simultaneous encouragement and control of aggressiveness, the early entry into the children's gang and the devotion of childhood to baby-tending and to the cooperative group of brothers and sisters, all are distinctive forms of behavior that, taken as a whole, represent an integrated cultural pattern. The Negro family should be analyzed as part of the social structure of Negro communities, but little analytic work has been done on American Negro social structure. What has been done suggests an unorganized network of loose social groupings with a high level of communication and a low level of authority and coercion. The Negro family is an internally consistent system that fits with this hypothesized social structure. Individual independence in sexual behavior and marriage, comparability of role of husband and wife, and the strengthening of the nuclear family by unpatterned use of the grandparental ties are consistent with such a social structure. Furthermore, the family functions well within a stable community, providing security for children and adjusting well to the high level of emotional expressiveness that is nurtured. We speak therefore of American Negro culture as an entity expressing itself in childrearing and family forms, and we assume it can be described in other aspects of Negro life, expecially small group structure. American White culture may dominate in the areas of life where Negroes participate in American institutions and many items of general American culture are used throughout Negro life, but in small groups and to some extent in any all-Negro group the organizational and behavioral styles of American Negro culture would be expected to be manifest.

Negro family styles are different enough from the White that psychoanalytic interpretations of modal personality would have to be modified for use in this culture. It is a task beyond the scope of this paper, but some relevant considerations emerging from this work may be summarized: early toilet training and the encouragement of autonomy are pursued together; love and aggression and control of aggression are linked in an unusual way; a mother with much authority is also indulgent and erotically provoking; the father's proper role vis-à-vis the baby is quite similar to the mother's in indulgence and erotic stimulation.

It also appears from this study of childhood that certain cultural styles are as significant as the parent-child drama, namely the elaboration of interpersonal contacts and the elimination of experience with the object world, the ever-present polarity of individuality and absorption in interpersonal and group experience, the cultivation of will and volition, even a valuing of arbitrariness, and also the playfulness of so many relationships. Cultural styles such as these as well as the institutional structure of American Negro society are the milieu for Negro personality formation.

Notes

[1] I wish to thank Dr. Conrad Arensberg for reading the manuscript and for making available to me some of his own related analytic work, which suggested some of the formulations contained in this article. Valuable as his insights have been to me, he is of course not responsible for the specific interpretations in this article.

[2] Census on the racial proportions of the population give approximately sixteen percent non-White in the county and nineteen percent in Georgiatown. Several Negro hamlets are

situated just beyond the town limits and their occupants are employed in the town. These persons, counted by the Census as county residents, are actually townspeople socioeconomically and are so counted in the estimate here.

[3] The behavioral forms discussed in this section were as fully exhibited among middle-class as among lower-class families. The class differences in general were not very great in this town and would not be expected to affect these fundamental styles of interpersonal behavior, except as different expectations of achievement did in some ways affect child training.

[4] Hylan Lewis notes that "individuality and idiosyncrasies of character flourish" (1967:169) and also "despite the overall conformity a striking fact about Kent Negro society is the manner in which everyone tends to be a 'character' " (1955:322 ff).

[5] The mother's way of directing household chores is similar to the call and response in music (see Lomax 1967).

References cited:

Bernard, Jessie. 1966. Marriage and family among Negroes. Englewood Cliffs: Prentice-Hall.

Davie, Maurice R. 1949. Negroes in American society. New York: McGraw-Hill.

Davis, Allison, and John Dollard. 1940. Children of bondage. American Council on Education. New York: Harper and Row (Torchbook edition).

Davis, Allison, and Robert J. Havighurst. 1946. Social class and color differences in child-rearing. American Sociological Review 2:698–710.

Frazier, E. Franklin. 1939. The Negro family in the United States. Chicago: University of Chicago Press.

Herskovits, Melville J. 1941. The myth of the Negro past. New York: Harper.

Johnson, Charles S. 1934a. Shadow of the plantation. Chicago: University of Chicago Press.

———. 1934b. Negro personality changes in a Southern community. In Race and culture contacts. E. B. Reuter, ed. New York: McGraw-Hill.

Kardiner, Abram, and Lionel Ovesey. 1951. The mark of oppression. New York: World.

Lewis, Hylan. 1955. Blackways of Kent. Chapel Hill: University of North Carolina Press.

———. 1960. The changing Negro family. In The nation's children. Eli Ginsberg, ed. White House Conference on Children and Youth.

———. 1967. Culture, class and family life among low-income urban Negroes. In Employment, race, and poverty. Arthur M. Ross and Herbert Hill, eds. New York: Harcourt, Brace and World.

Liebow, Elliot. 1967. Tally's corner. Boston: Little, Brown.

Lomax, Alan. 1967. The homogeneity of African-New World Negro musical style. Paper presented at the 66th Annual Meeting of the American Anthropological Association, Washington, November 30–December 6.

Moynihan, Daniel P. 1965. The Negro family: the case for national action. Washington: U.S. Department of Labor, Office of Policy Planning and Research.

Powdermaker, Hortense. 1939. After freedom. New York: Viking Press.

Rohrer, John H., and Munro S. Edmonson. 1960. The eighth generation. New York: Harper.

Smith, M. G. 1962. West Indian family structure. Seattle: University of Washington Press.

U.S. Department of Labor. 1965. Labor market report. Washington: U.S. Government Printing Office.

Valentine, Charles A. 1968. Culture and poverty. Chicago: University of Chicago Press.

Suggestions for
Further Reading

Additional readings include works by E. Franklin Frazier, which should be read in their entirety: *The Negro Family in Chicago* (Chicago: University of Chicago Press, 1932), *The Free Negro Family* (Nashville: Fisk University Press, 1932), *The Negro Family in the United States* (Chicago: University of Chicago Press, 1939; rev. and abrd., 1948), and *Negro Youth at the Crossways* (Washington, D.C.: American Council on Education, 1940). Article-length discussions have been included in G. Franklin Edwards (ed.), *E. Franklin Frazier on Race Relations* (Chicago: University of Chicago Press, 1968).

A pioneering work is W. E. B. Du Bois (ed.), *The Negro American Family* (Atlanta: Atlanta University Publications No. 13, 1908).

Relevant studies generally reflecting the Frazier approach are St. Clair Drake and Horace Cayton, *Black Metropolis* (New York: Harcourt, Brace & World, 1945), and the American Council on Education series: Allison Davis and John Dollard, *Children of Bondage* (Washington, D.C.: American Council on Education, 1940), Charles S. Johnson, *Growing Up in the Black Belt* (Washington, D.C.: American Council on Education, 1941), and Ira DeA. Reid, *In a Minor Key: Negro Youth in Story and Fact* (Washington, D.C.: American Council on Education, 1940).

The issues generated by the Moynihan report can best be approached through Lee Rainwater and William L. Yancey (eds.), *The Moynihan Report and the Politics of Controversy* (Cambridge, Mass.: M. I. T. Press, 1967). A critique of the report and its conclusions, by a black scholar, is to be found in Andrew Billingsley, *Black Families in White America* (Englewood Cliffs, N. J.: Prentice-Hall, 1968). Two recent useful anthologies are Charles V. Willie (ed.), *The Family Life of Black People* (Columbus, Ohio: Charles Merrill, 1970) and Robert Staples (ed.), *The Black Family: Essays and Studies* (Belmont, Calif.: Wadsworth, 1971).

A Wadsworth Series:
Explorations in the Black Experience

General Editors

John H. Bracey, Jr.
Northern Illinois University

August Meier
Kent State University

Elliott Rudwick
Kent State University

Robert C. Weaver, "The Villain—Racial Covenants"; Robert C. Weaver, "The Role of the Federal Government"; Herman H. Long and Charles S. Johnson, "The Role of Real Estate Organizations"; Loren Miller, "Supreme Court Covenant Decision—An Analysis"; Herbert Hill, "Demographic Change and Racial Ghettos: The Crisis of American Cities"; Roy Reed, "Resegregation: A Problem in the Urban South"

4 The Process of Ghettoization: Internal Pressures

Arnold Rose and Caroline Rose, "The Significance of Group Identification"; W. E. B. Du Bois, "The Social Evolution of the Black South"; Allan H. Spear, "The Institutional Ghetto"; Chicago Commission on Race Relations, "The Matrix of the Black Community"; E. Franklin Frazier, "The Negro's Vested Interest in Segregation"; George A. Nesbitt, "Break Up the Black Ghetto?"; Lewis G. Watts, Howard E. Freeman, Helen M. Hughes, Robert Morris, and Thomas F. Pettigrew, "Social Attractions of the Ghetto"

5 Future Prospects

Karl E. Taeuber and Alma F. Taeuber, "Is the Negro an Immigrant Group?"; H. Paul Friesema, "Black Control of Central Cities: The Hollow Prize"

Suggestions for Further Reading

Black Matriarchy: Myth or Reality?

Introduction

1 The Frazier Thesis

E. Franklin Frazier, "The Negro Family in America"; E. Franklin Frazier, "The Matriarchate"

2 The Question of African Survivals

Melville J. Herskovits, "On West African Influences"

3 The Frazier Thesis Applied

Charles S. Johnson, "The Family in the Plantation South"; Lee Rainwater, "Crucible of Identity: The Negro Lower-Class Family"; Elliot Liebow, "Fathers without Children"

4 The Moynihan Report

Daniel P. Moynihan, "The Negro Family: The Case for National Action"; Hylan Lewis and Elizabeth Herzog, "The Family: Resources for Change"

5 New Approaches

Herbert H. Hyman and John Shelton Reed, " 'Black Matriarchy' Reconsidered: Evidence from Secondary Analysis of Sample Surveys"; Virginia Heyer Young, "Family and Childhood in a Southern Negro Community"

Suggestions for Further Reading

Black Workers and Organized Labor

Introduction

Sidney H. Kessler, "The Organization of Negroes in the Knights of Labor"; Bernard Mandel, "Samuel Gompers and the Negro Workers, 1886–1914"; Paul B. Worthman, "Black Workers and Labor Unions in Birmingham, Alabama, 1897–1904"; William M. Tuttle, Jr., "Labor Conflict and Racial Violence: The Black Worker in Chicago, 1894–1919"; Sterling D. Spero and Abram L. Harris, "The Negro Longshoreman, 1870–1930"; Sterling D. Spero and Abram L. Harris, "The Negro and the IWW"; Brailsford R. Brazeal, "The Brotherhood of Sleeping Car Porters"; Horace R. Cayton and George S. Mitchell, "Blacks and Organized Labor in the Iron and Steel Industry, 1880–1939"; Herbert R. Northrup, "Blacks in the United Automobile Workers Union"; Sumner M. Rosen, "The CIO Era, 1935–1955"; William Kornhauser, "The Negro Union Official: A Study of Sponsorship and Control"; Ray Marshall, "The Negro and the AFL-CIO"

Suggestions for Further Reading

The Black Sociologists: The First Half Century

Introduction

1 Early Pioneers

W. E. B. Du Bois, "The Study of the Negro Problems"; W. E. B. Du Bois, "The Organized Life of Negroes"; George E. Haynes, "Conditions among Negroes in the Cities"

2 In the Robert E. Park Tradition

Charles S. Johnson, "Black Housing in Chicago"; E. Franklin Frazier, "The Pathology of Race Prejudice"; E. Franklin Frazier, "La Bourgeoisie Noire"; Charles S. Johnson, "The Plantation during the Depression"; Bertram W. Doyle, "The Etiquette of Race Relations—Past, Present, and Future"; E. Franklin Frazier, "The Black Matriarchate"; Charles S. Johnson, "Patterns of Negro Segregation"; E. Franklin Frazier, "The New Negro Middle Class"

3 Black Metropolis: Sociological Masterpiece

St. Clair Drake and Horace Cayton, "The Measure of the Man"

Conflict and Competition: Studies in the Recent Black Protest Movement

Introduction

1 Nonviolent Direct Action

Joseph S. Himes, "The Functions of Racial Conflict"; August Meier, "Negro Protest Movements and Organizations"; Lewis M. Killian and Charles U. Smith, "Negro Protest Leaders in a Southern Community"; Ralph H. Hines and James E. Pierce, "Negro Leadership after the Social Crisis: An Analysis of Leadership Changes in Montgomery, Alabama"; Jack L. Walker, "The Functions of Disunity: Negro Leadership in a Southern City"; Gerald A. McWorter and Robert L. Crain, "Subcommunity Gladiatorial Competition: Civil Rights Leadership as a Competitive Process"; August Meier, "On the Role of Martin Luther King"

2 By Any Means Necessary

Inge Powell Bell, "Status Discrepancy and the Radical Rejection of Nonviolence"; Donald von Eschen, Jerome Kirk, and Maurice Pinard, "The Disintegration of the Negro Non-Violent Movement"; Allen J. Matusow, "From Civil Rights to Black Power: The Case of SNCC, 1960–1966"; Joel D. Aberbach and Jack L. Walker, "The Meanings of Black Power: A Comparison of White and Black Interpretations of a Political Slogan"; David O. Sears and T. M. Tomlinson, "Riot Ideology in Los Angeles: A Study of Negro Attitudes"; Robert Blauner, "Internal Colonialism and Ghetto Revolt"; Charles V. Hamilton, "Conflict, Race, and System-Transformation in the United States"

Suggestions for Further Reading